AF712111

Competition Law in the United States

Competition Law in the United States

Third Edition

Howard Langer

This book was originally published as a monograph in the International Encyclopaedia of Laws/Competition Law.

General Editors: Roger Blanpain, Frank Hendrickx
Volume Editors: Francesco Denozza, Alberto Toffoletto

Wolters Kluwer

Published by:
Kluwer Law International B.V.
PO Box 316
2400 AH Alphen aan den Rijn
The Netherlands
Website: www.wklawbusiness.com

Sold and distributed in North, Central and South America by:
Wolters Kluwer Legal & Regulatory U.S.
7201 McKinney Circle
Frederick, MD 21704
United States of America
Email: customer.service@wolterskluwer.com

Sold and distributed in all other countries by:
Turpin Distribution Services Ltd.
Stratton Business Park
Pegasus Drive, Biggleswade
Bedfordshire SG18 8TQ
United Kingdom
Email: kluwerlaw@turpin-distribution.com

DISCLAIMER: The material in this volume is in the nature of general comment only. It is not offered as advice on any particular matter and should not be taken as such. The editor and the contributing authors expressly disclaim all liability to any person with regard to anything done or omitted to be done, and with respect to the consequences of anything done or omitted to be done wholly or partly in reliance upon the whole or any part of the contents of this volume. No reader should act or refrain from acting on the basis of any matter contained in this volume without first obtaining professional advice regarding the particular facts and circumstances at issue. Any and all opinions expressed herein are those of the particular author and are not necessarily those of the editor or publisher of this volume.

Printed on acid-free paper

ISBN 978-90-411-8546-4

e-Book: ISBN 978-90-411-8560-0
web-PDF: ISBN 978-90-411-8574-7

This title is available on www.kluwerlawonline.com

© 2016, Kluwer Law International BV, The Netherlands

All rights reserved. No part of this publication may be reproduced, stored in a retrieval system, or transmitted in any form or by any means, electronic, mechanical, photocopying, recording, or otherwise, without the prior written permission of the publisher.

Permission to use this content must be obtained from the copyright owner. Please apply to: Permissions Department, Wolters Kluwer Legal & Regulatory U.S., 76 Ninth Avenue, 7th Floor, New York, NY 10011-5201, USA. Website: www.wklawbusiness.com

Printed and Bound by CPI Group (UK) Ltd, Croydon, CR0 4YY.

The Author

Howard Langer is the senior partner of Langer Grogan & Diver, P.C., a litigation firm specializing in antitrust law, located in Philadelphia, Pennsylvania. He is also adjunct professor of law at the Law School of the University of Pennsylvania where he teaches antitrust law. He has been a visiting fellow at the Centre for Competition Law and Policy at the University at Oxford and a guest professor at the University of Tokyo Law School. Born November 28, 1950 in New York, Mr. Langer obtained his law degree from the University of Pennsylvania in 1977. He is member of the American Law Institute.

Mr. Langer acknowledges the assistance of his colleagues, Robert LaRocca and John Grogan, who reviewed the drafts of this work and provided much needed editorial assistance, and Daniel Simons who has assisted in the updates. He also would be remiss in not acknowledging the important work of his student, Jonathan Mincer, who reviewed the manuscripts and took the initial laboring oar in drafting the sections on the procedures of the Federal Trade Commission and Concentrations. Finally, and most of all, he acknowledges the special efforts of his assistant, Gina Gossett, who undertook to prepare the manuscript for publication. Without her help and sharp eye, this, like most of his professional efforts, would certainly never have been completed.

The Author

Table of Contents

Table of Contents

List of Abbreviations

The treatise uses standard nomenclature for American citations:

ALJ	Administrative Law Judge
AT&T	American Telephone & Telegraph
BMI	Broadcast Music Inc.
C.F.R.	Code of Federal Regulations
DAAG	Deputy Assistant Attorney General
DOJ	Department Of Justice
EU	European Union
F. Supp.	Federal Supplement
F. Supp.2d	Federal Supplement Second
F.2d and F.3d	Federal Reporter Second and Federal Reporter Third
FBI	Federal Bureau of Investigation
FCC	Federal Communications Commission
FERC	Federal Energy Regulatory Commission
FTC	Federal Trade Commission
HHI	Herfindahl-Hirschman Index
HSR	Hart-Scott-Rodino
ITC	International Trade Commission
L.Ed.	Supreme Court Reporter Lawyers Edition
N.J.S.A.	New Jersey Statutes Annotated
NFL	National Football League
NFLP	National Football League Properties
S.Ct.	Supreme Court Reporter (West)
TRU	Toys R Us
U.S.	United States Supreme Court Report
U.S.C.	United States Code
Wis. Stat.	Wisconsin Statutes
WL	West Law Reporter (online)

General Introduction

§1. Historical Background of American Antitrust Law

1. The Sherman Antitrust Act was adopted in 1890, just twenty-five years following the Civil War. The war established the dominance of the industrial might of the northern states and further enhanced the growing industrialization of what had been an agrarian society. The Sherman Act was intended to assure the economic liberty attendant to the political liberty preserved by the war, which remained the seminal event in the life of the country at the time the act was passed. Senator John Sherman, the primary author of the act, was the younger brother of the great Civil War general, William Tecumseh Sherman. Subsequent Court decisions have underscored the importance of the laws to the principles of justice, equality and democracy central to the country's conception of itself. A 1979 Supreme Court decision explained:

> The initial House debates concerning provisions related to private damages actions reveal that these actions were conceived primarily as "open(ing) the door of justice to every man, whenever he may be injured by those who violate the antitrust laws, and giv(ing) the injured party ample damages for the wrong suffered." 51 Cong.Rec. 9073 (1914).[1]

2. School children in the United States are taught that the growth of the country into the largest economy in the world was fueled in no small part by dynamic capitalism preserved by its antitrust laws. The laws were conceived, at least in part, as a substitute for the benefits other nations believe they derive from other economic systems such as socialism or communism. The US remains the epitome of a capitalist economy with an estimated 2014 Gross Domestic Product of USD 17.4 trillion. It teaches its children that the dynamic economy and society encouraged by the antitrust laws were a major lubricant of this great economic engine.

3. American antitrust laws sought to address concerns about the huge aggregations of capital that were generated as a rural society turned industrial. These concerns were

1. *Brunswick Corp. v. Pueblo Bowl-O-Mat, Inc.*, 429 U.S. 477, 486, 97 S. Ct. 690, 696, 50 L. Ed. 2d 701 (1977).

as much social and political as economic, and a focus only on the economic efficiency goals of the American antitrust laws leads to serious misunderstanding of their development. In contrast to the European Community, which first put in place an antitrust law in 1957 as part of the Treaty of Rome,[2] the key statutory provisions of American antitrust law were in place by 1914, when the Clayton Act and the Federal Trade Commission (FTC) Act were enacted in response to early decisions construing the Sherman Act.

4. The initial concerns were threefold: to protect the free market system with its attendant efficiencies; to protect democracy by limiting the size and power of economic organizations; and to protect a socially dynamic society. How these goals were to be achieved was left almost entirely to the courts. The two core statutory provisions, sections 1 and 2 of the Sherman Act, were intentionally left broad and vague. Section 1 prohibited all "contracts, combinations and conspiracies in restraint of trade"[3] and section 2 prohibited "monopolies."[4] No effort was made to define the key terms. Courts quickly recognized that virtually every contract was, in some sense, in restraint of trade. If I had one bicycle and I sold it to A when B also wanted it, by selling it to A, I was precluding a sale to B and thereby, in some sense, restraining trade. The courts developed the concept that only contracts in *unreasonable* restraint of trade were prohibited by the act. But this construction of the statute created such concern that judges would eviscerate the new antitrust law that it became the central issue of the 1912 presidential campaign and ultimately led to the passage of the Clayton Act.

5. Section 2's prohibition of "monopolies"[5] gave rise to similar concerns. At what level of the market was monopoly achieved? Was not the whole goal of the capitalist system to allow the winner in the competitive marketplace to reap the rewards of victory after vanquishing the competition? And were there not economies to be achieved from size alone? These views achieved considerable traction and led some – including the great Oliver Wendell Holmes – to dismiss the antitrust laws as humbug.

6. Economic efficiency, which came to dominate judicial interpretation of the antitrust laws beginning in the 1960s, was not a major goal of many of the most famous supporters of American antitrust law. Louis Brandeis, perhaps the greatest proponent of the antitrust laws, believed that the consumer should pay more to obtain the greater choice provided by a multiplicity of vendors and that assuring lower prices at the cost of that variety was not a goal of the antitrust laws. The Robinson-Patman Act of 1936 unsuccessfully sought to protect small business, particularly local groceries, by placing obstacles to the lower prices provided by the aggregation buying power in large supermarket chains.

> In 1945, Judge Learned Hand could explain the antitrust laws in social terms: The Act has wider purposes. Indeed, even though we disregard all but economic considerations, it would by no means follow that such concentration of producing

2. Treaty of Rome, Arts. 81–89, Mar. 25, 1957.
3. Sherman Act § 1, 26 Stat. 209, 15 U.S.C. § 1 (1890).
4. Sherman Act § 2, 26 Stat. 209, 15 U.S.C. § 2 (1890).
5. *Ibid.*

> power is to be desired, when it has not been used extortionately. Many people believe that possession of unchallenged economic power deadens initiative, discourages thrift and depresses energy; that immunity from competition is a narcotic, and rivalry is a stimulant, to industrial progress; that the spur of constant stress is necessary to counteract an inevitable disposition to let well enough alone. Such people believe that competitors, versed in the craft as no consumer can be, will be quick to detect opportunities for saving and new shifts in production, and be eager to profit by them. ...[Congress] did not condone "good trusts" and condemn "bad" ones; it forbad all. Moreover, in so doing it was not necessarily actuated by economic motives alone. It is possible, because of its indirect social or moral effect, to prefer a system of small producers, each dependent for his success upon his own skill and character, to one in which the great mass of those engaged must accept the direction of a few. These considerations, which we have suggested only as possible purposes of the Act, we think the decisions prove to have been in fact its purposes.[6]

And as late as 1972, Justice Marshall wrote in the *Topco* decision that the:

> Antitrust laws in general, and the Sherman Act in particular, are the Magna Carta of free-enterprise. They are as important to the preservation of economic freedom and our free-enterprise system as the Bill of Rights is to the protection of our fundamental personal freedoms. And the freedom guaranteed each and every business, no matter how small, is the freedom to compete.[7]

7. It is as a result of this heritage that the United States, almost entirely alone among Western nations, has jailed price fixers and continues to do so. Unlike in Europe, economic efficiency could never fully explain the passion that still lingers in criminal enforcement of the American antitrust laws. All this remains foreign to Europeans and others.

8. Economic analysis, in a particular form arising from Chicago School economics, came to dominate the construction of the American antitrust laws beginning in the 1970s. It continues to dominate analysis to the present day. Only with the most recent economic crisis, brought on by financial firms and insurance firms that were "too big to fail," has reexamination begun. Hopefully, the reappraisal will take into account developments such as behavioral economics, short-term and long-term incentives created by executive compensation, and other complexities of antitrust policy and economics, such as the case for a socially dynamic society, sloughed over in the past by a judiciary of limited economic expertise often seduced by the elegant simplicities of Chicago School economics.

9. The ensuing chapters summarize the complex array of doctrines that have emerged in the 130 years since the passage of the first American antitrust law.

---

6. *United States v. Aluminum Co. of Am.*, 148 F.2d 416, 427 (2d Cir. 1945).
7. *United States v. Topco Associates, Inc.*, 405 U.S. 596, 610, 92 S. Ct. 1126, 1135, 31 L. Ed. 2d 515 (1972).

§2. THE AMERICAN LEGAL SYSTEM

10. The federal government of the US is divided into executive, legislative and judicial branches. This is pertinent to the antitrust laws because the legislature, Congress, passed the acts that have spawned American antitrust law; two agencies of the executive – the Antitrust Division of the Department of Justice (DOJ) and the FTC – have responsibility for bringing enforcement actions; and the judiciary is responsible for ultimate interpretation and enforcement. Because the United States is a common law jurisdiction in which judicial decisions establish binding precedent and the legislature has intentionally left the antitrust statutes vague to allow for ongoing judicial interpretation, the major body of American antitrust law is founded upon judicial construction.

11. The federal judiciary is composed of the nine-member Supreme Court, thirteen circuit courts of appeal that serve as intermediate appellate courts, and district courts in every state that serve as the primary trial courts. All judges are appointed for life by the president and are confirmed by the Senate.[8]

12. On the federal judicial system's first rung are its district courts, which serve as the trial courts for both criminal and civil cases arising under *federal* law. This is an important concept to grasp because a far wider variety of cases arise under state law, including most criminal violations and almost all tort cases. However, federal courts have diversity jurisdiction, which enables them to hear many cases over which they would not otherwise have jurisdiction. A federal court has diversity jurisdiction in cases arising between citizens of different states involving sums above USD 75,000.[9] The diversity statute is quite technical in defining citizenship of corporations for purposes of the statute. As a result of diversity jurisdiction, a significant portion of very large commercial litigation is undertaken in federal court.

13. The federal antitrust laws grant exclusive jurisdiction to the federal courts to hear cases arising under those statutes.[10] All federal antitrust cases initiated by private plaintiffs begin in the district courts.

14. There is a broad right to jury trials in the federal court system, so major commercial cases, including antitrust cases, are generally heard by juries of laymen in the rare instances when they actually proceed to trial. Virtually all cases in which the plaintiff seeks monetary damages are heard by juries. Cases in which solely injunctive relief is sought – such as efforts to enjoin mergers – are heard by judges.

15. Cases in federal courts are governed procedurally by the Federal Rules of Civil Procedure. As a practical matter, the courts resolve most major antitrust cases after motion practice, based on a series of procedural devices. The cases that survive such motion practice are usually resolved through settlement by the parties. Those unresolved proceed to trial.

---

8. Parallel systems exist in each state: each has a similar three-part structure, but with a governor, instead of the president, at the helm of the executive branch. The legislative structures in the different states vary, as do the judicial branches. In contrast with the federal system, many states' judges are elected. There is considerable controversy about whether appointment or election is the better method of judicial selection.
9. 28 U.S.C. § 1332.
10. 15 U.S.C. § 4.

16. Cases begin with the filing of a complaint. Recently, the Supreme Court has raised the pleading requirement for initiating a lawsuit. American law requires notice pleading rather than fact pleading. A typical complaint traditionally contains very sparse factual averments. However, the Supreme Court, in a highly controversial decision, recently held that "we do not require heightened fact pleading of specifics, but only enough facts to state a claim to relief that is plausible on its face."[11] The language "plausible on its face" and other language in the opinion abolished a long-standing rule that a complaint "should not be dismissed for failure to state a claim unless it appears beyond doubt that the plaintiff can prove no set of facts in support of his or her claim which would entitle him or her to relief."[12] By rejecting the "no set of facts" standard, the Court has significantly changed civil practice. One result has been immense confusion and inconsistency in the district courts' rulings on the adequacy of pleadings.

17. The adequacy of the pleading to allege a cause of action is tested at an early stage by a motion to dismiss. The court judges the pleading based solely on the allegations in the complaint without reference to external material and must assume the facts alleged to be true. The case proceeds if the court decides that the matters alleged in the complaint, if proven, would state a cause of action.

18. In the US, in contrast to civil law jurisdictions and most common law jurisdictions, there are broad "discovery" rights. Discovery serves an investigatory role and usually constitutes the primary effort in American litigation. Discovery in a major antitrust case can proceed for a period of years, during which parties obtain both paper and electronic files of their adversaries, pose written questions in the form of interrogatories, and take oral sworn testimony of witnesses outside the courtroom in the form of depositions. It was, in large part, a concern with the cost and burden of this investigatory process that led the Supreme Court to impose a more rigorous standard for the initial pleading.[13]

19. At the conclusion of discovery, a party may file a motion for summary judgment. In contrast to a motion to dismiss, a motion for summary judgment allows the court to review evidence to determine whether it is sufficient to state a cause of action. The court may not weigh the evidence or make credibility determinations, but must determine whether evidence exists which, if credited by a jury, would meet all the elements of the cause of action. Summary judgment in antitrust cases has been a subject of much controversy, especially since the Supreme Court's decision in *Matsushita*. There, the Court held that:

> To survive a motion for summary judgment or for a directed verdict, a plaintiff seeking damages for a violation of § 1 must present evidence "that tends to exclude the possibility" that the alleged conspirators acted independently. … Respondents in this case, in other words, must show that the inference of conspiracy

11. *Bell Atl. Corp. v. Twombly*, 550 U.S. 544, 570, 127 S. Ct. 1955, 1974, 167 L. Ed. 2d 929 (2007).
12. *Conley v. Gibson*, 355 U.S. 41, 45–46 (1957).
13. *Bell Atl. Corp. v. Twombly*, 550 U.S. 544 (2007).

> is reasonable in light of the competing inferences of independent action or collusive action that could not have harmed respondents.[14]

Determining what constitutes such evidence has led to an immense body of case law.

20. Judgments entered by a district court – whether upon summary judgment or a verdict by a jury – are reviewed by a circuit court of appeals. The country is divided into eleven circuits by geography. There are also two more specialized appellate circuits, the US Court of Appeals for the Federal Circuit and the District of Columbia Circuit. The eleven circuits hear appeals of all cases arising in the district courts within the geographic areas covered by the circuits with very limited exception. Patent, trademark and other intellectual property cases are heard by the Federal Circuit regardless of the district court in which they arise. A party has a right to appeal all final judgments of a district court. The circuit courts of appeal usually sit in panels of three judges.

21. In contrast to the circuit courts of appeal, the US Supreme Court has a docket that is discretionary with very limited exceptions. The Supreme Court is composed of nine judges who always sit en banc. A petitioner starts by filing a petition for a writ of certiorari, which is a request that the Supreme Court hear the appeal. In recent years, the Court has granted fewer than 1% of such petitions. The most common reason the Supreme Court grants review is to resolve conflicts between decisions of different circuit courts of appeal to assure harmony in the interpretation of the nation's laws. Such conflicts are common, and it is considered a virtue of the system that the Supreme Court has the benefit of the views of various circuit courts of appeal and the records of different trial courts before it grants a petition for review of a particular question. As a result, the Court will usually wait until more than two circuit courts of appeal have provided disparate views on a question before it will grant a writ of certiorari to review that question.

22. Because the US is a common law jurisdiction, decisions of the Supreme Court establish binding precedent in all subsequent cases. Similarly, decisions of the circuit courts of appeal are binding on subsequent cases within the geographic jurisdiction of the circuit unless overruled by the Supreme Court and are generally viewed as important authority by other circuits even though they are not technically bound by their authority. Because of the sparseness of the antitrust statutes, development of American antitrust law has occurred almost exclusively within the judiciary. Early on, legislators expressed concern about the discretion the courts had in interpreting the antitrust laws. In more recent years, the flexibility provided by ongoing judicial construction of the laws has been viewed by some as a strength rather than a weakness, though this view should be viewed with some skepticism in light of the Court's lack of legislative expertise.

---

14. *Matsushita Elec. Indus. Co., Ltd. v. Zenith Radio Corp.*, 475 U.S. 574, 588, 106 S. Ct. 1348, 1356–1357, 89 L. Ed. 2d 538 (1986).

Part I. The Structure of American Antitrust Law and Its Enforcement

Chapter 1. Sources of American Antitrust Law

§1. National Sources

I. Federal Antitrust Laws

23. The primary statutory sources of antitrust law in the US are sections 1 and 2 of the Sherman Antitrust Act, passed in 1890, and the Clayton Act, which was originally passed in 1914 but was considerably amended subsequently. Of greater importance, however, is the vast body of judicial decisions interpreting the statutes and establishing an effective "common law" in the area.

24. Sections 1 and 2 of the Sherman Act are venerated in the US in a way that foreign attorneys find difficult to grasp. The Sherman Act is taught in American secondary schools. The National Archives, which holds the records of the federal government, even included the Sherman Act in the list of the 100 most important documents in American history.[15]

25. When the Sherman Act was passed, there was initially some question as to whether it created new law or merely codified an extensive body of common law in the area of monopolies and trade regulation. It is now clear that the act represented a radical departure from prior law:

(1) It has criminal sanctions, unlike any previous sanction for conspiring in restraint of trade or monopolizing.
(2) It provided a private cause of action for damages, unlike prior law, which generally provided solely injunctive relief.
(3) It included a treble damage remedy rather than merely damages arising from the injury itself.

26. The Sherman Act provisions are of sufficient importance, and sufficiently brief, to warrant quoting them:

15. *See* , <www.ourdocuments.gov/content.php?flash=true&page=milestone>.

> §1. Every contract, combination in the form of trust or otherwise, or conspiracy, in restraint of trade or commerce among the several States, or with foreign nations, is declared to be illegal. Every person who shall make any contract or engage in any combination or conspiracy hereby declared to be illegal shall be deemed guilty of a felony, and, on conviction thereof, shall be punished by fine not exceeding $100,000,000 if a corporation, or, if any other person, $1,000,000, or by imprisonment not exceeding 10 years, or by both said punishments, in the discretion of the court.[16]

> §2. Every person who shall monopolize, or attempt to monopolize, or combine or conspire with any other person or persons, to monopolize any part of the trade or commerce among the several States, or with foreign nations, shall be deemed guilty of a felony, and, on conviction thereof, shall be punished by [the same remedies as for violations of § 1].[17]

27. The second major statutory source of antitrust law is the Clayton Antitrust Act, which was first passed in 1914. It contains important provisions intended to clarify the scope of prohibited conduct, such as tying, interlocking directorates, and exclusive dealing. However, the Act includes a proviso that severely circumscribes its effectiveness by prohibiting such activities only where their effect "may be substantially to lessen competition, or to tend to create a monopoly."[18] The Act was subsequently amended substantively by the Robinson-Patman Act, which provided a detailed, but ultimately ineffective, statutory scheme governing price discrimination.

28. The most important provision of the Clayton Act is section 7, which governs mergers, and which now includes the technical rules governing merger reporting and enforcement.[19]

29. The FTC Act, also passed in 1914, created a major federal agency with considerable authority to enforce a prohibition on "unfair methods of competition"[20] and the antitrust laws. The FTC's Bureau of Competition enforces the antitrust laws through administrative proceedings and lawsuits in federal court. While the FTC may conduct elaborate administrative proceedings, it must petition courts to enforce its orders. Despite the broad language of the FTC Act, which courts have acknowledged,[21]

16. 15 U.S.C. § 1.
17. 15 U.S.C. § 2.
18. 15 U.S.C. § 18.
19. *Ibid.*
20. 15 U.S.C. § 45.
21. *FTC v. Sperry & Hutchinson Co.*, 405 U.S. 233, 244 (1972) ("Legislative and judicial authorities alike convince us that the Federal Trade Commission does not arrogate excessive power to itself if, in measuring a practice against the elusive, but congressionally mandated standard of fairness, it, like a court of equity, considers public values beyond simply those enshrined in the letter or encompassed in the spirit of the antitrust laws.").

in practice, courts have held the statute to provide little authority beyond that provided by the Sherman Act.[22]

30. A variety of statutes provide exemptions from the antitrust laws, such as the McCarran-Ferguson Act exempting the business of insurance,[23] the Capper-Volstead Act exempting agricultural cooperatives,[24] the Webb-Pomerene Act relating to foreign trading associations,[25] and several other technical statutes applying to particular industries.

II. State Antitrust Laws

31. In addition to the federal antitrust laws, distinct bodies of antitrust law have been promulgated by individual states. The complex relationship between state and federal antitrust laws is beyond the scope of this treatise. Many states have held that their substantive antitrust laws govern solely intrastate activity and that federal antitrust law governs interstate activity. However, there are important distinct state antitrust acts – particularly the Cartwright Act in California – which have given rise to extensive litigation. Certain major issues that arise as a result of distinctions between federal and state antitrust law are discussed in the course of this treatise.[26]

§2. International Sources

32. There are no international sources of American antitrust law. However, there is a procedural statute, the International Antitrust Enforcement Assistance Act of 1994,[27] and an Agreement Between the Government of the United States and the European Communities on the Application of Positive Comity Principles in the Enforcement of their Antitrust Laws[28] that are both intended to facilitate cooperation between American and foreign antitrust authorities.

22. *Official Airlines Guides v. FTC*, 630 F.2d 920 (2d Cir. 1980); *Boise Cascade Corp. v. FTC*, 637 F.2d 573 (9th Cir. 1980); *Ethyl Corp. v. FTC*, 729 F.2d 128 (2d Cir. 1984).
23. 15 U.S.C. §§ 1011–1015.
24. 7 U.S.C. §§ 291, 292.
25. 15 U.S.C. §§ 61–65.
26. For a recent discussion of this interplay *see*, *Sullivan v. DB Investments, Inc.*, 667 F.3d 273 (3d Cir. 2011).
27. 15 U.S.C. §§ 6201 et seq.
28. U.S. Department of Justice and Federal Trade Commission, "Agreement Between the Government of the United States and the European Communities on the Application of Positive Comity in the Enforcement of their Antitrust Laws," Jun. 4, 1998, *available at* <www.justice.gov/atr/public/international/docs/1781.pdf>.

§3. Secondary Sources

I. Regulations and Guidelines

33. Aside from the regulations governing procedure in administrative actions before the FTC, the most important secondary source of American antitrust laws is the Horizontal Merger Guidelines promulgated by the US DOJ and the FTC. These guidelines explain the federal agencies approach to merger enforcement and are discussed in detail in the merger section below.

§4. Sources' Relation and Hierarchy

34. This is not a concept pertinent to American antitrust law.

§5. Role and Authority of Precedents

35. The US is a common law jurisdiction, and judicial decisions are the most complete and dynamic source of American antitrust law. As discussed above, there are few antitrust statutes and they were left intentionally vague to allow courts flexibility in dealing with challenges arising from the marketplace.

36. Decisions of district courts are binding solely upon the parties, and only have precedential effect to the extent they prove persuasive. Decisions of the circuit courts of appeal are binding on all district courts and appeals within their circuits, but not outside their circuits. However, even outside their circuits, circuit court decisions carry significant persuasive authority.

37. Supreme Court decisions are binding on all courts. To an overwhelming extent, the antitrust laws of the US are defined by the body of Supreme Court decisions that interpret the antitrust statutes.

38. Within state court systems, a similar hierarchy exists, extending from the trial court to the highest appellate courts. The particular nomenclature often differs. For example, in New York, the trial court of general jurisdiction is known as the Supreme Court while the highest court is known as the Court of Appeals.

39. This common law system of binding precedent created by appellate courts has led to a complicated development of American antitrust laws in which courts have acted in what would seem a quasi-legislative capacity in establishing and changing basic tenets of antitrust law. For example, resale price maintenance conspiracies were held to be violations per se, of the Sherman Act in *Dr. Miles Med. Co. v. John D. Park & Sons Co.*[29] Almost a hundred years later in *Leegin Creative Leather Products, Inc. v. PSKS, Inc.*,[30] the Court overruled *Dr. Miles* and held that resale price maintenance was not illegal per se and was to be governed by the rule of reason. Similarly, price-squeeze allegations were held to be basic evidence of monopolization in *United States*

29. 220 U.S. 373, 31 S. Ct. 376, 55 L. Ed. 502 (1911).
30. 551 U.S. 877, 127 S. Ct. 2705, 168 L. Ed. 2d 623 (2007).

v. Aluminum Co. of Am.,[31] perhaps the leading monopolization decision under American antitrust law, but the Supreme Court seemed to cast such evidence aside in *Pac. Bell Tel. Co. v. Linkline Communications, Inc.*[32]

31. 148 F.2d 416 (2d Cir. 1945).
32. 555 U.S. 438, 452, 129 S. Ct. 1109, 1120, 172 L. Ed. 2d 836 (2009).

§1. Territorial Reach

40. The American antitrust laws reach any behavior, wherever in the world undertaken, so long as it has a significant effect in American commerce. The territorial reach of the antitrust laws of the US was circumscribed by the Foreign Trade Antitrust Improvements Act (FTAIA) of 1982, which excludes from the Sherman Act's reach anticompetitive conduct that causes injury only outside of the US. It states a general rule that the Sherman Act "shall not apply to conduct involving trade or commerce... with foreign nations."[33] But it creates vast exceptions to the general rule applicable for imports and where conduct significantly harms domestic commerce or exporters. Thus, the Act will reach antitrust violations occurring anywhere in the world that would violate American antitrust law so long as they significantly harm American commerce. As Justice Breyer explained in the Supreme Court decision construing the act:

> The issue before us concerns (1) significant foreign anticompetitive conduct with (2) an adverse domestic effect and (3) an independent foreign effect giving rise to the claim. In more concrete terms, this case involves vitamin sellers around the world that agreed to fix prices, leading to higher vitamin prices in the US and independently leading to higher vitamin prices in other countries such as Ecuador. We conclude that, in this scenario, a purchaser in the US could bring a Sherman Act claim under the FTAIA based on domestic injury, but a purchaser in Ecuador could not bring a Sherman Act claim based on foreign harm.[34]

Any conduct, anywhere in the world, undertaken in violation of the American antitrust laws that has an effect upon American commerce will fall within the reach of those laws.

§2. Special Sectors

41. There are numerous special sectors that are insulated from antitrust claims. These arise from a variety of sources, such as statutory exemptions for particular sectors of the economy; judicial doctrines that insulate particular forms of conduct, such as government petitioning activity;[35] and judicial doctrines that effectively insulate certain regulated areas of the economy.[36] Knowledge of the exemptions is crucial, since they allow conduct that might otherwise be the most egregious of antitrust violations.

33. 96 Stat. 1246, 15U.S.C. § 6a.
34. *F. Hoffmann-La Roche Ltd. v. Epigram S.A.*, 542 U.S. 155, 159; 124 S.Ct. 2359, 2363 (2004).
35. *See, e.g., United Mine Workers v. Pennington*, 381 U.S. 657 (1965).
36. *See, e.g., Cal. Liquor Dealers v. Midcal Aluminum, Inc.*, 445 U.S. 97 (1980).

However, there is no systematic statutory scheme listing the exemptions or, in many cases, even providing assurance that particular conduct is exempt.

42. Some sectors are immune as a result of a statute. For example, the McCarran-Ferguson Act provides an exemption for most activities relating to the business of insurance.[37] The Capper-Volstead Act provides an exemption for agricultural cooperatives.[38] The Export Trading Company Act of 1982 and the Webb-Pomerene Act both provide exemptions for organizations engaged solely in export trade that meet certain requirements.[39] Certain sports leagues' negotiations related to television contracts are exempt.[40] Though the limited scope of this exemption has been recognized in recent decisions.[41]

43. Judicial doctrines immunize other sectors. Federal and state rate regulation confers immunity where rates are actually filed and reviewed by a government agency.[42] Organized labor – the target of early antitrust lawsuits – is generally exempted by a combination of statutes and judicial decisions.[43] Pervasive government regulation in an area, such as Securities and Exchange Commission regulation of securities, can result in pre-emption of antitrust law.[44] Other sectors are discussed in the succeeding sections.

44. The complex system of both state and federal law can create a situation where state law may authorize or require conduct that would seemingly violate federal antitrust law. Depending on the degree of regulation, state regulation of an industry or a sector may confer immunity. A series of less-than-clear Supreme Court cases provides the basis for determining whether there is immunity. The Court has established a two-part test to determine whether action by a state exempts conduct from federal antitrust law:

(1) Is the restraint on competition "clearly articulated and affirmatively expressed as state policy?"
(2) Is the policy "actively supervised" by the state?[45]

---

37. 15 U.S.C. §§ 1011–1015.
38. 7 U.S.C. §§ 291, 292.
39. 15 U.S.C. §§ 4001–4021;15 U.S.C. §§ 61–65; *see, Int'l Raw Materials, Ltd. v. Stauffer Chem. Co.*, 978 F.2d 1318 (3d Cir. 1992).
40. Sports Broadcasting Act of 1961, 15 U.S.C. §§ 1291–1295.
41. *Laumann v. Nat'l Hockey League*, 907 F. Supp. 2d 465, 489 (S.D.N.Y. 2012) ("the term 'sponsored telecasting' under the SBA pertains only to network broadcast television and does not apply to non-exempt channels of distribution such as cable television, pay-per-view, and satellite television networks.") Quoting *Kingray, Inc. v. NBA, Inc.*, 188 F.Supp.2d 1177, 1183 (S.D.Cal.2002)).
42. *See, California Retail Liquors Association v. Midcal Aluminum Inc.*, 445 U. S. 97, 105 (1980).
43. The statutes include 15 U.S.C. § 17, 29 U.S.C.§ 52, and 29 U.S.C. § 104–105. The judicial decisions include *Meat Cutters v. Jewel Tea*, 381 U.S. 676 (1965); *Connell Constr. Co. v. Plumbers*, 421 U.S. 616 (1975); *Brown v. Pro Football*, 518 U.S. 231 (1996); and *United Mine Workers v. Pennington*, 381 U.S. 657 (1965).
44. *See, e.g., Silver v. N.Y. Stock Exchange*, 373 U.S. 341 (1963).
45. *California Retail Liquors Association v. Midcal Aluminum Inc.*, 445 U. S. 97, 105 (1980).

An example of such a regulation would be a utility rate actually reviewed and approved by a state public utility commission. Other circumstances are less clear. For example, in *Midcal*, a state statute required distributors to post certain prices for liquor and prohibited sales below the posted prices, effectively establishing price maintenance of liquor. But the state did not "actively supervise"[46] the scheme: it did not establish the prices or review the reasonableness of the price schedules, but left the posting of prices entirely to private parties. The Court found that this scheme did not confer immunity. The issue of what constitutes "a clearly articulated and affirmatively expressed state policy"[47] has been construed so that a state's authorization, but not compulsion, of the conduct has been held to satisfy the condition.[48] Two recent Supreme Court decisions have stressed need for both a genuine clearly articulated and affirmatively expressed state policy to displace competition – rather than mere state involvement,[49] as well the need for genuine active supervision.[50] Succeeding sections discuss the effects of these doctrines on state-owned enterprises and public utilities.

45. Another major area exempt from the antitrust laws is government petitioning. Collectively known as the *Noerr-Pennington* doctrine,[51] these decisions exempt attempts to obtain executive, legislative or judicial action. The doctrine does not exempt "sham" activity, but that term is read narrowly to mean petitioning activity not undertaken to achieve its purported goal but for an ulterior purpose. For example, a company that systematically filed oppositions to competitors' rate filings knowing that it lacked standing to do so or knowing that it lacked any basis for its opposition, but which did so simply to delay implementation of the rates or to impose costs on its competitors, would be considered to be engaging in sham petitioning.[52] By definition, a successful effort to obtain government action cannot be sham. This is true even if it was motivated solely by a desire to harm a competitor.[53] The Supreme Court has gone so far as to hold that where legislative action resulted from bribery, the bribery and attendant legislative action cannot give rise to an antitrust claim.[54] The Court will not second guess under the antitrust laws conduct leading to legislative action even if the conduct gives rise to criminal liability under some other statute.[55]

46. The concept of sham litigation has been much litigated. A sham lawsuit is one that is both objectively baseless and brought for the purpose of injuring competition.[56] The defendant must prove that a suit is objectively baseless before it can reach the

46. *Ibid.*
47. *Ibid.*
48. *Southern Rate Conf. v. United States*, 471 U.S. 48 (1985).
49. *F.T.C. v. Phoebe Putney Health Sys., Inc.*, 133 S. Ct. 1003(2013).
50. *N. Carolina State Bd. of Dental Examiners v. F.T.C.*, 135 S. Ct. 1101 (2015).
51. *See, United Mine Workers v. Pennington*, 381 U.S. 657 (1965); *Eastern Railroad Presidents Conference v. Noerr Motor Freight, Inc.*, 365 U.S. 127 (1961).
52. *See, California Motor Transport Co, v. Trucking Unlimited*, 404 U.S. 508 (1972); *MCI Communications Corp. v. AT&T Co.*, 708 F.2d 1081 (7th Cir. 1983), *cert. denied* 464 U.S. 891 (1983).
53. *Professional Real Estate Investors v. Columbia Pictures, Inc.*, 508 U.S. 49 (1993).
54. *City of Columbia v. Omni Outdoor Advertising, Inc.*, 499 U.S. 365, 377 (1991).
55. *Ibid.*
56. *See, Prof'l Real Estate Investors, Inc. v. Columbia Pictures Indus., Inc.*, 508 U.S. 49, 113 S. Ct. 1920, 123 L. Ed. 2d 611 (1993).

question of whether it was brought to injure competition. A successful lawsuit is by definition not a sham. Some questions remain as to the standard for evaluating a series of lawsuits that are brought for the purpose of injuring a competitor.

§3. State-Owned Enterprises and Public Utilities

47. Public utilities and certain government-owned enterprises may be subject to the antitrust laws while, as a result of doctrines deferring to regulatory and government review, much of their activity will be exempted. Thus, for example, the telephone monopoly of American Telephone & Telegraph Company (AT&T) was broken up as a result of a government antitrust action – and was subject to several private antitrust suits – even though both federal and state regulators extensively regulated the company.[57] Similarly, a major, extensively regulated, electrical utility was held liable under the antitrust laws for refusing to transfer electricity across its system.[58] Government-approved rates cannot form the basis of an antitrust claim. Even when courts analyze activity that is subject to some level of regulation from a non-regulatory perspective, they have been highly deferential to the regulatory schemes in question and reluctant to allow suits to proceed. A recent series of Supreme Court cases used this approach for cases involving utilities.[59]

48. Saying that an enterprise is state-owned can mean several things within the American federal system. An enterprise may be owned by the federal government, a federally created agency, a state, a state created agency, a city or municipality, or an agency created by a municipality. The distinction in ownership can be important. Direct action by a state is generally immune, but actions by a state authorizing activity by private parties or sub-agencies, such as hospital board or municipality are subject to a stricter test. Where the action is authorized by the state but carried out by private parties or other entities, a two-part test is applied. "The challenged restraint [must]... be one clearly articulated and affirmatively expressed as state policy and the policy must be actively supervised by the state."[60]

In *F.T.C. v. Phoebe Putney Health System, Inc,*[61] the Court emphasized that the "clear articulation test" required more than simple state authorization to participate in a market, it required that the anticompetitive effects of the state's grant be "clearly foreseeable." There, the Court held that the mere fact that the state had created an agency authorized to own and acquire hospitals, did not confer immunity where the acquisition would have created a monopoly. "When a State grants some entity general

57. *See, United States v. AT&T*, 524 F.Supp. 1336 (D. DC. 1981); *United States v. AT & T*, 552 F. Supp. 131 (D. DC. 1982); *MCI Communications Corp. v. AT&T Co.*, 708 F.2d 1081 (7th Cir. 1983), *cert. denied* 464 U.S. 891 (1983).

58. *Otter Tail Power Co. v. United States*, 410 U.S. 366, 381–382 (1973).

59. *Verizon Communications Inc. v. Law Offices of Curtis V. Trinko, LLP*, 540 U.S. 398 (U.S. 2004); *Pacific Bell Telephone Co. v. Linkline Communications, Inc.*, 129 S.Ct. 1109 (U.S. 2009); *see also Town of Concord, Mass. v. Boston Edison Co.*, 915 F.2d 17 (1st Cir. 1990).

60. *California Retail Liquor Dealers Association v. Midcal Aluminum, Inc.*, 445 U.S. 97, 105 (1980).

61. __U.S.__, 133 S.Ct. 1003 (2013).

power to act, whether it is a private corporation or a public entity like the Authority, it does so against the backdrop of federal antitrust law." And "'simple permission to play in a market' does not 'foreseeably entail permission to roughhouse in that market unlawfully.'"[62]

Similarly, in *N. Carolina State Bd. of Dental Examiners v. F.T.C.*, 135 S. Ct. 1101 (2015) the Court required that there be genuine, active state supervision, especially where the alleged regulating entity established by the state is composed of competitors active in an industry. There, a state board of dental examiners' principal duty is to create, administer, and enforce a licensing system for dentists. To perform that function it has broad authority over licensees. The Board's authority with respect to unlicensed persons, however, is more restricted: like 'any resident citizen,' the Board may file suit to 'perpetually enjoin any person from ... unlawfully practicing dentistry.'"The Board sought to eliminate entities performing teeth whitening services by sending the cease and desist letters. The Court explained that the board did not claim that the state exercised active, or indeed any, supervision over its conduct regarding non-dentist teeth whiteners. There was no supervision at all. The Court explained, It suffices to note that the inquiry regarding active supervision is flexible and context-dependent. Active supervision need not entail day-to-day involvement in an agency's operations or micromanagement of its every decision. Rather, the question is whether the State's review mechanisms provide 'realistic assurance' that a non-sovereign actor's anticompetitive conduct 'promotes state policy, rather than merely the party's individual interests.'"[63]

49. Municipalities, unlike states, are partially insulated from antitrust damages – but not injunctive actions – by the Local Government Antitrust Act of 1984.[64] Thus, as *Phoebe Putney* recognized, *Midcal* is applied in a modified form to activities by municipal-owned enterprises. On the one hand, a "clearly articulated state policy," generally a state statute, must exist authorizing the municipality's activity and at least contemplating the alleged restrictive activity under the foreseeability test. The state legislative scheme must expressly specify an intent to displace competition with regulation, but, as long as the restrictive activity is reasonably encompassed by the legislative scheme, the scheme need not specify the restrictive activity itself. Thus, for example, in *Town of Hallie v. City of Eau Claire*, a statute authorizing a city to provide sewage services and to determine the areas to receive these services was considered sufficient to insulate municipalities from suit by other municipalities claiming that the refusal to connect them to a new sewage treatment facility violated the antitrust laws.[65]

50. In *City of Columbia v. Omni Outdoor Adver., Inc.*, the Supreme Court held that even where a competitor may have bribed municipal officials to obtain favorable zoning ordinances limiting competing billboard companies from entering the market, the conduct was insulated from an antitrust claim.[66] Zoning ordinances, the Court explained, clearly entailed restriction of commercial activity and were necessarily

62. *Ibid.*, at 1013 quoting *Kay Elec. Cooperative v. Newkirk*, 647 F.3d 1039, 1043 (10th Cir. 2011).

63. 135 S. Ct. at 1116.

64. 15 U.S.C. §§ 34–36.

65. 471 U.S. 34, 47 (1985).

66. 499 U.S. 365, 367, 111 S. Ct. 1344, 1347, 113 L. Ed. 2d 382 (U.S. 1991).

immune under *Hallie*. The Court would not allow a federal court to review legislative acts – even those of a municipal body – under the antitrust laws.[67]

§4. Sensible Effect and De Minimis Effects

51. There are no concepts under American antitrust law directly analogous to sensible effects and *de minimis* as the terms are used in EU law, but there are concepts that deal with similar issues. For example, a violation under American law must effect competition rather than just competitors.[68] Eliminating a single competitor in a diffuse market may have no discernible effect on competition. Similarly, just replacing one distributor with another may only have an effect on the displaced competitor rather than on competition. Such circumstances provide no cause of action under federal antitrust law. While certain state franchise laws accord very strong protections in such circumstances[69] that is not a subject for this treatise.

52. The federal antitrust laws only reach interstate and foreign commerce. At one time, particularly in the early twentieth century, this limitation imposed considerable restrictions on the reach of federal antitrust laws. During the New Deal era of the 1930s, the Supreme Court greatly expanded the reach of federal law under the Commerce Clause of the Constitution[70] by giving an expansive definition to interstate commerce. However, similar provisions under the antitrust laws were not read quite as expansively.[71] Some judicial decisions have held that where all the anticompetitive acts and their effects occur solely within a single state, the interstate commerce requirement is not met.[72] However, it is rare for anticompetitive actions and effects to occur within a single state in an economy as integrated as that of the US.[73]

---

67. *Ibid.*
68. *Brown Shoe Co., Inc. v. United States*, 370 U.S. 294,320 (1962).
69. *See, e.g.*, New Jersey Franchise Practices Act, N.J.S.A. 56:10-1 et. seq.; *Beilowitz v. Gen. Motors Corp.*, 233 F. Supp. 2d 631 (D.N.J. 2002).
70. Art. I, s. 8, Cl. 3.
71. *Gulf Oil Corp. v. Copp Paving Co.*, 419 U. S. 186, 197, n. 12 (1974) ("The jurisdictional inquiry under general prohibitions like…§ 1 of the Sherman Act, turning as it does on the circumstances presented in each case and requiring a particularized judicial determination, differs significantly from that required when Congress itself has defined the specific persons and activities that affect commerce and therefore require federal regulation.").
72. *See, e.g., United States v. Yellow Cab Co.*, 332 U.S. 218 (1947).
73. *See, e.g., Cardio-Medical Assoc., Ltd. v. Crozer-Chester Medical Center*, 721 F.2d 68, 76 (3d Cir. 1983) (holding that plaintiffs had adequately alleged an effect on interstate commerce in alleging that a local cardiological services provider had interfered "with the interstate travel of patients, the interstate payment of fees, and the interstate purchase of medication are well-recognized methods for demonstrating an effect on interstate commerce in antitrust litigation."); *Anesthesia Advantage, Inc. v. Metz Group*, 912 F.2d 397, 401–404 (10th Cir. 1990) (refusing to dismiss a lawsuit even when plaintiffs only alleged some general effects on interstate commerce, such as interstate shipment of supplies and movement of patients, because "a plaintiff need not establish that the flow of interstate commerce is actually *diminished*; it is sufficient to show that such commerce is affected in more than a *de minimis* way.").

Chapter 3. Overview of Substantive Provisions

§1. Restrictive Agreements

53. Restrictive agreements are governed by section 1 of the Sherman Act, which prohibits "every contract, combination ... or conspiracy, in restraint of trade." Certain restraints are deemed so clearly anticompetitive that they are considered illegal per se. The courts will not entertain an argument that a circumstance could exist in which such a restraint was reasonable. These restraints include horizontal restraints among competitors such as price-fixing,[74] restrictions on output,[75] geographic division of markets,[76] or allocation of customers.[77] When a per se violation has occurred, say price-fixing, the court will not inquire into its economic justification or effect on the market. Thus, if two competing gasoline stations in a city agree upon the price they charged for gasoline, they are subject to a criminal sanction even if they are just two of one hundred gasoline stations in the city and their agreement has no real power to affect prices. Of course, in a civil damage suit a plaintiff would still have to prove it was damaged by their conduct, which might prove difficult in this example.

54. Other restrictive agreements are governed by what is known as the rule of reason. Under the rule of reason, a court will weigh the competitive harm arising from the agreement against the economic justifications for it. Courts apply the rule of reason to such agreements as exclusive dealing arrangements,[78] vertical price-fixing,[79] allocation by manufacturers of distributors' markets,[80] and a wide variety of restrictive agreements among competitors not touching directly upon price. Where the rule of reason is applied, various justifications can be offered, and are often found persuasive by the courts. Thus, for example, a computer manufacturer can justify creating exclusive geographic territories for its distributors by arguing that doing so prevents a high volume internet discounter from invading a territory in which a distributor has expended large sums on advertising and retail showrooms to build market share and maintain service for the computers. Such a discounter would be "free riding" upon the efforts of the distributor if it were allowed to invade the distributor's territory. A court might consider the relative market shares of participants and the interbrand competition (between the manufacturer's distributors and others) that exists in weighing the economic justifications for restrictions on intrabrand competition (between the manufacturer's distributors themselves).

---

74. *United States v. Socony-Vacuum Oil Co.*, 310 U.S. 150 (1940).
75. *In re Linerboard Antitrust Litig.*, 305 F.3d 145 (3d Cir. 2002).
76. *United States v. Topco Associates*, 405 U.S. 596 (1972).
77. *Palmer v. BRG of Georgia, Inc.*, 498 U.S. 46 (1990).
78. *See, e.g., Tampa Elec. Co. v. Nashville Coal Co.*, 365 U.S. 320, 81 S.Ct. 623, 5 L.Ed. 2d 580 (1961).
79. *Leegin Creative Leather Products, Inc. v. PSKS, Inc.*, 551 U.S. 877, 127 S. Ct. 2705, 168 L. Ed. 2d 623 (2007).
80. *Continental TV, Inc. v. GTE Sylvania Inc.*, 433 U.S. 36, 97 S.Ct. 2549, 53 L.Ed.2d 568 (1977).

55. Restrictive agreements among sports teams are, as a rule, adjudicated under the rule of reason because courts recognize that sports, by necessity, require some level of collusion among the competing teams to establish rules of the games.[81] Thus, a rule restricting baseball teams to twenty-five players may be found reasonable, since, after all, the concept of a "team" assumes some limit on the number of players. However, agreements by leagues to establish pay schedules for assistant coaches have been found to violate antitrust law because there is no offsetting rationale for the restrictions.[82]

56. As discussed in more detail below, some agreements present a complex initial question as to whether they are properly characterized as a per se violation or are better considered under a rule of reason analysis.

§2. Monopolies (Dominant Undertakings)

57. The concept of "dominant undertakings" or "undertaking" does not exist in American antitrust law. Rather, the Sherman Act speaks of contracts, combinations and conspiracies in restraint of trade.[83] Such violations may be brought against individuals, corporations, partnerships and other legal entities, including universities, trade organizations and other not-for-profit entities.

58. The closest analog to a dominant undertaking is section 2 of the Sherman Act, which prohibits monopolization, attempts to monopolize, and conspiracies to monopolize.[84] A primary distinction between section 1 and section 2 is that section 1 in almost all circumstances requires multiple actors to establish a violation while section 2 reaches unilateral activity. The term "monopolize" is not defined within the statute. Courts generally define it as the power to control prices and exclude competition. As in the analysis of dominance, a determination of monopolization requires defining a relevant market and usually an assessment of market share. Sufficient market share is strong evidence of the power to control prices and exclude competition.

59. Size alone is not a violation. A natural monopoly, such as certain public utilities, is allowed,[85] as is a monopoly obtained legitimately through superior products or services or through patents.[86] In addition, some markets are not large enough to allow for multiple sellers. Courts consider monopoly power the reward for success in the marketplace and the potential to obtain it a major stimulus to competition.[87] For these reasons, the plaintiff must establish an abuse of some kind, either in the acquisition

81. *National Collegiate Athletic Association v. Board of Regents of University of Oklahoma*, 468 U.S. 85 (1984).
82. *Law v. National Collegiate Athletic Association*, 134 F.3d 1010 (10th Cir. 1998).
83. 15 U.S.C. § 1.
84. 15 U.S.C. § 2.
85. *American Football League v. National Football League*, 323 F.2d 124, 131 (4th Cir. 1963) ("When one has acquired a natural monopoly by means which are neither exclusionary, unfair, nor predatory, he is not disempowered to defend his position fairly").
86. *United States v. Aluminum Co. of Am.*, 148 F. 2d 416, 430 (2nd Cir. 1945) ("A single producer may be the survivor out of a group of active competitors, merely by virtue of his superior skill, foresight and industry" and the antitrust laws do not condemn this).
87. *Ibid.* ("The successful competitor, having been urged to compete, must not be turned upon when he wins.")

of the monopoly power or in the wielding of the monopoly power once acquired, to establish a violation of section 2. For example, in *United States v. Microsoft*, Microsoft was found, among other things, to have entered into restrictive agreements with various outlets for software development and distribution that served no economic purpose other than to foreclose these outlets to competitors.[88] In other cases, policies under which monopolists would only lease their products for extended periods of time, but would not sell or offer shortened leases for them, were held to be violations because the necessary effect of such policies was to foreclose the market to others.[89]

60. Efforts to reach industry-wide behavior that does not involve concerted activity that would rise to the level of conspiracy, however loosely defined under the antitrust laws, have not been successful. In 1982, for example, the FTC abandoned a challenge it had pursued throughout the 1970s to the breakfast cereal industry based on a "shared monopoly" theory.[90] The industry had been highly concentrated, characterized by high prices, and several of the major manufacturers were located within a single, relatively small city. However, the government found that in the absence of evidence of conspiracy, there was no violation of the antitrust laws.

§3. Mergers (Concentrations)

61. In American antitrust law, the term "mergers and acquisitions" covers the field described as concentrations in European Union (EU) law.

62. The law governing mergers, section 7 of the Clayton Act, is closely related to the concept of monopolization. However, the language of section 7 contrasts sharply with that of section 2 in that it allows far greater latitude for government intervention:

> No person engaged in commerce or in any activity affecting commerce shall acquire, directly or indirectly, the whole or any part of the stock or other share capital and no person subject to the jurisdiction of the FTC shall acquire the whole or any part of the assets of another person engaged also in commerce or in any activity affecting commerce, where in any line of commerce or in any activity affecting commerce in any section of the country, the effect of such acquisition may be substantially to lessen competition, or to tend to create a monopoly.[91]

Rather than discussing markets, the statute creates its own, much broader terminology, "line of commerce." Rather than requiring a showing of monopolization, the standard is simply that "the effect may be substantially to lessen competition." As a result, in the 1960s, the Supreme Court affirmed government actions prohibiting mergers of

88. 253 F.3d 34 (D.C. Cir. 2001).

89. *United States v. United Machinery Corp.*, 110 F.Supp. 295 (D.Mass. 1953).

90. *Kellogg Co.*, [1970–1973 Transfer Binder] Trade Reg. Rep. (CCH) No. 8883 ¶ 19,898 (Apr. 26, 1972), complaint dismissed, 3 Trade Reg. Rep. (CCH) ¶ 21,864 (Sep. 10, 1981), dismissal affirmed, 99 F.T.C. 8 (1982).

91. 15 U.S.C. § 18.

entities with extremely small market shares – sometimes even less than 10% of a market.[92] Today, a different, supposedly more sophisticated, standard is used and embraced in the Merger Guidelines promulgated by the Justice Department and the FTC. These standards are discussed in the section devoted to mergers below. All acquisitions of a sufficient size[93] must be initially reported to the Antitrust Division of the DOJ and the FTC before the proposed transaction can be consummated.[94]

§4. Other Prohibitions

63. American antitrust law contains a comprehensive statutory scheme governing price discrimination, known as the Robinson-Patman Act.[95] This statute, which was passed to protect small business from discrimination based upon concessions that larger rivals are able to extract from suppliers, generally has been viewed as unsuccessful. It advances policies that are sometimes viewed as contrary to the goals of other antitrust laws in that it may penalize a seller for providing an entity prices that are too low. It prohibits discrimination in the sale of commodities of like grade and quality to similarly situated customers. The primary defenses to price discrimination claims are that the lower price is cost justified or that it has been given to meet competition from another supplier.

§5. Tests of Illegality

I. Per se Prohibitions and Naked Restraints

64. The doctrine of per se antitrust violations finds its roots in the earliest jurisprudence under the Sherman Act. The doctrine holds that certain activities in restraint of trade are so clearly economically pernicious that they violate the law per se and the court will not consider any evidence of their reasonableness in a particular circumstance. An 1898 decision by William Howard Taft, a Sixth Circuit judge who later became the President of the US and then the Chief Justice of the Supreme Court, defined certain activities – which today would be termed systematic bid-rigging – as so clearly economically harmful that no economic justification would be considered by the court.[96] The defendants, who were manufacturers of pipes for major sewage and water systems, argued that their prices were reasonable and their agreement

92. *See, e.g., Brown Shoe Co., Inc. v. United States*, 370 U.S. 294 (1962); *United States v. Von's Grocery Co.*, 384 U.S. 270 (1966).
93. The triggering size is at least USD 200 million in stock or assets or of at least USD 50 million when one party makes at least USD 100 million in annual revenues and the other makes at least USD 10 million in annual revenues (all dollars amounts are indexed for inflation).
94. Hart-Scott-Rodino Act, 15 U.S.C. § 18A.
95. 15 U.S.C.. § 13 *et seq*.
96. *Addyston Pipe & Steel Co. v. United States*, 85 F. 271 (6th Cir. 1898), *aff'd as modified*, 175 U.S. 211, 20 S. Ct. 96, 44 L. Ed. 136 (1899).

necessary, to avoid ruinous competition that had previously prevailed in the industry. The court would hear none of it: "[W]e do not think that at common law there is any question of reasonableness open to the courts with reference to such a contract."[97] The Supreme Court has put it more bluntly: "price-fixing agreements are unlawful per se under the Sherman Act and ... no showing of so-called competitive abuses or evils which those agreements were designed to eliminate or alleviate may be interposed as a defense."[98]

65. *United States v. Socony-Vacuum* underscored the power of the per se doctrine. The conduct at issue was an arrangement, originally encouraged by the federal government early in the Great Depression, to alleviate a glut in oil production that had driven prices below cost. A government program, under a statute later held unconstitutional, encouraged independent oil companies lacking storage to sell their excess oil systematically to major companies that had sufficient storage. The program's goal was to better control distribution and eliminate the oversupply that was severely depressing prices. The Court found that the agreement's purpose was to restrict supply and thereby to elevate prices. Therefore, the Court would not entertain a defense based on the distressed market conditions.

66. Certain agreements among horizontal competitors, such as agreements to fix prices or production[99] or to allocate customers or territories[100] or to boycott, have all been held to be per se violations, as has the tying of goods in certain circumstances. These violations are known as "naked restraints." Once horizontal competitors have been found to have engaged in these activities, courts will entertain no defenses to them.

67. The per se doctrine is powerful, particularly with regard to conduct deemed criminal, since the government need only prove the existence of a conspiracy or agreement – not any economic effects. The doctrine is somewhat less dramatic in civil cases, where parties still need to prove causation and damages resulting from the illegal conduct. Still, the doctrine prevents courts from excusing conduct based on economic exigencies or competing concerns as they could under the "rule of reason" standard described below.

68. A good example of the power of the doctrine is *Monsanto Co. v. Spray-Rite Serv. Corp.* [101] At the time the case was decided, vertical price-fixing conspiracies were illegal per se. The Court sustained a verdict in favor of a distributor who claimed a manufacturer had ceased to sell its products as part of a conspiracy to maintain resale prices among the manufacturer and other distributors. The Court based its decision on a finding that the plaintiff had produced sufficient evidence of such a conspiracy. Had the case been decided under the rule of reason, the standard applied today to vertical price-fixing, the plaintiff would also have had to refute economic justifications that the manufacturer could have advanced for seeking to maintain resale prices, such as

---

97. *Ibid.* at 293.
98. *United States v. Socony-Vacuum Oil Co.*, 310 U.S. 150, 218, 60 S. Ct. 811, 842, 84 L. Ed. 1129 (1940).
99. *United States v. Trans-Missouri Freight Ass'n*, 166 U.S. 2290, 17 S.Ct. 540, 41 L.Ed. 1007 (1897).
100. *United States v. Topco Associates*, 405 U.S. 596 (1972).
101. 465 U.S. 752, 768, 104 S. Ct. 1464, 1473, 79 L. Ed. 2d 775 (1984).

providing distributors with sufficient margins to provide adequate service for the product.

69. For many years, courts favored per se analysis because it provided certainty and consistency and simplified antitrust cases. Courts sought to include a wider variety of conduct within its purview. However, more recently, courts have cut back the doctrine and shifted their focus to characterizing the conduct in question. Certain antitrust violations, such as vertical price-fixing,[102] have been removed entirely from the ambit of per se analysis.[103] Other violations, such as boycotts and tying, continue to be subjected to per se analysis only in a narrow set of instances.[104] In many circumstances, the question has shifted to determining whether the particular conduct is, in fact, price-fixing. This subject is taken up in Part II Chapter 1 §1IA3 below.

II. Balancing Tests

70. Under American antitrust law, the balancing test is known as the rule of reason. The rule of reason weighs the harm of the restraint against any pro-competitive justification for it. As Justice Breyer put it:

> (1) What is the specific restraint at issue? (2) What are its likely anticompetitive effects? (3) Are there offsetting procompetitive justifications? (4) Do the parties have sufficient market power to make a difference?[105]

California Dental v. FTC involved advertising restrictions imposed by a dental organization through its ethical code. The code forbade advertising of across-the-board discounts on dental services, requiring dental providers to provide a list price and a discounted price for each procedure, and forbade any quality claims, such as gentle dentistry. The Court held that the trial court had inadequately considered the possibility that the restrictions in the sensitive area of advertising of professional services had increased, rather than decreased, competition by assuring the accuracy of the advertising.

71. The particular issue before the Court in *California Dental* was the extent to which a court had to inquire into the effects of the restraint when applying the rule of reason analysis. Before *California Dental*, the Court had created a series of truncated forms of the rule of reason analysis. If the anticompetitive nature of the restraint was obvious, a court could undertake a "quick look"; otherwise, the court would be required to undertake a full-blown inquiry with extensive expert evidence. Determining the appropriate inquiry for the particular case had proven difficult. Justice Souter, writing for the majority in *California Dental*, canvassed prior authority:

---

102. This violation is also known as resale price maintenance.
103. *Leegin Creative Leather Products, Inc. v. PSKS, Inc.*, 551 U.S. 877, 127 S. Ct. 2705, 168 L. Ed. 2d 623 (2007).
104. *Illinois Tool Works Inc. v. Indep. Ink, Inc.*, 547 U.S. 28, 126 S. Ct. 1281, 164 L. Ed. 2d 26 (2006).
105. *California Dental Ass'n v. FTC*, 526 U.S. 756, 782, 119 S. Ct. 1604, 1618, 143 L. Ed. 2d 935 (1999) (Breyer, J. dissenting).

> In National Collegiate Athletic Assn. v. Board of Regents of Univ. of Okla., 468 U.S. 85, 104 S.Ct. 2948, 82 L.Ed.2d 70 (1984), we held that a "naked restraint on price and output requires some competitive justification even in the absence of a detailed market analysis."Id., at 110, 104 S.Ct. 2948. Elsewhere, we held that "no elaborate industry analysis is required to demonstrate the anticompetitive character of horizontal agreements among competitors to refuse to discuss prices, National Soc. of Professional Engineers v. United States, 435 U.S. 679, 692, 98 S.Ct. 1355, 55 L.Ed.2d 637 (1978), or to withhold a particular desired service, FTC v. Indiana Federation of Dentists, 476 U.S. 447, 459, 106 S.Ct. 2009, 90 L.Ed.2d 445 (1986) (quoting National Soc. of Professional Engineers, supra, at 692, 98 S.Ct. 1355)." In each of these cases, which have formed the basis for what has come to be called abbreviated or "quick-look" analysis under the rule of reason, an observer with even a rudimentary understanding of economics could conclude that the arrangements in question would have an anticompetitive effect on customers and markets. In National Collegiate Athletic Assn., the league's television plan expressly limited output (the number of games that could be televised) and fixed a minimum price. 468 U.S., at 99-100, 104 S.Ct. 2948. In National Soc. of Professional Engineers, the restraint was "an absolute ban on competitive bidding." 435 U.S., at 692, 98 S.Ct. 1355. In Indiana Federation of Dentists, the restraint was "a horizontal agreement among the participating dentists to withhold from their customers a particular service that they desire." 476 U.S., at 459, 106 S.Ct. 2009. As in such cases, quick-look analysis carries the day when the great likelihood of anticompetitive effects can easily be ascertained.[106]

72. In certain areas, primarily the learned professions,[107] sports and education, courts have required application of the rule of reason to what would generally be deemed naked restraints. An exception was adopted for sports because of the recognition that the concept of a league requires rules and other decisions to which competitors must agree. A rule limiting the number of players on a team has direct and immediate effects on the labor market, but may be a necessary requirement to assure fairness in a sport. However, in *National Collegiate Athletic Assn.*, the Court undertook little analysis to determine that a rule limiting member schools' television programing violated the antitrust laws.[108] Similarly, in *Law v. Nat'l Collegiate Athletic Ass'n*,[109] the court applied a quick look in finding a rule restricting coaches' salaries to violate the antitrust laws. More recently, a court suggested that issues relating to a broadcasting

106. *California Dental Ass'n v. FTC,* 526 U.S. 756, 769–770, 119 S. Ct. 1604, 1612–1613, 143 L. Ed. 2d 935 (1999).

107. *Nat'l Soc. of Prof'l Engineers v. United States,* 435 U.S. 679, 696 (1978).

108. *National Collegiate Athletic Assn. v. Board of Regents of Univ. of Okla.*, 468 U.S. 85, 104 S.Ct. 2948, 82 L.Ed.2d 70 (1984).

109. 134 F.3d 1010 (10th Cir. 1998).

geographic market allocation scheme among professional sports teams could be resolved by application of a quick look.[110]

In contrast, in *United States v. Brown University*, the court required a full, rule of reason analysis where the government charged that coordinated efforts among major universities to distribute financial aid to needy students amounted to a form of price-fixing.[111]

73. The problem with the rule of reason, which goes back to the earliest period of American antitrust jurisprudence, is that it renders the law highly uncertain. The doctrine leaves it for courts to determine the legality of conduct on a case-by-case basis, almost always after the fact. It was precisely this concern that originally led courts to provide certainty to the law by expanding the conduct held to be per se violations.

III. Merger Tests

74. Just as the courts have moved from per se rules to more complex, economics-based analyses, the federal agencies that enforce the antitrust laws have moved to more complex and less predictable analyses of mergers in recent years. In 2010, these agencies, the Antitrust Division of the DOJ and the FTC, promulgated a new iteration of the Horizontal Merger Guidelines, which are non-binding but highly influential guidelines for enforcing section 7 of the Clayton Act and other statutes pertaining to mergers.[112] The guidelines focus less on market structure and concentration and more on the specific effects of a merger on consumers:

> These Guidelines should be read with the awareness that merger analysis does not consist of uniform application of a single methodology. Rather, it is a fact-specific process through which the Agencies, guided by their extensive experience, apply a range of analytical tools to the reasonably available and reliable evidence to evaluate competitive concerns in a limited period of time. Where these Guidelines provide examples, they are illustrative and do not exhaust the applications of the relevant principle.
>
> The unifying theme of these Guidelines is that mergers should not be permitted to create, enhance, or entrench market power or to facilitate its exercise. For simplicity of exposition, these Guidelines generally refer to all of these effects as enhancing market power. A merger enhances market power if it is likely to encourage one or more firms to raise price, reduce output, diminish innovation, or otherwise harm customers as a result of diminished competitive constraints or incentives. In evaluating how a merger will likely change a firm's behavior,

110. *Laumann v. Nat'l Hockey League,* 56 F. Supp. 3d 280, 307 (S.D.N.Y.).
111. 5 F.3d 658, 677–678 (3d Cir. 1993).
112. *FTC & U.S. Dep't of Justice, Horizontal Merger Guidelines* (2010).

> the Agencies focus primarily on how the merger affects conduct that would be most profitable for the firm.[113]

The guidelines describe the kinds of evidence that the agencies use in determining whether a proposed merger is expected to be anticompetitive. This evidence includes comparisons with similar mergers, concentration in the relevant market, head-to-head competition between the merging parties, and the disruptive role, if any, that the would-be merger target plays in the market. The agencies interview and obtain documents from the merging parties, customers, competitors, and other industry participants. If, after its investigation, the agency determines that the merger will harm consumers, it will challenge the merger in court.

75. Since the 2010 Merger Guidelines courts continue to use criteria drawn from merger analysis under the previous iteration of the guidelines, released in 1992 and revised in 1997. However, the government has presented more sophisticated effects analysis, for example, showing the effect of competition by comparing the lower prices in markets in which there are multiple competitors to prices in markets dominated by one seller.[114] In these guidelines, the analysis starts with defining a market and determining the concentration in that market. The more concentrated the market is, the less evidence of anticompetitive effects the agencies must find before challenging a merger. While the new guidelines deemphasize market concentration analysis and increase the amounts of concentration necessary before the agencies will presume that a proposed merger is anticompetitive, the guidelines maintain those general concepts. Courts continue to rely on market concentration metrics even more heavily.

76. Market concentration is measured using the Herfindahl-Hirschman Index (HHI). The HHI is calculated by summing the squares of the individual market shares of all the participants in a particular market. In this way, it gives proportionately greater weight to the market shares of the larger firms. The *2010 Guidelines* state that a market with an HHI of below 1,500 is considered unconcentrated, and that a merger resulting in a market with that concentration is allowed to be consummated without further analysis. The agencies consider a market with an HHI of 1,500-2,500 points to be moderately concentrated. The agencies will usually scrutinize a merger that will increase the HHI in such market by more than 100 points for potential anticompetitive effects. If a merger in a highly concentrated market, one with an HHI over 2,500, would raise its HHI by over 200 points, then the agencies will presume the merger to be anticompetitive and will likely challenge it unless the merging parties can provide "persuasive evidence showing that the merger is unlikely to enhance market power."[115] The guidelines emphasize that the HHI thresholds are not "a rigid screen" and are only "one way to identify some mergers unlikely to raise competitive concerns and some others for which it is particularly important to examine whether other competitive factors confirm, reinforce, or counteract the potentially harmful effects of increased concentration."[116]

---

113. *Ibid.*, at § 1.
114. *See* , e.g. *F.T.C. v. Staples, Inc.,* 970 F. Supp. 1066 (D.D.C. 1997) and *Federal F.T.C. v. Whole Foods Mkt., Inc.*, 548 F.3d 1028 (D.C. Cir. 2008).
115. *Ibid.*, at § 5.3.
116. *Ibid.*

77. These issues are discussed in greater detail in Chapter 3 below.

Chapter 4. Overview of Main Notions

§1. Undertaking

78. There is no concept in American antitrust law comparable to the term "undertaking," as used in EU law. Both natural persons and legal entities can be sued for violations of the antitrust laws. These include corporations, partnerships, joint ventures, not-for-profit institutions, and certain governmental entities. The question under American antitrust law, particularly under section 1 of the Sherman Act, is the degree of separateness and independence that two entities who are allegedly conspiring have from each other. Certain entities are too closely associated to be independent actors for purposes of section 1. For example, a corporation and its wholly owned subsidiary cannot conspire under section 1 despite the fact that they are separate legal entities.[117] The Court explained:

> [T]he coordinated activity of a parent and its wholly owned subsidiary must be viewed as that of a single enterprise for purposes of § 1 of the Sherman Act. A parent and its wholly owned subsidiary have a complete unity of interest. Their objectives are common, not disparate; their general corporate actions are guided or determined not by two separate corporate consciousnesses, but one. They are not unlike a multiple team of horses drawing a vehicle under the control of a single driver. With or without a formal "agreement," the subsidiary acts for the benefit of the parent, its sole shareholder. If a parent and a wholly owned subsidiary do "agree" to a course of action, there is no sudden joining of economic resources that had previously served different interests, and there is no justification for § 1 scrutiny.[118]

79. Similarly, two oil companies that formed a formal joint venture to market gasoline in a market in which they formerly competed were held not to have violated the antitrust laws because of the absence of a plurality of actors necessary under section 1:

> Price-fixing agreements between two or more competitors, otherwise known as horizontal price-fixing agreements, fall into the category of arrangements that are per se unlawful. [citation] These cases do not present such an agreement, however, because Texaco and Shell Oil did not compete with one another in the relevant market-namely, the sale of gasoline to service stations in the western United States-but instead participated in that market jointly through their

117. *Copperweld Corp. v. Independence Tube Corp.*, 467 U.S. 752, 104 S. Ct. 2731, 81 L. Ed. 2d 628 (1984).
118. *Ibid.*, at 771.

> investments in Equilon. In other words, the pricing policy challenged here amounts to little more than price setting by a single entity-albeit within the context of a joint venture-and not a pricing agreement between competing entities with respect to their competing products. Throughout Equilon's existence, Texaco and Shell Oil shared in the profits of Equilon's activities in their role as investors, not competitors. When "persons who would otherwise be competitors pool their capital and share the risks of loss as well as the opportunities for profit ... such joint ventures [are] regarded as a single firm competing with other sellers in the market."[citation] As such, though Equilon's pricing policy may be price fixing in a literal sense, it is not price fixing in the antitrust sense.[119]

The separateness issue can be complex. In its most recent analysis of the subject, *American Needle*, the Supreme Court rejected an argument that the otherwise separately incorporated teams of the National Football League (NFL) were effectively a single entity when they all assigned their intellectual property rights to a third entity, National Football League Properties (NFLP), for the purposes of marketing clothing and trademarked items. The Court explained: *[D]ecisions by the NFLP regarding the teams separately owned intellectual property constitute concerted action. Thirty-two teams operating independently through the vehicle of the NFLP are not like the components of a single firm that act to maximize the firm's profits. The teams remain separately controlled, potential competitors with economic interests that are distinct from NFLP's financial well-being.... Unlike typical decisions by corporate shareholders, NFLP licensing decisions effectively require the assent of more than a mere majority of shareholders. And each team's decision reflects not only an interest in NFLP's profits but also an interest in the team's individual profits.... The 32 teams capture individual economic benefits separate and apart from NFLP profits as a result of the decisions they make for the NFLP. NFLP's decisions thus affect each team's profits from licensing its own intellectual property. "Although the business interests of" the teams "will often coincide with those of the" NFLP "as an entity in itself, that commonality of interest exists in every cartel."... In making the relevant licensing decisions, NFLP is therefore "an instrumentality" of the teams.* [120]

The Court cited to a line of cases in which it had found that competitors that engaged in concerted activity through a separate corporation they had formed did not escape liability:

> [W]e have repeatedly found instances in which members of a legally single entity violated § 1 when the entity was controlled by a group of competitors and served, in essence, as a vehicle for ongoing concerted activity. In United States v. Sealy, Inc., 388 U.S. 350, 87 S.Ct. 1847, 18 L.Ed.2d 1238 (1967), for example, a group of mattress manufacturers operated and controlled Sealy, Inc., a company that licensed the Sealy trademark to the manufacturers, and dictated that each operate within a specific geographic area. Id., at 352-353, 87 S.Ct. 1847. The Government

119. *Texaco Inc. v. Dagher*, 547 U.S. 1, 5–6, 126 S. Ct. 1276, 1279–1280, 164 L. Ed. 2d 1 (2006).
120. *Am. Needle, Inc. v. Nat'l Football League*, 130 S. Ct. 2201, 2215, 176 L. Ed. 2d 947 (2010) (citations omitted).

> alleged that the licensees and Sealy were conspiring in violation of § 1, and we agreed. Id., at 352-354, 87 S.Ct. 1847. We explained that "[w]e seek the central substance of the situation" and therefore "we are moved by the identity of the persons who act, rather than the label of their hats."Id., at 353, 87 S.Ct. 1847. We thus held that Sealy was not a "separate entity, but ... an instrumentality of the individual manufacturers."[121]

80. But it is difficult to make the distinction the Court drew into a general rule. Even in *American Needle,* the Court struggled to articulate a general rule:

> Because the inquiry is one of competitive reality, it is not determinative that two parties to an alleged § 1 violation are legally distinct entities. Nor, however, is it determinative that two legally distinct entities have organized themselves under a single umbrella or into a structured joint venture. The question is whether the agreement joins together "independent centers of decision-making."Id., at 769, 104 S.Ct. 2731. If it does, the entities are capable of conspiring under § 1, and the court must decide whether the restraint of trade is an unreasonable and therefore illegal one.[122]

§2. Relevant Market

81. Defining the relevant market is the first step in three basic kinds of antitrust analysis: determining the effects of a merger; analyzing whether monopolization has occurred; and assessing the impact of a restrictive activity under the rule of reason. The concept of relevant market is composed of two parts: relevant geographic market and relevant product market.

82. Key recent merger decisions have turned on the definition of the relevant market. For example, *FTC v. Whole Foods Mkt., Inc.*, turned on the government's ability to persuade the court that "premium, natural, and organic supermarkets" represented a relevant market distinct from supermarkets generally.[123] Similarly, *FTC v. Staples, Inc.*, turned on the government's ability to prove that a market existed for "the sale of consumable office supplies through office superstores" that was distinct from the general market for consumable office supplies.[124]

83. Relevant market is most commonly proved by establishing what is known as the "cross elasticity of demand," i.e., are practical substitutes for the product at issue available at comparable prices? If there are, the market is defined to include those substitutes. If not, the market is confined to the product at issue. A good illustration of the relevance of this test came from an effort many years ago by the producers of coconut oil to cartelize the sale of coconut oil. The cartelization was effective and once the prices were raised and fixed, all of the customers shifted their purchases from

121. *Ibid.*, at 2209–2210.

122. *Ibid.*, at 2212.

123. 548 F.3d 1028 (D.C. Cir. 2008).

124. 970 F. Supp. 1066, 1073 (D.D.C. 1997).

coconut to other vegetable oils, many of which were perfect substitutes for coconut oil. Coconut oil was not a relevant market. Rather the market included a wide variety of vegetable oils all suitable for similar uses, all substitutes for each other.

84. By contrast, in the *Staples* case mentioned above, the government was able to prove that a distinct market existed for "the sale of consumable office supplies through office superstores."[125] This market was different from the general market for consumable office supplies because prices at Staples and the two other major office superstores did not respond to price changes at such general merchandisers as Wal-Mart or K-Mart, but responded to price changes at the other office superstores. The government demonstrated that prices were lower in markets in which multiple superstores competed with one another. In contrast, the presence of a Wal-Mart or K-Mart near an office superstore had no effect on prices.

85. So how is the cross-elasticity of demand test applied? Many courts look to the test provided in the Horizontal Merger Guidelines. There, the government describes what is known as the Small but Significant and Non-transitory Increase in Price (SSNIP) test. The guidelines define a relevant product market as a set of goods or services over which a hypothetical monopolist could impose an SSNIP (usually 5%–10%) without losing so many customers that the SSNIP would be unprofitable.[126] If a significant number of customers are lost to other products after the price increase, those other products must be included within the relevant market. If the number of customers lost is not so significant as to make the increase unprofitable, the set of goods or services in question constitute the relevant product market.

86. This test derives from *United States v. E.I. du Pont de Nemours & Co.*, the famous *Cellophane* case, in which the Supreme Court included cellophane and brown wrapping paper within a single product market by blindly applying its primitive understanding of the cross-elasticity of demand.[127] The Court found that the two products were in the same market because some customers would switch between the products in response to price changes. The Court committed what became known as the "*Cellophane* fallacy" by ignoring the fact that a monopolist charges its profit-maximizing price. That is, du Pont's price for cellophane was an inflated monopolistic price that was the maximum premium it could extract for the unique characteristics of cellophane without losing customers. Cellophane was much more expensive than brown paper. The fact that du Pont could not raise its price further without losing customers to brown paper wrapping sellers did not mean that the products' prices were competitive. DuPont was already extracting a monopoly price. The Court neglected the absolute differences in price between cellophane and brown paper from which its switching analysis began. As Chief Justice Warren explained in his dissent, "We cannot believe that buyers, practical businessmen, would have bought cellophane in increasing amounts over a quarter of a century if close substitutes were available at from one-seventh to one-half cellophane's price. That they did so is testimony to cellophane's distinctiveness."[128]

---

125. *Ibid.*
126. *FTC & U.S. Dep't of Justice, Horizontal Merger Guidelines* § 4.1 (2010).
127. 351 U.S. 377 (1956).
128. *United States v. E.I. du Pont de Nemours & Co.*, 351 U.S. 377, 417 (1956) (C.J. Warren, dissenting).

87. Six years later, Chief Justice Warren had an opportunity to correct the *Cellophane* analysis in *Brown Shoe Co. v. United States*,[129] in which he discussed the more general indicia that could be used to define a relevant market:

> The outer boundaries of a product market are determined by the reasonable interchangeability of use or the cross-elasticity of demand between the product itself and substitutes for it. However, within this broad market, well-defined submarkets may exist which, in themselves, constitute product markets for antitrust purposes…The boundaries of such a submarket may be determined by examining such practical indicia as industry or public recognition of the submarket as a separate economic entity, the product's peculiar characteristics and uses, unique production facilities, distinct customers, distinct prices, sensitivity to price changes, and specialized vendors.[130]

It is through a combination of these factors and price analysis that modern courts have reached their definitions of relevant market. Thus, in *Staples*, in addition to the price data that the court found persuasive, the court looked to the uniqueness of the office superstores, the unique product mix and varieties of office products they sold, the customers who frequented the stores, and similar characteristics.[131] In *Whole Foods*, the court acknowledged that a variety of products sold by "premium, natural, and organic supermarkets" were sold in general supermarkets.[132] However, the court found that the wide variety of organic perishables sold by the former could not be sold profitably to the customer base at typical supermarkets, and a core customer group existed for the product mix only available at the premium, natural, and organic supermarkets. From this finding, the court derived a more general rule:

> a core group of particularly dedicated, "distinct customers," paying "distinct prices," may constitute a recognizable submarket, … whether they are dedicated because they need a complete "cluster of products,"… because their particular circumstances dictate that a product "is the only realistic choice,"… or because they find a particular product "uniquely attractive."[133]

---

129. 370 U.S. 294 (1962).
130. *Ibid.*, at 325.
131. *FTC v. Staples, Inc.*, 970 F. Supp. 1066, 1073 (D.D.C. 1997). In 2016 Staples and Office Depot again sought to merge, arguing that market conditions had changed. The FTC obtained a preliminary injunction blocking the merger. It agreed that the market had changed and shifted the focus persuading the court that detrimental effects would occur in the market for large business to business customers. *Fed. Trade Comm'n v. Staples, Inc.*, No. CV 15-2115 (EGS), 2016 WL 2899222 (D.D.C. May 17, 2016).
132. *FTC v. Whole Foods Mkt,. Inc.*, 548 F.3d 1028 (D.C. Cir. 2008).
133. *Ibid.*, at 1039.

§3. Market Power/Dominant Position

88. Market power is often used synonymously with "monopoly power" in analysis under the American antitrust laws. Monopoly power is defined as the power to control prices and exclude competition. Market power has also been defined as, "the ability to raise prices above those that would be charged in a competitive market."[134] The concept is most often relevant to merger cases, in which a regulator will be assessing the ability of the post-merger entity to raise prices. It is also relevant for analysis in monopolization cases under section 2 of the Sherman Act and for analysis under the rule of reason in section 1 cases.

89. Market power, or monopoly power, can be proven in two ways – or by a combination of the two ways. It may be demonstrated directly by showing that it is effectively exercised. For example, if a drug company that has a patent for a drug with unique therapeutic properties can be shown to have been able to raise prices repeatedly without losing significant sales or profits, that would be strong evidence of monopoly power.

90. Market power can also be demonstrated "indirectly" by showing that the defendant has a major market share in a market with significant barriers to entry. The extreme is a single company that entirely controls a market: "When a product is controlled by one interest, without substitutes available in the market, there is monopoly power."[135] In *Nat'l Collegiate Athletic Ass'n*, the Court elaborated:

> It inexorably follows that if college football broadcasts be defined as a separate market – and we are convinced they are – then the NCAA's complete control over those broadcasts provides a solid basis for the District Court's conclusion that the NCAA possesses market power with respect to those broadcasts.[136]

91. There is no bright-line test for the market share percentage that confers monopoly power. Also, any market share percentage is generally considered in conjunction with a measure of the ease of entry into the market. Market shares above 75% certainly support an inference of market power, so long as there are barriers to entry.[137] Market shares below 60% generally would indicate an absence of monopoly power.[138] High market share alone, however, in the absence of barriers to entry, will not prove market power. The two must be considered together.

92. Barriers to entry are most often conceived of as economic barriers, such as the enormous sunk costs of existing participants that would have to be matched by new entrants, patents, environmental approval, zoning restrictions, permitting

134. *Nat'l Collegiate Athletic Ass'n v. Bd. of Regents of Univ. of Oklahoma*, 468 U.S. 85, 136 (1984).
135. *United States v. E.I. du Pont de Nemours & Co.*, 351 U.S. 377, 394 (1956).
136. *Nat'l Collegiate Athletic Ass'n v. Bd. of Regents of Univ. of Oklahoma*, 468 U.S. at 112.
137. *United States v. E.I. du Pont de Nemours & Co.*, 351 U.S. 377, 391 (1956) (finding that since du Pont had a 75% market share in cellophane, "it may be assumed it does have monopoly power over that 'market.'")
138. *United States v. Aluminum Co. of Am.*, 148 F.2d 416, 424 (2d Cir. 1945) ("it is doubtful whether sixty or sixty-four percent [market share] would be enough" to constitute a monopoly).

requirements, or "network effects." Network effects, a modern economic concept, relate to the barriers that arise from the pervasive acceptance and use of a particular product. In its challenge to Microsoft's dominance in the operating systems market, the government argued that the pervasiveness of the Windows operating system led the overwhelming majority of software producers to write their programs in Windows compatible modes, creating an enormous barrier to entry for new entrants into the operating system market.[139]

93. Even a company with a relatively small market share can have market power. For example, in *United States v. Visa U.S.A., Inc.*, the court found that MasterCard possessed significant market power even though it controlled only a 26% share of the relevant market.[140] The Court explained:

> In this regard, plaintiff has proven through the testimony of merchants that they cannot refuse to accept Visa and MasterCard even in the face of significant price increases because the cards are such preferred payment methods that customers would choose not to shop at merchants who do not accept them. ... In addition, both Visa and MasterCard have recently raised interchange rates charged to merchants a number of times, without losing a single merchant customer as a result. [141]

94. A second case involving the credit card companies discussed the issue of MasterCard's market power despite its relatively small market share at greater length and emphasized the importance of barriers to entry:

> Market share is not the only factor in a court's analysis of whether the evidence supports an inference of the defendant's monopoly power; rather, courts consider it in the context of all of the evidence of the relevant market's dynamics.... In addition to information about market share, information about entry barriers, the strength of competition, the nature of the challenged conduct and the probable development of the industry, among other factors, can shed light on whether a defendant has acquired "the kind of competitive advantage about which the antitrust laws should be concerned."...
>
> Generally, a defendant with a low degree of power in the relevant market cannot successfully wield monopoly power; customers dissatisfied with the defendant's prices can and do simply turn to other suppliers. ... Evidence of a defendant's high market share indirectly suggests that the defendant has the power to control prices if only because it demonstrates that there are few competitors and that

---

139. *United States v. Microsoft*, 253 F.3d 34 (D.C. Cir. 2001).

140. 163 F. Supp. 2d 322 (S.D.N.Y. 2001) *modified*, 183 F. Supp. 2d 613 (S.D.N.Y. 2001) aff'd, 344 F.3d 229 (2d Cir. 2003) and *aff'd*, 344 F.3d 229 (2d Cir. 2003) and *enforced*, 98 CIV. 7076 (BSJ), 2007 WL 1741885 (S.D.N.Y. Jun. 15, 2007).

141. *Ibid.*, at 340.

> customers' alternatives are limited in the event they decide the defendant's prices are too high. Where the structure of the market as a whole prevents a customer's ability to purchase lower-priced alternatives to the defendant's product, however, a defendant's market share may be less probative of its monopoly power. For example, a market with high entry barriers would to some extent suppress competition: whereas a seller in a market with low entry barriers could not raise its prices without the risk that a new seller would enter the market and offer the same product for a lower price, a competitor in a market with high entry barriers could raise its prices unfettered by the prospect of a new entrant into the market who would undercut prices. …
>
> The Individual Plaintiffs allege that the entry barriers to the General Purpose [credit card] Market are so high that there have not been new competitors in over 20 years. … Moreover, they claim that MasterCard's conduct has neutralized the ability of market forces to correct supra-competitive pricing and that the rules it imposes on merchants force them to purchase network services at prices they would not pay if they had economically feasible alternatives.[142]

95. Often, proof of relevant market and market power go hand-in-hand and the proof adduced to prove relevant market goes far towards establishing market power. This was the case in *Staples* discussed in the preceding section, where evidence of the ability of office superstores to price without regard to other outlets for similar products helped establish both the existence of a separate market and significant market power.[143]

§4. Agreements and Concerted Practices

96. Under American antitrust law, concerted practices are only subject to intervention if an agreement exists among the parties to engage in the concerted practice. Outright agreements among horizontal competitors that affect price are per se violations, even if the agreements relate to matters other than strictly price. Agreements on contractual terms,[144] credit terms,[145] output,[146] and territories[147] have all been held to be per se violations. The leading Supreme Court case on the per se rule, *United States v. Socony-Vacuum*, involved an agreement among competitors to absorb excess production of oil to stabilize prices, rather than a direct agreement on prices.[148] The Court had little difficulty finding that such an agreement was a per se violation.

142. *In re Payment Card Interchange Fee & Merch. Disc. Antitrust Litig.*, 562 F. Supp. 2d 392, 401–402 (E.D.N.Y. 2008)(citations omitted).
143. *FTC v. Staples, Inc.*, 970 F. Supp. 1066 (D.D.C. 1997).
144. *Paramount Famous Lasky Corp. v. United States*, 282 U.S. 30 (1930).
145. *Catalano, Inc. v. Target Sales, Inc.*, 446 U.S. 643 (1980).
146. *United States v. Andreas*, 216 F.3d 645 (7th Cir. 2000).
147. *United States v. Topco Associates, Inc.*, 405 U.S. 596 (1972).
148. 310 U.S. 150 (1940).

97. While each of the cases cited above involved outright agreements, courts have also inferred implicit agreements from the parties' conduct. Inferring agreement requires something more than simply finding parallel business conduct.[149]

98. Agreements among those in a vertical relationship – such as manufacturers and wholesalers or wholesalers and retailers – are judged under the more lenient "rule of reason." Thus, for example, an agreement by a manufacturer to allocate territories among its distributors is governed by the rule of reason,[150] while an agreement among retailers to allocate territories among themselves is a violation per se.[151]

99. A variety of agreements discussed below in the joint-venture section create effectively new entities or products. There are instances where the court will judge what appears to be a horizontal agreement among competitors under a rule of reason analysis where the agreement can be "characterized" as something other than an agreement directed to affect price.

§5. Restrictions on Competition

100. Restrictions on competition frequently arise from joint-venture agreements and covenants not to compete. These restrictions are often analyzed under what has become known as the "ancillary restraints doctrine." The particular contract clauses that give rise to antitrust concerns are usually contained as part of broader agreements to achieve ends other than to restrain trade. The contracting parties will usually argue that the restriction on competition is necessary to achieve the primary purpose of the contract.

101. Most commonly, such terms take the form of a covenant not to compete. For example, in an employment contract an employer may seek to protect its particular business secrets from being exploited by an employee who leaves the employer and attempts to compete with it. Often cases involving such clauses arise under state law, rather than federal antitrust law because, as a practical matter, they are part of contracts enforced in state courts. In addition to employment agreements, such clauses are frequently encountered in agreements to sell businesses and in franchise agreements. So long as they are ancillary to a legitimate agreement, they are generally judged using a rule of reason analysis that focuses on the reasonableness of the time, scope and geographic area of the restriction on competition.[152]

102. Usually, the context in which the "ancillary restraint" analysis arises in federal cases is in joint ventures, such as in *United States v. Topco Associates, Inc.*[153] Topco was a cooperative made up of regional supermarket chains that was created to provide these chains with private-label products to allow them to better compete with national chains that had store brands. There it was argued that a territorial allocation

---

149. *Bell Atlantic Corp. v. Twombly*, 550 U.S. 544, 556–557 (2007).

150. *Continental T.V., Inc. v. GTE Sylvania Inc.*, 433 U.S. 36 (1977).

151. *United States v. Topco Associates, Inc.*, 405 U.S. 596 (1972).

152. This is a venerable doctrine going back to *United States v. Addyston Pipe& Steel Co.*, 175 U.S. 211 (1899). *See , e.g.*, *Volunteer Firemen's Ins. Services, Inc. v. CIGNA Prop. & Cas. Ins. Agency*, 693 A.2d 1330 (Pa. Super. Ct. 1997).

153. 405 U.S. 596, 92 S. Ct. 1126, 31 L. Ed. 2d 515 (1972).

– enforced by a clause providing members with effective veto power over admitting a new member within the allocated territory – was necessary to protect the value of the private-label products.[154] The supermarket chains that had entered into the agreement argued that it was necessary to enable their own products to compete with "nationally advertised brands."[155] Because the restrictive clause in *Topco* created a territorial allocation among competitors, it was considered per se illegal. The Court would not consider the justifications advanced for the clause. *General Leaseways v. National Truck Leasing Association* followed *Topco* to find that a clause precluding members of a national truck leasing group from competing within each other's territories was per se illegal.[156] However, the court acknowledged that the pure per se rule of *Topco* may have been eroded, so it went on to analyze the justifications advanced, under the rule of reason, but found them unpersuasive.

103. Often, courts will find that the restraint does not fall within the per se domain. Instead, they will judge the restraint under a rule of reason analysis that considers the degree to which the overall contract increases economic efficiency and the degree to which the ancillary restraint is necessary to the contract or contributes to the efficiency it provides.

104. The most frequently cited case in this area is Judge Robert Bork's decision in *Rothery Storage & Van Co. v. Atlas Van Lines, Inc.*[157] There, a national moving van company, Atlas, contracted with "agencies" that were themselves moving companies to create a national network of home moving service providers. The court accepted that the national network provided economic benefits such as avoiding what would otherwise have been empty freight hauls on return trips, allowing for the local companies to participate in a nationwide service, and allocating and balancing receipts among the participants. When a regulatory change permitted the local moving companies to engage in interstate moving services themselves, Atlas prohibited any of its members from engaging in interstate services while serving as agencies for Atlas. The court did not apply a per se rule to the prohibition for many reasons. First, the primary allegation was that the prohibition was a concerted boycott of the companies that refused to accede to the new rule. As discussed in Part II, the application of per se doctrine to boycotts had been significantly eroded. More to the point, the court adopted the ancillary restraint analysis articulated in *Addyston Pipe.*[158]

105. Because the rule restricting Atlas agencies' competition with Atlas was "ancillary" to the broader purpose of creating a national moving network, the court applied the rule of reason. That is, it balanced the competitive efficiencies attendant to the overall scheme against the harm of the alleged anticompetitive restraints. First, the court found that any genuine anticompetitive effect was unlikely in the home moving market since Atlas represented barely 6% of the market and was only the sixth largest moving company in the country. The court also found that even if there were any anticompetitive effects, they were far outweighed by the risk that members would

154. *United States v. Topco Associates, Inc.*, 405 U.S. 596, 604–605 (1972).

155. *Ibid.*, at 604.

156. 744 F.2d 588, 589 (7th Cir. 1984).

157. 792 F.2d 210 (D.C. Cir. 1986).

158. *United states v. addyston pipe & steel co*, 85 f. 271 (6th Cir, 1898) *aff'd* 175 U.S. 211, 20 S.Ct 96 (1898).

"free-ride" by accepting the advantages of the Atlas network and then using many of those benefits to compete against the network without compensating Atlas for the benefits. For example, Atlas provided training that members could use in their competing businesses.

106. In addition to joint ventures, other contracts that often raise concerns under the antitrust laws are exclusive purchase agreements, output agreements, and reciprocal dealing agreements. These agreements are discussed in detail in Part II below. While such agreements can also be challenged under section 1 of the Sherman Act or section 3 of the Clayton Act, they are usually addressed as evidence of a monopolization violation under section 2 of the Sherman Act. Generally the courts will analyze the amount of commerce foreclosed by the agreement and will uphold the agreement only if that amount is not great and can be justified appropriately.[159]

§6. Monopolization and Abuse of Dominance

107. Section 2 of the Sherman Act prohibits monopolizations, attempts to monopolize, and conspiracies to monopolize. Actions under section 2 may be brought by the government or by entities injured by an alleged violation. An injured party may recover triple the damages incurred as a result of the violation.

108. The offense of monopolization has two elements: (1) the possession of monopoly power in a relevant market; and (2) the willful acquisition, maintenance, or use of that power by anticompetitive or exclusionary means or for anticompetitive or exclusionary purposes.[160] The first element is the more easily defined. The possession of monopoly power is the power to control prices or exclude competition in the relevant market. Relevant market was discussed in section 2 above. While determining whether the first element is violated often involves complex analysis, the concepts of monopoly power and relevant market underlying it are susceptible to tests.

109. The same cannot be said for the second element of a monopolization violation. That element confronts the central antitrust paradox. The economic system depends upon competition. The goal of each competitor is sufficient dominance over rivals to enable it to obtain a lucrative return on sales, i.e., a level of monopoly power under which it can control prices or exclude competitors. The second element of the test for monopolization tries to distinguish the legitimate achievement of the goal from the illegitimate achievement of the goal, or the abuse of the goal once achieved. This distinction is based on the idea that it is beneficial to reward the inventor of the best product or most efficient means of distribution with profits, even monopoly profits. Conversely, monopolization law seeks to prevent a person from exercising monopoly power who has obtained it illegitimately or obtained it legitimately but then maintained it through abuse.

110. Classic illegitimate exercise of monopolistic power includes discriminatory or predatory pricing, in which the monopolist lowers prices in a territory in which it faces competition using profits obtained by charging high prices in areas in which it

159. *United States v. Dentsply Int'l, Inc.*, 399 F.3d 181 (3d Cir. 2005).

160. *Aspen Skiing Co. v. Aspen Highlands Skiing Corp.*, 472 U.S. 585, 595–596, 105 S. Ct. 2847, 2854, 86 L. Ed. 2d 467 (1985).

possesses a monopoly. This was the issue in the classic *Standard Oil v. United States* case[161] and was also core evidence in *United States v. Grinnell Corp.*[162] The nature of the conduct deemed unacceptable has varied substantially. In *Conwood Co., L.P. v. U.S. Tobacco Co.*,[163] a dominant entity had its sales force sabotage its competitor's display racks in convenience stores. In *LePage's Inc. v. 3M*,[164] "bundled discounts," i.e., discounts that could only be achieved if a specific quantity of a variety of products were purchased, and exclusive purchase contracts provided a basis for finding illegal monopolization when employed by a dominant firm.

111. So, how can one know whether particular conduct will run afoul of monopolization law? In *United States v. Microsoft Corp.*,[165] the District of Columbia Circuit used a multi-tiered analysis. First, the plaintiff must establish that the monopolist's challenged conduct had an anticompetitive effect, i.e., that it harmed the competitive process. The effect had to be upon consumers, not merely upon competitors. Harm to competitors could, of course, also be shown to harm consumers.

112. Once the plaintiff establishes that the conduct had an anticompetitive effect, the monopolist may proffer a pro-competitive justification – that is, that the conduct benefits consumers by providing greater efficiency or enhanced consumer appeal. It then falls upon the plaintiff to either rebut the pro-competitive justification or, alternatively, to show the anticompetitive harm of the conduct outweighs its pro-competitive effects. The District of Columbia Circuit held that the analysis should be directed entirely to the effect on competition, rather than to the monopolist's intent. "Evidence of the intent behind the conduct…is relevant only to the extent it helps us understand the likely effect of the … conduct."[166]

113. The *Microsoft* case centered upon Microsoft's efforts to restrict distribution of Netscape, an internet browser that competed with Microsoft's own browser, Internet Explorer. Microsoft's ultimate goal was to protect the monopoly of its Windows product in the desktop computer operating system market. The fear was that the Netscape browser would allow access to methods of computing that would diminish the significance of the Windows operating system.

114. Applying the standard described above, the court first found that a number of Microsoft's license restrictions, with both computer manufacturers and software developers, constituted anticompetitive conduct. For example, Microsoft prevented manufacturers of computers who necessarily installed the Windows operating system (without which the computer could not function) from removing visible access to the Internet Explorer browser that was included within Windows. The government proffered evidence that this conduct was anticompetitive because it effectively precluded computer manufacturers from distributing alternative browsers, such as Netscape. Computer manufacturers found that if they provided two browsers on their computers, computer users at that time would get confused and call customer support; this increased volume

161. *Standard Oil Co. of New Jersey v. United States*, 221 U.S. 1 (1911).
162. 384 U.S. 563 (1966).
163. 290 F.3d 768 (6th Cir. 2002).
164. 324 F.3d 141 (3d Cir. 2003).
165. 253 F.3d 34 (D.C. Cir. 2001).
166. *Ibid.*, at 59.

of support calls was extremely expensive for computer manufacturers. Therefore, computer manufacturers would not install a second browser.

115. Microsoft sought to justify the restrictions in two ways. First, it argued that the license provisions were protected by copyright law – an argument the court dismissed out of hand. Second, Microsoft argued that allowing a computer manufacturer to alter the Windows software to hide visible access to Internet Explorer would threaten Windows's stability. The sole document Microsoft produced to support this justification was an internal Microsoft memorandum voicing concern that allowing such tampering by computer manufacturers could lead to user confusion. The court found that the cost of such consumer confusion would be borne not by Microsoft, but by computer manufacturers, and rejected Microsoft's justification. The sole threat Microsoft was addressing was a threat to its monopoly.

116. Microsoft undertook a variety of other actions that the court discussed. These are covered in part II below.

§7. Mergers (Concentrations)

117. Concentrations is a term foreign to American antitrust law. The subject is entirely subsumed within merger law. As discussed above, in section 3 under "Scope of Application," mergers are governed by section 7 of the Clayton Act.

118. As previously discussed, the act contains broader language than the monopolization statute and was intended to provide a wider reach that the existing jurisprudence under section 2 of the Sherman Act. Thus, the Clayton Act replaces "market" with "any line of commerce" and prohibits not "monopolization," but activity whose effect "may be substantially to lessen competition." The goal of the act was to provide the government with greater flexibility to regulate proposed mergers.

119. The technical requirements for merger pre-reporting are discussed in greater detail in the "Merger Control" section below. Under the Hart-Scott-Rodino Act, companies that intend to merge must report their proposed merger to the government before consummating merger if the transaction or the companies meet certain size thresholds.

§8. Joint Ventures

120. Courts generally use a rule of reason analysis to judge joint ventures. Joint ventures present several thorny questions for antitrust analysis. The first question is whether the creation of the joint venture – a separate unified entity – negates the requirement of multiple actors for a claim under section 1 of the Sherman Act. The second question is whether, if the joint venturers engage in conduct that normally would be judged under the per se rule if undertaken by horizontal competitors, the conduct will be judged under the per se rule when undertaken by a joint venture. Certain joint ventures are governed by 15 U.S.C. § 4301, which provides for a rule of reason analysis.

121. The Supreme Court answered the first question in *American Needle*,[167] where it outlined the criteria for determining whether joint venturers' conduct was to be judged as that of single entity or multiple entities. The Court rejected the argument that the joint venture created a unified entity that shielded the entity from scrutiny under section 1 of the Sherman Act. It held that NFLP, a consortium of the thirty-two NFL teams to which each team assigned certain trademark rights, did not merge the thirty-two teams into a single entity with regard to its licensing of the trademarks separately owned by each of the thirty-two teams. The NFLP had entered into a ten-year, exclusive license with Reebok to sell hats bearing the trademarks of each of the thirty-two NFL teams. An entity that had formerly manufactured hats for certain of the teams sued the NFLP for conspiring to license all of its trademarks to Reebok alone. The Court of Appeals had held that the thirty-two teams were incapable of conspiring under the antitrust laws because they acted jointly as a single entity, the NFLP. The Supreme Court reversed, holding "that concerted action under § 1 does not turn simply on whether the parties involved are legally distinct entities. Instead, we have eschewed such formalistic distinctions in favor of a functional consideration of how the parties involved in the alleged anticompetitive conduct actually operate."[168]

122. The Court established criteria to determine when a court would look beyond the joint-venture structure to find the requisite plurality of actors. "The question is whether the agreement joins together independent centers of decision-making." If it does, the entities are capable of conspiring under section 1, and the court must decide whether the restraint of trade is an unreasonable and therefore illegal one.[169] The Court determined that the teams were independent centers of decision-making based on the fact that the teams were actual competitors for fans, players, and in the market for intellectual property. The sale of intellectual property redounded in profits to the individual teams. The teams retained individual ownership of the intellectual property that was merely jointly managed by the NFLP. The teams remained separate profit-maximizing enterprises whose interests in marketing their intellectual property were not necessarily aligned. The Supreme Court held that the existence of the NFLP did not shield the pooling teams from liability by eliminating the plurality of actors necessary to a claim under section 1 of the Sherman Act.

123. The Court did not establish an overall standard for judging the activities of joint venturers. It applied a rule of reason standard because, as it had previously held in the case of sports, some "restraints on competition are essential if the product is to be available at all."[170] That is, a sport cannot exist without some rules. But the Court did not reject per se treatment entirely in the case of joint ventures, citing

167. *Am. Needle, Inc. v. Nat'l Football League,* 130 S. Ct. 2201, 2206, 176 L. Ed. 2d 947 (2010).
168. *Ibid.*, at 2209.
169. *Ibid.*, at 2212 (citation omitted).
170. *Ibid.*, at 2216 (citation omitted).

decisions in which the Court had applied per se treatment to horizontal competitors' naked territorial allocations through joint ventures.[171]

124. In *Texaco Inc. v. Dagher*,[172] the Court held that a separate entity created by two major oil companies – Texaco and Shell – to sell gasoline to the gasoline stations, which continued operating under the respective company's former brand name, was a genuine separate economic entity:

> As a single entity, a joint venture, like any other firm, must have the discretion to determine the prices of the products that it sells, including the discretion to sell a product under two different brands at a single, unified price. If Equilon's price unification policy is anticompetitive, then respondents should have challenged it pursuant to the rule of reason.[173]

The plaintiffs had not challenged the restraint under the rule of reason and so the Court did not have an opportunity to reach the issue of whether the pricing would have survived rule of reason analysis.[174]

125. Under 15 U.S.C. § 4301, certain joint ventures in research and development or production are governed by a rule of reason standard. The specific types of joint ventures governed by this statute are defined at 15 U.S.C. §§ 4301(a)(6)(A)-(G).

126. The distinction between the application of the per se rule or the rule of reason in the case of joint ventures may not be as sharp as it is in other areas. In *American Needle*, the Court reiterated that "depending upon the concerted activity in question, the Rule of Reason may not require a detailed analysis; it 'can sometimes be applied in the twinkling of an eye.'"[175]

127. Chapter 1 of Part II below discusses various other applications of the different standards.

---

171. These decisions are *United States v. Sealy, Inc.*, 388 U.S. 350, 351, 87 S. Ct. 1847, 1849, 18 L. Ed. 2d 1238 (1967) and *United States v. Topco Associates, Inc.*, 405 U.S. 596, 597, 92 S. Ct. 1126, 1128, 31 L.Ed. 2d 515 (1972). In addition, the Court cited its decision refusing to apply the per se rule for certain conduct by a joint venture, *Texaco Inc. v. Dagher*, 547 U.S. 1, 3, 126 S. Ct. 1276, 1278, 164 L. Ed. 2d 1 (2006), merely as a "*see also*," suggesting it too did not control in all joint venture cases.
172. 547 U.S. 1, 3, 126 S. Ct. 1276, 1278, 164 L. Ed. 2d 1 (2006).
173. *Ibid.*, at 7.
174. *Dagher* also involved an entity that had been reviewed and approved by the relevant antitrust regulatory agency before it began operations.
175. *Am. Needle*, 130 S. Ct. at 2216–17.

Chapter 5. Consequences of Violations and Enforcement Institutions

§1. Administrative Enforcement

I. The Antitrust Authorities

128. There are two primary antitrust authorities in the US: The Antitrust Division of the DOJ and the FTC

A. The Antitrust Division

129. The Antitrust Division of the DOJ is not, in most respects, an administrative agency at all. It is the prosecutorial arm of the federal government and prosecutes criminal violations of the antitrust laws. It also has the authority, though infrequently used outside the area of merger enforcement, to bring civil enforcement actions. The Antitrust Division and the FTC have concurrent jurisdiction to enforce civil antitrust law, including reviewing mergers. The agencies decide which of them will review a merger at the time it is filed, based mostly on which agency has the most experience reviewing related mergers. Because so much of American antitrust activity by the federal government is in the form of criminal proceedings and because only the Antitrust Division can bring criminal actions under the antitrust laws, the Antitrust Division is the most potent of American antitrust authorities. The Antitrust Division acts in a quasi-administrative capacity in its merger review function, at least prior to bringing suit. It also acts as a quasi-administrative agency when, under its Business Review Procedure, it provides businesses advice regarding the Antitrust Division's views of particular contemplated business activity.[176]

B. The FTC

130. The FTC, an independent federal agency, shares responsibility for enforcing the civil antitrust laws with the Antitrust Division. As an independent agency, the FTC is controlled by a bipartisan group of five commissioners whom the President appoints to seven-year terms. Its policies on particular issues of antitrust may differ from those of the Justice Department, which reports directly to the President. A stark example of this disagreement occurred in 2005 when the FTC sought review of a recent decision in the controversial area of "reverse payments" in patent cases. The Justice Department refused to file a petition for certiorari, that is, for Supreme Court review, on behalf of the FTC, despite its normal practice of doing so for federal agencies. When the FTC

176. *See*, 28 C.F.R. § 50.6; 28 CFR § 50.6 Antitrust Division Business Review Procedure, *available at* <www.justice.gov/atr/public/busreview/201659c.htm>.

filed a petition for certiorari on its own behalf in the case,[177] and the Supreme Court sought the views of the Justice Department's Solicitor General regarding the propriety of its review, the Solicitor General opposed review.[178]

131. Unlike the Antitrust Division, the FTC has an administrative mechanism for resolving legal disputes between the agency and the companies allegedly violating antitrust law. The FTC's administrative adjudication process is discussed in the final chapter.

1. Formation, Composition

a. The Antitrust Division

132. The first Assistant Attorney General (AAG) for Antitrust was appointed by President Theodore Roosevelt in 1903. The Antitrust Division itself, however, was established in 1933. It is a division within the Justice Department. It has grown into an enormous organization including more than 360 attorneys, 55 economists, and 180 paralegals. The Division is headquartered in Washington D.C. and has field offices in Atlanta, Cleveland, Chicago, Dallas, New York City, Philadelphia, and San Francisco.

133. The AAG in charge of the Antitrust Division is nominated by the President and confirmed by the Senate. Five Deputy Assistant Attorneys General, who may be either career employees or appointed officials, oversee the five sections of the office: criminal enforcement, international enforcement, economic analysis, regulatory matters, and civil enforcement. The Director and Deputy Director of Operations, the Director of Criminal Enforcement, and the Economic Director of Enforcement have additional supervisory authority for their respective programs and are career employees. The AAG may be assisted by several special counsel.

134. The various sections and divisions of the Antitrust Division litigate criminal and civil cases, engage in merger review, coordinate competition policy with other federal agencies, coordinate efforts with state and foreign regulators, and comment on proposed legislation.

b. The FTC

135. In 1914, Congress passed the FTC Act[179] establishing the FTC to prevent "unfair methods of competition."[180] Courts have found that the FTC Act "was designed to supplement and bolster the Sherman Act and the Clayton Act, to stop in their incipiency acts and practices which, when full-blown, would violate those Acts, as well as to condemn as 'unfair method of competition' existing violations of them."[181] The FTC has the authority to enforce the antitrust laws.

177. *See,* Brief for Petitioner, *FTC v. Schering-Plough Corp.*, 126 S.Ct. 2929 (No. 05-273), 2005 WL 2105243 (U.S. Aug. 29, 2005).
178. *See,* Brief for the United States as Amicus Curiae, *FTC v. Schering-Plough Corp.*, 126 S.Ct. 2929 (No. 05-273), 2006 WL 1358441 (U.S. May 17, 2006).
179. 15 U.S.C. §§ 41–58, as amended.
180. 15 U.S.C. § 45(2).
181. *FTC v. Motion Picture Advertising Serv. Co.*, 344 U.S. 392, 394–395 (1953) (citations omitted).

136. Unlike the Antitrust Division, the FTC is an independent agency. The FTC has five Commissioners, no more than three of whom can be members of the same political party. The President appoints each Commissioner to a seven-year term and chooses one Commissioner to be the FTC Chairman, who leads the Commission.[182] The President can terminate Commissioners only for cause.[183]

137. The FTC's Bureau of Competition is dedicated to antitrust enforcement. The bureau is led by a director, who is appointed by the chairman. The bureau is divided into units that divide responsibility based on the stage of enforcement, the industry involved, and the conduct at issue. Other FTC divisions assist the Bureau of Competition with merger enforcement. The Bureau of Economics, staffed by economists, collaborates closely with the attorneys in the Bureau of Competition. The Bureau of Competition also may work with the Office of Policy Planning, the Office of International Affairs, the Office of General Counsel, and the Bureau of Consumer Protection.

2. Investigating Powers

a. The Antitrust Division

138. The Antitrust Division has full criminal investigatory powers. It can call upon the Federal Bureau of Investigation (FBI) for assistance in its investigations. It may convene grand juries, issue subpoenas for documents and testimony before a grand jury, and even conduct raids together with the FBI. It can compel testimony before the grand jury through grants of immunity. These powers are in addition to the full gamut of powers it holds pursuant to its civil investigatory authority. The FTC, whose authority is limited to civil investigations, has fewer and less coercive powers at its disposal.

b. The FTC

139. The FTC has only civil investigative procedures at its disposal. The main investigative tools that the FTC uses, aside from reviewing the pre-merger filings mandated by the Hart-Scott-Rodino Act, are subpoenas and civil investigative demands (CIDs). Section 9 of the FTC Act authorizes the agency to issue subpoenas, which may compel witness testimony or production of documents.[184] Section 20 of the FTC Act authorizes the agency to issue CIDs, which may reach more broadly than subpoenas.[185] The FTC can use CIDs to compel production of documents or tangible things and require recipients to provide answers to questions or to provide written reports. CIDs can even be served on entities outside the US.[186]

182. *Ibid.*
183. 15 U.S.C. § 41 ("Any Commissioner may be removed by the President for inefficiency, neglect of duty, or malfeasance in office").
184. 15 U.S.C. § 49.
185. 15 U.S.C. § 57b-1.
186. 15 U.S.C. § 57b-1(c)(7)(B).

140. The FTC's other investigative tools include the power to require the filing of reports or answers to questions about an organization, practices, or individuals.[187] Also, pharmaceutical drug manufacturers are required to file certain agreements with the FTC and the Antitrust Division.[188]

3. Adjudicating Powers (Ascertaining and Sanctioning)

a. The Antitrust Division

141. The only area in which the Antitrust Division has quasi-adjudicative powers is in the area of merger review. There, it may approve a merger or, alternatively, challenge a merger in the courts. It lacks authority to prohibit a merger on its own.

b. The FTC

142. The FTC has its own adjudicative process. However, if the FTC wants to stop corporate action quickly, such as blocking a merger, it must seek a preliminary injunction from a federal district court.[189] The court's decision whether to grant a preliminary injunction is crucial because, if it is granted, the companies are unlikely to continue pursuing their intended merger, and if is not granted, and the merger goes forward, the FTC is unlikely to challenge a completed merger.

143. However, in the rare instances when either the companies or the FTC decide to continue pursuing a merger that a court has either accepted or rejected at the preliminary injunction stage, a mechanism of administrative adjudication is available within the FTC. This process is also followed when the FTC undertakes other enforcement actions such as price-fixing investigations. The first step in the FTC's adjudicative process is a hearing before an Administrative Law Judge (ALJ). ALJs are FTC employees, but they are independent decision-makers and their role is to adjudicate complaints by the FTC against allegedly anticompetitive actors. ALJs are the FTC's initial fact-finders – the equivalent of a trial judge in the federal court system. Either party has the right to appeal an ALJ's decision. The FTC's five Commissioners, collectively known as the Commission, preside over the appeal. The FTC's Rules of Practice for Adjudicative Proceedings provides the FTC's rules of procedure and evidence for hearings presided over by ALJs and the Commission.[190]

144. The losing party in a Commission decision may appeal to a federal Court of Appeals. An order by the Commission becomes final and enforceable sixty days after it is served, unless the Commission or a federal Court of Appeals stays the order.[191]

---

187. 15 U.S.C. § 46.
188. Medicare Prescription Drug Improvement and Modernization Act of 2003, Pub L. 108–173.
189. 15 U.S.C. § 53(b) authorizes the FTC to seek injunctions to end or prevent the violation of a law enforced by the FTC.
190. FTC Rules of Practice for Adjudicative Proceedings, 16 C.F.R. Part 3 (known as "Part 3 Rules").
191. 16 C.F.R. § 3.56.

4. Other Institutional Tasks

145. Both the Antitrust Division and the FTC must sue in court to enforce a finding that an action is anticompetitive. Judges make the final determinations of an action's legality under the antitrust laws; the agencies can do no more than try to persuade them. The DOJ is generally responsible for conducting litigation on behalf of a federal government agency,[192] but the FTC also has authority to represent itself in court in certain kinds of cases as well.[193]

146. In addition, the FTC has authority to promulgate rules to regulate trade.[194] Both agencies also promulgate guidelines and policy statements, most notably the Horizontal Merger Guidelines, which explain the agencies' merger policy in detail.[195] While the merger guidelines are not binding on the courts, they do inform the antitrust court's analysis of mergers. The agencies also act as advocates for competition, both in the U.S. and through partnerships with government agencies abroad.

II. Government Direct Enforcement Activities

147. The Antitrust Division and the FTC cannot enforce the antitrust laws directly. Instead, if they find, after investigation, that an action harms or is likely to harm competition, they can sue to prevent that action from occurring. A federal judge or ALJ will hear the arguments of the government and its opponents and decide whether the action is anticompetitive. As described above, that adjudicative decision can be appealed.

148. However, both agencies have the authority to undertake investigations directly: they can both issue subpoenas and civil investigative demands, and the Antitrust Division can conduct grand jury investigations and enforce other criminal investigative procedures.

III. Other Administrative Agencies Applying Antitrust Rules

149. A number of other statutes require government agencies besides the Antitrust Division and FTC to provide competitive review, such as merger review. The principal such statutes are discussed below.

150. The Bank Merger Act creates a procedure under which the Office of the Comptroller of the Currency, the Board of Governors of the Federal Reserve System, the Federal Deposit Insurance Corporation, or the Office of Thrift Supervision review

192. 28 U.S.C. § 516 (providing this authority to the Attorney General, who heads the Department of Justice).
193. 15 U.S.C. § 56.
194. 15 U.S.C. § 57a.
195. United States Dep't of Justice and Federal Trade Comm'n, Horizontal Merger Guidelines (2010), *available at* <www.ftc.gov/os/2010/08/100819hmg.pdf>.

mergers relating to banks in consultation with the Antitrust Division.[196] Mergers falling under the Bank Mergers Act are exempt from reporting and review under the Hart-Scott-Rodino Act. Similarly, The Bank Holding Act of 1956, requires competitive review by the Federal Reserve of certain bank acquisitions by bank holding companies.[197] While the statute does not require formal consultation with the Attorney General, it is the practice of the Federal Reserve to seek comment by the Attorney General in its reviews.

151. The Federal Communications Commission (FCC) regulates interstate and foreign commerce in communication by wire and radio.[198] Its authority encompasses telecommunications common carriers, radio and television broadcasting, and cable communications. The US, represented by the Antitrust Division, is automatically a party respondent, separate from the FCC, in proceedings for review of most FCC orders (except licensing and license transfer orders) in the courts of appeals.

152. The experience of AT&T in its efforts to acquire T-Mobile provides a good example of how such procedures work in tandem. The Justice Department brought suit to enjoin the merger but the merger also required approval by the FCC. The FCC ultimately announced that it would undertake a full-scale review of the merger – a process that could take years. AT&T sought to short circuit matters by withdrawing the petition for approval from the FCC and obtaining a prompt decision from the court in the antitrust case. However, the government argued that there was no longer a case or controversy for the court to consider in the absence of a request for approval from the FCC since there could be no merger without such approval. Once the court accepted that argument, AT&T abandoned its merger efforts.

153. The International Trade Commission (ITC) governs issues related to import trade into the US. The ITC evaluates claims of unfair trade practices involving the importation of articles into the US. The ITC must seek the Justice Department's advice before making a final determination. The Justice Department may also participate in the interagency group that advises whether to approve the ITC's findings and proposed relief. Under various other acts, the ITC has responsibilities relating to dumping and tariffs. Private parties are authorized to bring complaints before the ITC.

154. The Department of Energy Organization Act established the Federal Energy Regulatory Commission (FERC).[199] Under the Federal Power Act[200] and Natural Gas Act,[201] FERC regulates mergers and acquisitions involving electric utilities and similar energy related entities.

---

196. 12 U.S.C. § 1828(c) (the statute provides for consultation with the Attorney General, who heads the Department of Justice, of which the Antitrust Division is a part).
197. 12 U.S.C. §§ 1841–1850, 1971–1978.
198. 47 U.S.C. § 151.
199. 42 U.S.C. §§ 7101–7352.
200. 16 U.S.C. §§ 791–828c.
201. 15 U.S.C. §§ 717 et seq.

IV. Administrative Fines

155. The antitrust agencies usually do not issue fines themselves. They can enter into consent agreements with the private parties whose conduct is in question requiring payment of fines or they can ask federal courts to impose fines. Also, by statute, a respondent that violates an outstanding order of the FTC is liable "for a civil penalty of not more than USD 10,000 for each violation."[202]

V. Administrative Injunctions and Other Restrictive Orders

156. Under the FTC Act, the FTC has authority to issue cease and desist orders after an administrative proceeding before the Commission, which would occur after an appeal from a decision by an Administrative Law Judge.[203] The Commission's order becomes final sixty days after it is issued, unless it is stayed by the Commission or the reviewing federal Court of Appeals.[204]

157. Both antitrust agencies can negotiate consent agreements with the private parties ordering, limiting, or directing certain conduct. Often, a consent decree will require a party to divest assets attendant to a merger to prevent competitive harm. The antitrust agencies can seek injunctive or similar relief in the courts. This is the general procedure when the agencies seek to block a merger.

VI. Preliminary Injunctions (Interim Measures)

158. As an interim measure, the antitrust agencies can file a motion for a preliminary injunction in federal court enjoining a proposed merger or other anticompetitive conduct. A preliminary injunction prevents the merger from being consummated during proceedings on the final merits that determine whether the merger would or would not harm competition.

§2. Civil Enforcement

159. The private civil suit is a major component of American antitrust law, in part because the Clayton Act provides significant inducements to private enforcement. The statute provides the prevailing plaintiff with a mandatory award of treble damages and an award of attorneys' fees and the litigation costs.[205] This is a major departure from the general American rule that each party bears its own cost and attorneys' fees. It is also far more favorable to plaintiffs than the rule in non-American jurisdictions since it works in only one direction: a prevailing plaintiff, but not a prevailing defendant, may recover its attorneys' fees.

202. 15 U.S.C. § 45(l).
203. *Ibid.*, at § 45(b).
204. *Ibid.*, at § 45(g).
205. 15 U.S.C. § 15(a).

160. The Clayton Act provides additional inducements: a private plaintiff may use a judgment in a government action against a defendant as evidence of the defendant's liability, collaterally estopping the defendant from challenging the finding of liability.[206] This both assists government enforcement, since many defendants will accept pleas instead of risking entry of a formal judgment against them, and is an obvious boon to a civil plaintiff. The Supreme Court has referred to counsel bringing private civil enforcement actions as "private attorneys general."[207] American antitrust enforcement relies extensively on such suits.

161. These provisions under the antitrust statutes are greatly augmented by the class action provision of Rule 23 of the Federal Rules of Civil Procedure, which allows victims of antitrust violations to aggregate their claims in a single representative action. This vastly increases the total size of the potential award of damages to the victims. It is most commonly used to aggregate the claims of victims of price-fixing. All the claims of the direct customers of the conspiring defendants can be brought in a single action. The damages can be very high – recoveries in the hundreds of millions of dollars are not uncommon.[208] For example, in *In re NASDAQ Mkt.-Makers Antitrust Litig.*,[209] a class action alleging collusion among certain brokerage firms, resulted in recovery of USD 1.027 billion for victims.

162. In the litigation that followed the government's successful monopolization case against Microsoft, a wide array of private plaintiffs were able to aggregate their claims in class actions as well as to take advantage of the government's having established Microsoft's monopolization.

I. Competent Civil Courts

163. Actions to enforce federal antitrust laws can only be brought in the federal court system, since it has exclusive jurisdiction over claims brought under the federal antitrust laws. This means, as a practical matter, that the suit must be commenced in a US District Court. These courts are divided among the fifty states and the District of Columbia; the specific locale in which a case must be brought is determined by statutory jurisdiction and venue provisions. These provisions are not very restrictive when it comes to the cases brought under the antitrust laws. Section 12 of the Clayton Act, which governs service of process in antitrust suits, has been construed by most courts to permit service worldwide. It has also been construed to apply a minimum

206. 15 U.S.C. § 16(a).

207. *Hawaii v. Standard Oil Co. of Cal.*, 405 U.S. 251, 262, 92 S. Ct. 885, 891, 31 L. Ed. 2d 184 (1972).

208. *See, e.g.*, *In re Vitamins Antitrust Litig.*, 305 F. Supp. 2d 100, 104 (D.D.C. 2004) (USD 1.05 billion); *In re Linerboard Antitrust Litig.*, 321 F. Supp. 2d 619, 624 (E.D. Pa. 2004)(USD 202.5 million); *In re Brand Name Prescription Drugs Antitrust Litig.*, 94 C 897, 1996 WL 167347 (N.D. Ill. Apr. 4, 1996) (USD 408 million).

209. 187 F.R.D. 465, 470 (S.D.N.Y. 1998).

contacts test that bases jurisdiction on a foreign corporation's aggregate contacts with the entire US, rather than with any particular state.[210]

164. While normally the venue in which a case can be brought is further restricted by limiting venue statutes, courts generally hold that the venue provision of section 12 of the Clayton Act is supplemented by the general federal venue statute,[211] which permits an "alien corporation" to be sued in any district. An "alien corporation" is a corporation incorporated in a state other than the state in which the suit is brought, not a corporation domiciled in a foreign country. Thus, as a practical matter, a corporation is susceptible to suit in virtually any district in the US.

165. Under section 4 of the Clayton Act "any person who shall be injured in his business or property by reason of anything forbidden in the antitrust laws may sue ..." Because of this broad statutory grant, courts have created a number of doctrines that limit the persons and entities that can sue: antitrust injury, antitrust standing, the direct purchaser rule, and statutes of limitation.

A. Antitrust Injury

166. First, the injury must be an "antitrust injury," i.e., an injury that the antitrust laws were passed to address. In *Brunswick Corp. v. Pueblo Bowl-O-Mat, Inc.*,[212] a well-financed company acquired the plaintiff's local competitor which, absent the acquisition, would have gone out of business. The acquisition fell under the merger restrictions of section 7 of the Clayton Act, and the plaintiff sued, claiming that it lost profits as a result of the illegal acquisition. The jury found for the plaintiff and awarded damages based on the difference between the profits the plaintiff had earned and the profits it would have earned had the competing business left the market. The Supreme Court rejected the claim because the plaintiff's injury resulted from *the addition of competition*, rather than from any restriction on competition. The Court held that the plaintiff was required to prove "injury of the type the antitrust laws were intended to prevent and that flows from that which makes defendants' acts unlawful."[213]

B. Antitrust Standing

167. An antitrust violation may have significant impact on many different persons and many different levels in the chain of distribution. For example, a boycott of a competing discounter may affect the boycotted competitor that will suffer lost profits from the inability to obtain a necessary product, the customers of the competitor that cannot obtain the lower-priced product, and even the customers of the competitors organizing the boycott, who may claim that the boycott increased prices by reducing competition from the lower-priced discounter. If the discounter were driven from the market, its landlord may suffer loss of rental income, its creditors loss of any financing they provided, and its shareholders loss of the value of their shares. Each of these

210. *In re Auto. Refinishing Paint Antitrust Litig.*, 358 F.3d 288, 293 (3d Cir. 2004) (acknowledging a split of authority on the issue).
211. 28 U.S.C. § 1391.
212. 429 U.S. 477, 489, 97 S. Ct. 690, 697, 50 L. Ed. 2d 701 (1977).
213. *Ibid.*

different groups was injured, and, without further restrictions, each might be entitled to treble damages. Similarly, price-fixing may affect various levels in the chain of distribution, from the distributor to the retailer to the end user. The laws of standing are intended to determine who may sue. The Supreme Court, in a series of cases, has created various criteria to determine which entities are too "remote" to claim damages from an antitrust violation.

168. In *Associated Gen. Contractors of California, Inc. v. California State Council of Carpenters,*[214] and *Blue Shield of Virginia v. McCready,*[215] the Court set out the broad rules governing standing. *Associated General Contractors* set forth five criteria under which standing is to be considered: (1) the causal connection between the antitrust violation and the harm to the plaintiff and the intent by the defendant to cause that harm; (2) whether the plaintiff's alleged injury is of the type for which the antitrust laws were intended to provide redress; (3) the directness of the injury, which addresses the concern that liberal application of standing principles might produce speculative claims; (4) the existence of more direct victims of the alleged antitrust violations; and (5) the potential for duplicative recovery or complex apportionment of damages.[216] *Associated General Contractors* involved claims by a labor union that it lost union dues because an association of contractors conspired to force developers and landowners to use nonunion labor in their construction projects. While the Court recognized a causal connection between the alleged violation and the plaintiff's harm, it held that the union lacked standing. First, the Court questioned whether the union's claims met the *Brunswick* test, which requires that this loss of union dues be the type of injury the antitrust laws were intended to redress. The violation and injury were protected by American labor law, which addressed the issue directly. Antitrust law had assiduously avoided involvement in labor disputes. The alleged restraint was in the housing construction market. The union was neither a competitor nor customer in that market. Its success in the suit would not clearly affect the level of competition in the construction market. The union's injury was also indirect:

> [D]efendants applied coercion against certain landowners and other contracting parties in order to cause them to divert business from certain union contractors to nonunion contractors. As a result, the Union's complaint alleges, the Union suffered unspecified injuries in its "business activities." It is obvious that any such injuries were only an indirect result of whatever harm may have been suffered by "certain" construction contractors and subcontractors.[217]

The landowners and developers who were the subject of the coercion were more likely to bring suit if there was a genuine restraint upon competition. As a result, there was great risk of complexity and need for apportionment of damages. The Court denied standing.

---

214. 459 U.S. 519, 103 S. Ct. 897, 74 L. Ed. 2d 723 (1983).
215. 457 U.S. 465, 102 S.Ct. 2540, 73 L.Ed.2d 149 (1982).
216. *See In re Lower Lake Erie Iron Ore Antitrust Litig.*, 998 F.2d 1144, 1165–1166 (3d Cir. 1993); *Chemi SpA v. GlaxoSmithKline*, 356 F. Supp. 2d 495, 501 (E.D. Pa. 2005).
217. *Associated Gen. Contractors*, 459 U.S. at 540–541, 103 S. Ct. at 909–910, 74 L. Ed. 2d 723.

169. Blue Shield of Virginia v. McCready,[218] the Court's second major standing case, involved allegations of boycott. Blue Shield, a prepaid medical plan made up of doctors, refused to reimburse subscribers for psychological services provided by psychologists rather than psychiatrists. Mrs. McCready, who had visited and paid a psychologist and was denied reimbursement by Blue Shield, sued, claiming that she was a victim of Blue Shield's boycott of psychologists. Blue Cross argued that she lacked standing to bring suit because she was neither a purchaser of the plan – it had been purchased by her employer – nor an object of the boycott, since she was not a psychologist. The Supreme Court held that she had standing. It applied a somewhat different test than that in *Associated General Contractors*, but both tests share certain criteria. The *Blue Shield* analysis ran as follows. First, the concern for duplicative damages being awarded was absent. Mrs. McCready was seeking the unreimbursed payment she had made to her psychologist. Her psychologist had been paid, so he lacked a cause of action for those damages that Mrs. McCready was seeking.[219] Second, her loss was exactly that which the antitrust laws were intended to prevent:

> Denying reimbursement to subscribers for the cost of treatment was the very means by which it is alleged that Blue Shield sought to achieve its illegal ends. The harm to McCready and her class was clearly foreseeable; indeed, it was a necessary step in effecting the ends of the alleged illegal conspiracy. Where the injury alleged is so integral an aspect of the conspiracy alleged, there can be no question but that the loss was precisely "the type of loss that the claimed violations...would be likely to cause."[220]

170. As to the argument that Mrs. McCready was not a participant in the relevant markets because she neither purchased insurance nor provided psychological services, the Court explained that she, as a consumer of psychological services, was *directly* injured by the boycott:

> [S]ubscribers were compelled to choose between visiting a psychologist and forfeiting reimbursement, or receiving reimbursement by forgoing treatment by the practitioner of their choice. In the latter case, the antitrust injury would have been borne in the first instance by the competitors of the conspirators, and inevitably-though indirectly-by the customers of the competitors in the form of suppressed competition in the psychotherapy market; in the former case, as it happened, the injury was borne directly by the customers of the competitors. McCready did not yield to Blue Shield's coercive pressure, and bore Blue Shield's sanction in the form of an increase in the net cost of her psychologist's services. Although McCready was not a competitor of the conspirators, the injury she

---

218. 457 U.S. 465, 102 S.Ct. 2540, 73 L.Ed.2d 149 (1982).

219. The Court acknowledged that the psychologists were suing in a separate action for the different damages they incurred as a result of the boycott. They had lost the profits they would have made had patients been able to obtain reimbursement for their services.

220. 457 U.S. at 479, 102 S. Ct. at 2548 (citation omitted).

suffered was inextricably intertwined with the injury the conspirators sought to inflict on psychologists and the psychotherapy market.[221]

171. Taken together, *McCready* and *Associated General Contractors* replaced a hodgepodge of various tests created by the lower courts. However, they fail to provide anything approaching a litmus test, though succeeding cases have established certain basic principles. For example, it is generally accepted that landlords,[222] suppliers,[223] and stockholders[224] of victims lack standing to sue even though they incur losses in the form of lost rent, lost sales, or decline in stock value. An interesting issue that has split the courts is whether an employee who is fired for failing to cooperate in an antitrust violation has standing. The prevailing view is that, except in the limited circumstances, the fired employee lacks standing.[225]

C. *The Direct Purchaser Rule*

172. In one area, the Supreme Court has fashioned a bright-line rule of standing known as the *Illinois Brick*, or direct purchaser, rule. Only a victim dealing directly with an antitrust violator may recover damages. Thus, for example, in a price-fixing case, only a person purchasing from a conspirator may sue. This is the case even if the direct purchaser is a distributor who merely passes on the increased prices caused by the conspiracy to its downstream customers and suffers no actual damage itself. In *Illinois Brick Co. v. Illinois*,[226] the Court held that only the direct purchaser from a conspirator can sue for damages under federal antitrust law.

173. While the Court provided various rationales for this rule, the decision seemed to have been mandated by its prior decision in *Hanover Shoe, Inc. v. United Shoe Machinery Corporation*.[227] There, the Court had held that a violator could not assert, as a defense, that a victim had "passed on"[228][229] any injury to its customers and was therefore not injured itself. Having eliminated the defense and essentially provided

221. 457 U.S. at 483–484, 102 S. Ct. at 2550–2551.
222. *Southaven Land Co. v. Malone & Hyde, Inc.*, 715 F.2d 1079, 1085–1088 (6th Cir. 1983).
223. *SAS of P.R. v. P.R. Tel. Co.*, 48 F.3d 39, 44 (1st Cir. 1995).
224. *Loeb v. Eastman Kodak*, 183 F. 704, 710 (3d Cir. 1910).
225. *See Vinci v. Waste Mgmt., Inc.*, 80 F.3d 1372, 1376 (9th Cir. 1996)("*Ostrofe II* recognized a limited exception to the general rule that a terminated employee lacks antitrust standing.... limited to those cases in which a dismissed employee is an 'essential participant' in an antitrust scheme, the dismissal is a 'necessary means' to accomplish the scheme, and the employee has the greatest incentive to challenge the antitrust violation.")
226. 431 U.S. 720, 723, 97 S. Ct. 2061, 2063, 52 L. Ed. 2d 707 (1977).
227. 392 U.S. 481, 483, 88 S. Ct. 2224, 2226, 20 L. Ed. 2d 1231 (1968).
228. *Ibid.*, at 488.
229. *Illinois Brick* itself had created an exception in the case of a pre-existing, fixed quantity, cost-plus contract. *Ibid.*, at 494. However, the rareness of contracts meeting all three of these criteria has severely circumscribed the effect of the exception. Courts have repeatedly rejected attempts to circumvent the rule by merely alleging that a distributor was itself a co-conspirator and have required that the distributor actually be sued as a co-conspirator if a downstream plaintiff is seeking to avoid the *Illinois Brick* bar. *Fontana Aviation, Inc. v. Cessna Aircraft Co.*, 617 F.2d 478 (7th Cir. 1980).

a right to recovery of all overcharges to the direct purchaser without diminution for any overcharge that it had passed on, the Court, to avoid risks of duplicative damages and complex apportionment, placed the entire cause of action in the hands of the most directly affected party. By doing so, the Court placed the damages in the hands of the party likely to have had the largest purchases. It thereby created great incentive for that purchaser to sue and created the greatest deterrence to would be violators who would face claims by the parties with the greatest damages.

174. Except for one limited circumstance, the courts have been loathe to create exceptions to the *Illinois Brick* rule. The exception, which has been invoked in several cases, is where a purchaser has bought a product incorporating the price-fixed product from a company that was engaged in the price-fixing conspiracy. Thus, purchasers of candy from a sugar manufacturer that had been engaged in a conspiracy to fix the price of sugar were found to have standing to sue to recover the overcharges to the candy resulting from inclusion of the price-fixed sugar.[230] Similarly, purchasers of corrugated boxes from paper manufacturers who had engaged in a conspiracy to raise the price of the paper from which boxes were made were found to have standing to sue to recover the overcharges for the boxes resulting from inclusion of the price-fixed paper.[231]

175. One would have thought that since the focus of the *Illinois Brick* rule was upon concern for duplicative damages and apportionment of damages at different levels in the supply chain, the Supreme Court would have held that state antitrust laws specifically granting damage remedies to indirect downstream purchasers were pre-empted by federal law. However, the Court has held the opposite: that such statutes are valid and that indirect purchasers in states having such laws may sue under state antitrust laws even though direct purchasers may be suing for the same violations under federal law.[232]

176. Because *Illinois Brick* only pertains to damages actions and still allows an indirect victim to sue for an injunction, plaintiffs have brought class actions for injunctive relief under the federal antitrust laws in federal court and, under the supplementary jurisdiction of the court,[233] coupled their federal claims with damage claims under various state laws on behalf of classes of indirect purchasers residing in states having such statutory remedies.[234] Such cases present complexity, as anticipated in *Illinois Brick*.[235] But those complexities are being resolved as courts have come to construe the state laws of the states having such indirect purchaser statutes.[236]

230. *In re Sugar Industry Antitrust Litig.*, 579 F.2d 13, 18 (3d Cir. 1978).
231. *In re Linerboard Antitrust Litig.*, 305 F.3d 145, 159–160 (3d Cir. 2002).
232. *See, California v. ARC Am. Corp.*, 490 U.S. 93, 96, 109 S. Ct. 1661, 1663, 104 L. Ed. 2d 86 (1989).
233. 28 U.S.C. § 1367.
234. *See, e.g.*, *In re Flonase Antitrust Litig.*, 692 F. Supp. 2d 524, 533 (E.D. Pa. 2010); *In re Wellbutrin XL Antitrust Litig.*, 260 F.R.D. 143, 147 (E.D. Pa. 2009).
235. *See, e.g.*, *In re Wellbutrin XL Antitrust Litig.*, CIV.A. 08-2433, 2011 WL 3563835 (E.D. Pa. Aug. 15, 2011).
236. *See* , e.g., *Sullivan v. DB Investments, Inc.*, 667 F.3d 273 (3d Cir. 2011).

D. Limitations of Actions

177. Suit must be brought within four years of the date of the injury from the violation.[237] Two doctrines exist that may toll, i.e., extend, the limitations date. First, the doctrine of fraudulent concealment allows a party to extend the limitations date by proving that the defendants engaged in activity to conceal their violation. Such proof requires an act of concealment by the defendant that prevented discovery of the violation by a duly diligent plaintiff.[238] Some conspiracies, such as price-fixing, are often considered "self-concealing" and require little proof of actual concealment.[239]

178. A second doctrine is that of a continuing violation. A violation may continue over an extended period of time. A price-fixing conspiracy may extend over many years, and each sale made using the inflated prices under the agreement is a violation that revives the plaintiff's claim.[240] The fact that a conspirator began fixing prices more than four years before the plaintiff brought suit would not bar the suit if the price-fixing had continued into the limitations period. However, absent proof of fraudulent concealment, a plaintiff may be limited to damages for the four years prior to its suit. In other contexts, such as refusals to deal, courts have found that a continued passive refusal does not necessarily revive the action and that the statute of limitations will not be revived unless the refusal is reiterated.[241]

II. Sanctions

A. Nullity

179. Nullity is not a common concept in American antitrust law. A party may seek to enjoin enforcement of an agreement that violates the antitrust laws.[242] A court may refuse to enforce a restrictive agreement because it restrains competition, and a court cannot be used to enforce the very activity that the Sherman Act was intended to prevent.[243] However, "[a]s a defense to an action based on contract, the plea of illegality based on violation of the Sherman Act has not met with much favor" since "it creates a very strange class of private attorneys general," i.e., a party to a contract claiming its own contract is illegal.[244] Thus, in *Kelly*, the Court explained that a court would not enforce an agreement between a buyer and seller restricting the sale of the onions since that restriction violated the antitrust law. However, the Court refused to

237. 15 U.S.C. § 15b.
238. *In re Linerboard Antitrust Litig.*, 305 F.3d 145, 161 (3d Cir. 2002).
239. *See, State of N.Y. v. Hendrickson Bros.*, 840 F.2d 1065, 1083–1085 (2d Cir. 1988).
240. *Zenith Radio Corp. v. Hazeltine Research*, 401 U.S. 321, 388 (1971).
241. *See , e.g., Rx.com v. Medco Health Solutions, Inc.*, 322 F. App'x 394, 397 (5th Cir. 2009) cert. denied, 130 S. Ct. 512, 175 L. Ed. 2d 350 (U.S. 2009)("Rx.com failed to offer evidence that Defendants reiterated their refusals to admit Rx.com to their networks during the limitations period.").
242. *See, e.g., United States v. Dentsply Int'l, Inc.*, CIV.A. 99-005(SLR), 2006 WL 2612167 (D. Del. Apr. 26, 2006) (enjoining exclusive dealer contracts of monopolist).
243. *Kaiser Steel Corp. v. Mullins,* 455 U.S. 72, 82, 102 S. Ct. 851, 859, 70 L. Ed. 2d 833 (1982).
244. *Kelly v. Kosuga,* 358 U.S. 516, 518, 520, 79 S. Ct. 429, 431, 3 L. Ed. 2d 475 (1959).

recognize as a defense to an action for the payment for the sale of the onions that the onions were the subject of a price-fixing arrangement. "Past the point where the judgment of the Court would itself be enforcing the precise conduct made unlawful by the Act, the courts are to be guided by the over-riding general policy, as Mr Justice Holmes put it, 'of preventing people from getting other people's property for nothing when they purport to be buying it.'"[245]

B. Damages

180. The Clayton Act provides for mandatory treble damages as well as for an award of attorneys' fees and the costs of the litigation to the prevailing plaintiff.[246] As discussed earlier, the amount of a damages remedy can be significantly amplified by the class action procedural device, which allows victims to aggregate their claims in a single proceeding.

181. A very powerful weapon of plaintiffs in antitrust cases is the concept of joint and several liability. While in conspiracy cases it is common to sue all members of the conspiracy, a victim need not sue or obtain a judgment against all the conspirators to recover full damages. Conspirators are held jointly and severally liable for all of the damages flowing from a conspiracy.[247] This means that any person proven to be part of a conspiracy is liable for all of the damages flowing from the conspiracy.

182. This rule becomes a potent weapon where all the conspirators have been sued in, say, a price-fixing case. A plaintiff could settle with one defendant for a nominal amount and still pursue the full damages flowing from the conspiracy from the remaining defendants.[248] The defendants themselves have no right of contribution against their co-defendants.[249] Thus, the law as it stands places great pressure on defendants to settle early – or at least not to be left among the final defendants to settle.

183. To ameliorate these pressures, defendants often enter into "sharing agreements," sometimes known as "sales out" agreements. Under these agreements, defendants agree that if any of them settle, they will obtain a settlement provision from the plaintiff reducing the damages the plaintiff will seek against the remaining defendants by the percentage of all defendants' sales that the settling defendant controls, i.e., to take the settling defendants' sales out of the remaining case. The agreement provides that if such a provision is not obtained, the settling defendant will be liable to its co-defendants for any portion of their judgment based on the sales of the settling defendant.

184. Damages in antitrust cases take many different forms, depending upon the case. In price-fixing or market-allocation cases, the damages are generally the amount of the resulting overcharge, i.e., the difference between the price actually charged and

245. *Ibid.*, at U.S. at 520–521, 79 S. Ct. at 432.

246. 15 U.S.C. § 15(a).

247. *Texas Indus., Inc. v. Radcliff Materials, Inc.*, 451 U.S. 630, 646, 101 S. Ct. 2061, 2070, 68 L. Ed. 2d 500 (1981).

248. The amounts obtained in settlement are deducted from any judgment *after* trebling. *See, William Inglis & Sons Baking Co. v. Cont'l Baking Co., Inc.*, 981 F.2d 1023, 1024 (9th Cir. 1992).

249. *Texas Indus., Inc. v. Radcliff Materials, Inc.*, 451 U.S. 630, 646, 101 S. Ct. 2061, 2070, 68 L. Ed. 2d 500 (1981).

the price that would have prevailed in a competitive market.[250] The competitive market may be measured by a temporal period in which the market was believed to be competitive or by a market in an analogous product the price of which was not fixed. In *In re Linerboard Antitrust Litig.*, the court cited three different types of benchmarks that might be used:

> "[B]enchmarking," which uses "competitive prices for other comparable products to estimate the pattern of prices but-for the alleged misconduct[,]" could be effectively employed in this situation. Another proffered model would "compare[] prices during non-conspiratorial periods with product prices during the alleged conspiracy," and yet a third approach would use revenue, production and profit data to derive prices that are consistent with "yardstick" competitive performance levels.[251]

These analyses often involve highly complex statistical models.[252]

185. Where a competitor is suing, damages generally take the form of lost profits.[253] In broad concept, lost profit calculations may use methods similar to those described above. Is there a market in which the plaintiff operated that was not subject to the violation to which its profits in the area subject to the violation can be compared?[254] Is there a period before the violation that allows for comparison of the plaintiff's profits and business growth with the period in which the violation allegedly occurred? Are there other products the plaintiff sold not affected by violation that would allow for comparison? Is there a date prior to the violation on which the business can be valued, applying standard forms of business valuation, in comparison to the value of the business after the violation occurred? For example, a generic drug company excluded from the market may be able to construct a damages theory based upon its experience with other comparable generic drugs.

186. In theory, several classic Supreme Court decisions have broken the "injury" element of damages into two parts: causation, or "injury," and damages, i.e. the amount of damages suffered. "The courts have always distinguished between proof of *causation*

---

250. *In re Linerboard Antitrust Litig.*, 305 F.3d 145, 154 (3d Cir. 2002) ("suggested as a potential benchmark, the potential prices charged … during a competitive period when there would be no effects of the conspiracy."); *In re Plywood Antitrust Litig.*, 655 F.2d 627, 632 (5th Cir. 1981); *In re Corrugated Container Antitrust Litig.*, 756 F.2d 411, 417 (5th Cir. 1985).

251. 305 F.3d at 154–155 (citations omitted).

252. *See, e.g.*, *ibid.*, at 305 F.3d at 154; *In re High Fructose Corn Syrup Antitrust Litig.*, 295 F.3d 651, 660 (7th Cir. 2002).

253. *William Inglis & Sons Baking Co. v. Cont'l Baking Co., Inc.*, 981 F.2d 1023, 1024 (9th Cir. 1992)("net damage is the difference between the lost profit stream and the proceeds [the plaintiff] did receive.").

254. *See , e.g.*, In *Zenith Radio Corp. v. Hazeltine Research, Inc.*, 395 U.S. 100, 123–124, 89 S.Ct. 1562, 1576, 23 L.Ed.2d 129 (1969).

of damages and proof of the *amount* of damages. Once liability is established, a plaintiff's proof of damages is evaluated under a more lenient standard."[255]

187. The standard for proof of causation has generally been strict. The plaintiff must prove by a preponderance of the evidence that it was in some fashion injured by the defendant's antitrust violation. Many decisions, however, have given lip service to the proposition that once some causation has been proven, a standard for calculating the actual damages caused should be more lenient because it was the defendant, by engaging in the violation that disrupted the competitive conditions in the market, that caused the difficulty in proving damages with precision.[256]

188. However, courts have been strict when it comes to proving causation, so much so that the advantages flowing from the more lenient standard for calculating damages have been limited. They have required strict proof that the damages ultimately calculated were caused by the antitrust violation. When there are multiple causes for damages and the damages from the antitrust violation have not been sufficiently isolated, courts have reversed.[257] In *Comcast Corp. v. Behrend*,[258] a sharply divided Court vacated certification of a class action where the economic expert had opined on the damages caused by multiple alleged violations collectively and the court had certified a class based on only one of the multiple alleged violations. The Supreme Court felt that there was an insufficient record attributing the damages that were the subject of the expert testimony to the one violation rather than to the violations collectively.

C. *Class Actions*

189. Whether an antitrust case can go forward as a class action is governed by Rule 23(b)(3) of the Federal Rules of Civil Procedure. Because class actions are so important to antitrust litigation, it is important to understand that rule. By aggregating the claims of all victims damages in class actions can be very high. Recently, a Court of Appeals affirmed a judgment of USD 1.2 billion against Dow Chemical Company in a price-fixing case.[259] Generally, class action treatment is appropriate in horizontal conspiracy cases involving price-fixing and customer or geographic allocation schemes.

255. *In re Scrap Metal Antitrust Litig.*, 527 F.3d 517, 533 (6th Cir. 2008); *J. Truett Payne Co., Inc. v. Chrysler Motors Corp.*, 451 U.S. 557, 568, 101 S. Ct. 1923, 1930, 68 L. Ed. 2d 442 (1981) ("Once a violation has been established, that burden is to some extent lightened.").

256. *Bigelow v. RKO Radio Pictures*, 327 U.S. 251, 264–265, 66 S. Ct. 574, 580, 90 L. Ed. 652 (1946) ("Any other rule would enable the wrongdoer to profit by his wrongdoing at the expense of his victim. It would be an inducement to make wrongdoing so effective and complete in every case as to preclude any recovery, by rendering the measure of damages uncertain. Failure to apply it would mean that the more grievous the wrong done, the less likelihood there would be of a recovery."); *In re Lower Lake Erie Iron Ore Antitrust Litig.*, 998 F.2d 1144, 1176 (3d Cir. 1993) ("Once causation is determined, however, the actual amount of damages may result from a 'reasonable estimate, as long as the jury verdict is not the product of speculation or guess work.'").

257. *See, e.g., Coleman Motor Co. v. Chrysler Corp.*, 525 F.2d 1338 (3d Cir. 1975); *MCI Communications Corp. v. Am. Tel. & Tel. Co.*, 708 F.2d 1081, 1161 (7th Cir. 1983).

258. 133 S. Ct. 1426 (2013).

259. *In re Urethane Antitrust Litig.*, 768 F.3d 1245 (10th Cir. 2014).

Class actions have also been found appropriate in monopolization cases, but the class certification issues in those cases are more complex. Class certification had in the past sometimes been denied in certain cases involving tying, resale price maintenance or vertical price-fixing where courts have found the questions involved were too particular to individuals to allow class treatment, but the present trend is to allow such claims to proceed on a class basis.[260]

190. A case is filed as a class action by one or more representative parties filing a suit on behalf of a class of persons similarly situated. For example, a purchaser of widgets may bring suit for price-fixing of widgets against the major widget manufacturers and define a class as all purchasers of widgets from one or more of the defendants. However, a case can only proceed to judgment as a class action if a court has subsequently "certified" the case as a class action in response to a pretrial motion usually filed by the plaintiff. The court must find that the plaintiff meets the requirements of Rules 23(a) and (b)(3). Rule 23(a) sets out four "prerequisites" for class certification. The plaintiff must show that the class is so numerous that it would be impracticable to join all members of the class as parties (sometimes known as "the numerosity requirement"); that there is at least one question of law or fact common to all members of the class (the "commonality" requirement); that the claims of the class representatives are typical of the claims or defenses of the class (the "typicality" requirement); and that the representative parties will fairly and adequately represent the interests of the class (the "adequacy of representation" requirement). In practical terms, numerosity is met by classes of as few as thirty and as many as several million. In a price-fixing case, the question of whether the defendants conspired will often be held a sufficient common question. The typicality requirement often overlaps with the commonality requirement. The adequacy of representation requirement generally looks to the quality of the attorneys retained to represent the class and the similarity between the situations of the representative plaintiffs and the other plaintiffs.

191. In addition to establishing "prerequisites" of Rule 23(a), the plaintiffs must establish that the case meets the requirements of Rule 23(b)(3). The most difficult hurdle in that rule is the requirement that questions of law or fact common to the class predominate over any questions involving only individual members. This "predominance" requirement is generally met in horizontal conspiracy cases since every purchaser has a common interest in maximizing damages and each would have to prove the existence of an effective conspiracy.[261] Since the goal of a conspiracy in such a case is to raise prices, plaintiffs are generally able to persuade courts that causation also represents a common question that predominates.[262]

192. While class certification is determined on a case-by-case basis, and the grounds for certifying the case as a class action must be clearly articulated by the

260. *See , e.g., In re Visa Check/Mastermoney Antitrust Litig.,* 192 F.R.D. 68, 71 (E.D.N.Y. 2000) *aff'd, In re Visa Check/MasterMoney Antitrust Litig.,* 280 F.3d 124 (2d Cir. 2001).

261. *See , e.g., In re Linerboard Antitrust Litig.,* 305 F.3d 145, 148 (3d Cir. 2002).

262. *See , e.g., Sullivan v. DB Investments, Inc.,*667 F.3d 273 (3d Cir. 2011).

court,[263] courts have overwhelmingly found that cases alleging horizontal conspiracies meet the criteria of Rule 23.[264]

193. Class certification has also been held appropriate in tying cases. The plaintiffs in *In re Visa Check/Mastermoney Antitrust Litigation* alleged that requiring stores to accept debit cards on the same terms as credit cards as a condition for authorizing credit cards represented an illegal tying arrangement.[265] The class representatives in that case were among the largest corporations in the world, including Wal-Mart Stores. The case ultimately was settled for over USD 3 billion.[266] That case also involved claims of attempted monopolization that had been certified for class adjudication.[267]

194. Once certified, Rule 23 requires that notice be sent to class members describing the litigation and giving class members the opportunity to "opt-out," i.e., to request exclusion by notifying the court of their desire not to participate. All class members who do not actively "opt-out" are included in the class and are bound by any judgment.[268] Any final judgment will describe the class, such as "All purchasers of widgets from defendants between date X and date Y" and will list the class members that have requested exclusion.

195. The case then proceeds on a class basis. This can favor defendants as well as plaintiffs because defendants can obtain a final judgment resolving all the claims against them arising from the activity in a single action. Defendants have sometimes obtained summary judgment against classes in antitrust cases.[269] On rare occasions plaintiffs have obtained summary judgment as well.[270]

---

263. *See , e.g., In re Hydrogen Peroxide Antitrust Litig.,* 552 F.3d 305 (3d Cir. 2008).

264. *See , e.g., In re Linerboard Antitrust Litig.,* 305 F.3d 145, 148 (3d Cir. 2002); *In re NASDAQ Mkt.-Makers Antitrust Litig.,* 169 F.R.D. 493, 518 (S.D.N.Y. 1996)("Courts repeatedly have held that the existence of a conspiracy is the predominant issue in price fixing cases, warranting certification of the class even where significant individual issues are present.").

265. 192 F.R.D. 68, 71 (E.D.N.Y. 2000) *aff'd,* 280 F.3d 124 (2d Cir. 2001).

266. *Wal-Mart Stores, Inc. v. Visa U.S.A., Inc.,* 396 F.3d 96 (2d Cir. 2005).

267. The Supreme Court's most recent decision of a class action in the antitrust context, *Comcast v. Behrend,* __U.S.__, 133 S. Ct 1426 (2013) vacated certification of a class in a monopolization case because of a failure of the evidentiary showing. There, the plaintiffs' expert had conceded that his regression model showing damages to the class included damages that may have resulted from actions that were not the subject of the claims the court had certified for classwide adjudication. The Court was sharply divided on the issue. On remand the trial court has sought to mold a narrower class consistent with the Supreme Court's decision. See, *Glaberson v. Comcast Corp.* 2013 WL 5988966 (E.D. Pa. Nov. 12, 2013).

268. Companies have availed themselves of the opportunity to opt-out and then have filed their own individual non-class action suits. *See , e.g., In re Linerboard Antitrust Litig.,* 292 F. Supp. 2d 644, 651 (E.D. Pa. 2003) ("Of the 140 Requests for Exclusion, several groups of opt outs subsequently filed tag-along actions against defendants.").

269. *See, e.g., Blomkest Fertilizer, Inc. v. Potash Corp. of Saskatchewan,* 203 F.3d 1028, 1031 (8th Cir. 2000); *In re Citric Acid Litig.,* 191 F.3d 1090 (9th Cir. 1999); *In re Baby Food Antitrust Litig.,* 166 F.3d 112, 116 (3d Cir. 1999).

270. *See Law v. Nat'l Collegiate Athletic Ass'n,* 134 F.3d 1010 (10th Cir. 1998).

196. Antitrust cases have also proceeded to trial on a class basis. In some cases, the plaintiffs have prevailed.[271] For example, in *In re Corrugated Container Antitrust Litigation*:

> [T]he jury returned a verdict in favor of the plaintiff class and both subclasses against The Mead Corporation (Mead), finding that Mead had participated in a conspiracy to fix, raise, maintain, or stabilize prices of corrugated containers and corrugated sheets sold throughout the United States during a period beginning before January 1, 1964, and continuing at least until December 31, 1975; that nineteen other corrugated manufacturers had participated in the conspiracy with Mead; and that the conspiracy caused financial damage in the amount of 5% of the purchase price to purchasers of corrugated containers and corrugated sheets in both subclasses throughout the United States.[272]

In others class actions, the defendants have prevailed.[273]

197. As with most cases brought in the US, the majority of antitrust class actions are settled before trial. Settlement of a class action requires notice to the class and approval of the settlement by the court. The notice describes the nature of the settlement to the class members and advises them of the opportunity to object to the settlement. More recent amendments to Rule 23 also give the court discretion to provide class members a second opportunity to opt-out of a proposed settlement. There are criteria under which the fairness of a settlement is considered.[274] Special considerations arise when class action certification is sought at the same time that the court's approval of the parties' settlement is sought.[275] In the settlement context, the plaintiff and defendant cease to be adversaries. Both seek the court's approval of a settlement. This heightens the need to assure that the interests of the absent class members are adequately protected and that there has been no collusion between plaintiffs and defendants in reaching the settlement.

---

271. *See In re Plywood Antitrust Litig.,* 655 F.2d 627 (5th Cir. 1981); *In re Corrugated Container Antitrust Litig.,* 556 F. Supp. 1117, 1125 (S.D. Tex. 1982) *aff'd,* 687 F.2d 52 (5th Cir. 1982).

272. *In re Corrugated Container Antitrust Litig.,* 556 F. Supp. 1117 (S.D. Tex. 1982) *aff'd,* 687 F.2d 52 (5th Cir. 1982).

273. *See, e.g., In re Brand Name Prescription Drug Antitrust Litigation,* 186 F.3d 781 (7th Cir. 1999).

274. *See, e.g., In re Linerboard Antitrust Litig.,* 321 F. Supp. 2d 619, 628 (E.D. Pa. 2004):

In Girsh[v. Jepson, 521 F.2d 153 (3d Cir.1975)], the Court of Appeals adopted a nine-factor test to guide district courts in evaluating whether a class action settlement is fair, adequate and reasonable, as follows:

(1) the complexity, expense and likely duration of the litigation...; (2) the reaction of the class to the settlement...; (3) the stage of the proceeding and the amount of discovery completed...; (4) the risks of establishing liability...; (5) the risks of establishing damages...; (6) the risks of maintaining the class action through the trial...; (7) the ability of the defendants to withstand a greater judgment; (8) the range of reasonableness of the settlement fund in light of the best possible recovery...; (9) the range of reasonableness of the settlement fund to a possible recovery in light of all the attendant risks of litigation....

275. *Amchem Products, Inc. v. Windsor,* 521 U.S. 591, 117 S. Ct. 2231, 138 L. Ed. 2d 689 (1997).

D. Preliminary Injunctions (Interim Measures)

198. Interim measures under American antitrust law are known as "preliminary injunctions." The Clayton Act provide for preliminary injunctive relief:

> Any person, firm, corporation or association shall be entitled to sue for and have injunctive relief, in any court of the United States having jurisdiction over the parties, against threatened loss or damage by a violation of the antitrust laws,... when and under the same conditions and principles as injunctive relief against threatened conduct that will cause loss or damage is granted by courts of equity, under the rules governing such proceedings, and upon the execution of proper bond against damages for an injunction improvidently granted and a showing that the danger of irreparable loss or damage is immediate, a preliminary injunction may issue.[276]

The statute incorporates the general requirements under federal procedure for obtaining a preliminary injunction, and, despite the statutory mandate, federal courts generally require a party to meet the formal requirements for a preliminary injunction. A party seeking such relief must show that it faces a danger of irreparable harm and a likelihood of success on the merits of the case. The actual standards for preliminary relief vary among federal circuit courts. If the motion is granted, the plaintiff is required to post a bond covering the defendant's losses resulting from the injunction in the event the plaintiff does not ultimately prevail.

199. The preliminary injunction is most commonly used in merger enforcement. Generally, either the Antitrust Division or the FTC will seek a preliminary injunction to block the merger they oppose. The FTC has independent statutory authority that is more expansive than that of the Clayton Act. Section 13(b) of the FTC Act provides that "[u]pon a proper showing that, weighing the equities and considering the Commission's likelihood of ultimate success, such action would be in the public interest, ... a preliminary injunction may be granted."[277] The District of Columbia Circuit has explained the difference between the general standard for preliminary relief and that under the FTC Act (FTCA):

> Whenever the Commission has reason to believe that a corporation is violating, or is about to violate, Section 7 of the Clayton Act, the FTC may seek a preliminary injunction to prevent a merger pending the Commission's administrative adjudication of the merger's legality. [The FTCA] provides for the grant of a preliminary injunction where such action would be in the public interest – as determined by a weighing of the equities and a consideration of the Commission's likelihood of success on the merits. The Congress intended this standard to depart from what it regarded as the then-traditional equity standard, which it characterized as requiring the plaintiff to show: (1) irreparable damage, (2) probability of

276. 15 U.S.C. § 26.
277. 15 U.S.C. § 53(b).

> success on the merits and (3) a balance of equities favoring the plaintiff. The Congress determined that the traditional standard was not appropriate for the implementation of a Federal statute by an independent regulatory agency where the standards of the public interest measure the propriety and the need for injunctive relief. The courts had evolved an approach to cases in which government agencies, acting to enforce a federal statute, sought interim relief. The agency, in such cases, was not held to the high thresholds applicable where private parties seek interim restraining orders. The FTC is not required to establish that the proposed merger would in fact violate Section 7 of the Clayton Act.[278]

Generally, though not always, litigation of the preliminary injunction phase is determinative of merger litigation brought by the government. The substantive merger law is discussed elsewhere. This section deals solely with the standards applied by the courts in the context of a preliminary injunction motion.

200. "Likelihood of success on the merits" measures:

> The probability that, after an administrative hearing on the merits, the Commission will succeed in proving that the effect of the...merger "may be substantially to lessen competition, or to tend to create a monopoly" in violation of Section 7 of the Clayton Act. This court and others have suggested that the standard for likelihood of success on the merits is met if the FTC "has raised questions going to the merits so serious, substantial, difficult and doubtful as to make them fair ground for thorough investigation, study, deliberation and determination by the FTC in the first instance and ultimately by the Court of Appeals."[279]

201. The second prong, the weighing of equities, is loaded in favor of the government, especially once likelihood of success on the merits has been established. "[T]he FTC's showing of likelihood of success creates a presumption in favor of preliminary injunctive relief" and "the principal public equity weighing in favor of issuance of preliminary injunctive relief is the public interest in effective enforcement of the antitrust laws."[280] As a practical matter, mergers, once consummated, cannot be easily undone. By contrast, if a merger is enjoined preliminarily, and that decision is later found to be erroneous, a new deal can be struck. Therefore, once likelihood of success is proven, the equities are almost invariably found to favor the government.

202. But there are exceptions. For example, in *FTC v. Whole Foods Market., Inc.*, the trial court denied a preliminary injunction because the FTC had failed to prove a likelihood of success on the merits.[281] The Court of Appeals refused to stay the merger pending the FTC's appeal. The parties consummated the merger. The Court of Appeals then reversed the trial court's denial of the preliminary injunction, finding that the government *had* shown a likelihood of success. It remanded the case for a weighing of the equities. Because the merger had already been consummated, the Court of

278. *FTC. v. H.J. Heinz Co.*, 246 F.3d 708, 714 (D.C. Cir. 2001) (citations omitted).
279. *Ibid.*, at 714–715 (citation omitted).
280. *Ibid.*, at 726.
281. 548 F.3d 1028 (D.C. Cir. 2008).

Appeals found that the court could fashion a remedy mitigating the harm to competition from the merger.[282]

203. There are numerous decisions, some granting[283] and some denying[284] preliminary relief in the merger context.

204. Preliminary injunctions outside the area of mergers are rare, except where a defendant has allegedly cut off supply to a customer after the customer brought suit alleging an antitrust violation. For example, in *Rochester Drug Co-Operative, Inc. v. Braintree Laboratories*, a pharmaceutical manufacturer cut off a drug wholesaler that had filed a patent-antitrust case against it.[285] The court articulated the traditional standard for preliminary relief:

> The moving party for injunctive relief must establish: (1) a likelihood of success on the merits; (2) that it will suffer irreparable harm if the injunction is denied; (3) that granting preliminary relief will not result in even greater harm to the nonmoving party; and (4) that the public interest favors such relief. The burden lies with the movant to establish every element in its favor or the grant of a preliminary injunction is inappropriate. If either or both of the fundamental requirements – likelihood of success on the merits and probability of irreparable harm if relief is not granted – are absent, an injunction cannot issue. The decision to grant or deny… injunctive relief is an act of equitable discretion by the district court. The grant of a preliminary injunction is considered an "extraordinary" remedy that should be granted only in limited circumstances.[286]

205. However, following *Bergen Drug Company, Inc. v. Parke, Davis & Company*, the courts have applied a more lenient standard.[287] Citing *Bergen Drug*, the court in *Rochester Drug* found that "a defendant's termination of its business relationship with an antitrust plaintiff would make it difficult, if not impossible, for the plaintiff to prosecute the action successfully."[288] That court required the defendant to continue to sell to the plaintiff during the litigation. The general harm discussed in *Bergen Drug*, aside from the inability to prosecute the litigation, was that a full-line drug wholesaler must have access to all major drugs in order to satisfy its retailer customers' needs and would, in the absence of a preliminary injunction ensuring it continued supply, lose customers and intangible goodwill, which would result in irreparable harm. In *Rochester Drug Co-Operative*, the court required that a bond be posted,[289] although it is difficult

282. *Ibid.*, at 1034.
283. *See, e.g.*, *FTC v. Staples, Inc.*, 970 F. Supp. 1066 (D.D.C. 1997); *FTC v. CCC Holdings Inc.*, 605 F.Supp.2d 26 (2009); *F.T.C. v. Swedish Match*, 131 F.Supp.2d 151 (D.D.C. 2000); *U.S. v. Microsoft*, 980 F. Supp. 537 (D.D.C. 1997).
284. *See, e.g.*, *FTC v. Laboratory Corp. of America*, 2011 WL 3100372 (C.D. Cal., Mar. 11, 2011); *FTC v. Arch Coal, Inc.*, 329 F.Supp.2d 109 (D.D.C. 2004).
285. CIV. 07-142-SLR, 2011 WL 2669208 (D. Del. Jul. 7, 2011).
286. *Ibid.*, at 4 (citations omitted).
287. 307 F.2d 725 (3d Cir.1962).
288. *Rochester Drug Co-op., Inc. v. Braintree Labs.*, 2011 WL 2669208, *6 (D.Del. 2011).
289. *Ibid.*

to imagine what harm the defendant would suffer by being required to sell to the plaintiff.

§3. Criminal Enforcement

I. Criminal Sanctions for Antitrust Enforcement

206. In the US, people are sentenced to jail for criminal violations of the antitrust laws. In 2010, the Antitrust Division reported that thirty-seven defendants were sentenced to jail terms, averaging thirty months, for violations of the antitrust laws. The Sherman Act itself provides for penalties of up to ten years imprisonment.[290] In addition, significant fines and restitutionary remedies may be imposed. As the Antitrust Division puts it on its website:

> The Division's long-standing belief is that holding culpable individuals accountable by seeking jail sentences is the most effective way to deter and punish cartel activity. The Division's enforcement statistics continue to demonstrate that individuals prosecuted by the Division are being sent to jail with increasing frequency and for longer periods of time.[291]

The Sherman Antitrust Act is primarily a criminal statute. It presently reads:

> Every contract, combination in the form of trust or otherwise, or conspiracy, in restraint of trade or commerce among the several States, or with foreign nations, is declared to be illegal. Every person who shall make any contract or engage in any combination or conspiracy hereby declared to be illegal shall be deemed guilty of a felony, and, on conviction thereof, shall be punished by fine not exceeding $100,000,000 if a corporation, or, if any other person, $1,000,000, or by imprisonment not exceeding 10 years, or by both said punishments, in the discretion of the court.[292]

207. The public anger at antitrust violations in the US often astonishes those abroad. A recent court decision imposing four-year sentences on participants in a local cartel to fix the prices of concrete gives a sense of the vengeance with which sentences are sometimes imposed:

290. 15 U.S.C. § 1.
291. Dep't of Justice, Antitrust Division, *Division Update Spring 2011: Criminal Program*, <www.justice.gov/atr/public/division-update/2011/criminal-program.html> (last visited Nov. 17, 2011).
292. 15 U.S.C. § 1.

> The defendants, although dressed in the attire of hard-working businessmen, were nothing more than common thieves, and serial ones at that. Like a neighborhood thief, they stole from friends, acquaintances, businesses and local governments. The defendants 'tools of their trade were not dark clothing worn in midnight burglaries facilitated by pry bars and screw drivers. Instead, in ordinary business attire and in the glare of broad daylight, they used the ordinary communication tools of modern commerce and business, cell phones, Blackberries, and e-mail to rob their victims. Unlike the neighborhood thief who values high end TVs, computers, jewelry, and furs, the defendants specialized in cold hard cash. Unlike the neighborhood thief whose victims immediately recoiled in shock at the loss of their property, the defendants stole from their victims without them ever knowing it. Their actions [... were] clever and cunning, but taken with full knowledge and intent to violate this Nation's criminal antitrust laws.[293]

208. The overwhelming number of criminal cases brought by the federal government involve cartel behavior: either price-fixing, output restrictions, customer allocation, or division of markets among horizontal competitors.

209. As discussed in section II below, the government has aggressively pursued violations of other statutes by cartels, such as obstruction of justice, perjury, mail and wire fraud, and money laundering.

210. The Government has also pursued foreign nationals, many of whom have served prison time as a result of their violations. In 2016, in a case involving manipulation of U.S. dollar and Japanese yen LIBOR interest rates, two British nationals were found guilty and received jail terms of one and two years respectively.[294] Notably, the two were sentenced for conduct they undertook in London.

211. The federal government has been able to extend the reach of the antitrust laws, even to those areas where clear extradition treaties do not exist, by stopping travel by an indicted person. Once an international warrant has been issued, a defendant is subject to detention almost anywhere in the world. Thus, a Japanese traveler to Bolivia, may be detained as he or she passes through passport control. He or she may be jailed for many months in a Bolivian prison pending resolution of the detention. As a result, perpetrators outside the technical jurisdictional reach of the US will often agree voluntarily to submit to the jurisdiction of American courts.

212. In addition to incarceration, the Sherman Act provides for fines, "not exceeding USD 100,000,000 if a corporation, or, if any other person, USD 1,000,000."[295] In 2015, the Government collected over USD 3.6 billion in criminal fines from corporations, though that year's numbers were inflated by the huge fines arising from the LIBOR manipulation cases.[296] In 2014, it collected USD 2 million in fines imposed on individuals. The largest fine ever imposed was a USD 925,000,000 fine imposed

---

293. *United States v. Vandebrake*, 771 F. Supp. 2d 961, 965–966 (N.D. Iowa 2011).

294. Dep't of Justice, Antitrust Division, *Division Update Spring 2011: Criminal Program*, <www.justice.gov/atr/public/division-update/2011/criminal-program.html> (last visited Nov. 17, 2011).

295. 15 U.S.C. § 1.

296. *See* , https://www.justice.gov/atr/criminal-enforcement-fine-and-jail-charts.

on Citibank in 2015 relating to the LIBOR manipulation cases.[297] Significantly, most of largest fines levied on corporations by the Antitrust Division were levied on corporations domiciled outside the US.[298]

II. Other Application of Criminal Law to Relevant Conduct

213. Other statutes have been applied to antitrust violators. These include conspiracy, aiding and abetting, fraud, money laundering and tax offenses. They also include offenses arising from the investigative process, such as obstruction, perjury and false statements, and criminal contempt.[299]

214. For example, in 2009, the Antitrust Division obtained a guilty plea from a defendant who had, among other things, rigged prices on sales of environmental cleanup services to the federal government. The defendant had obtained the bids of competitors before setting its own bid, thereby allowing it to inflate its bids. The defendant pleaded guilty to defrauding the government and providing kickbacks. A

---

297. *See* , https://www.justice.gov/atr/division-operations/division-update-2016/milestones-financial-industry-cleanup.

298. *See* , https://www.justice.gov/atr/sherman-act-violations-yielding-corporate-fine-10-million-or-more

299. The *Antitrust Division Manual, Statutory Provisions and Guidelines of the Antitrust Division, available at* <www.justice.gov/atr/public/divisionmanual/chapter2.pdf>, lists the following statutes: under Conspiracy, Aiding and Abetting, it lists 18 U.S.C. § 2 (Principals [aiding and abetting]), 18 U.S.C. § 371 (Conspiracy to commit offense or defraud the United States), 18 U.S.C. § 1349 (Attempt and conspiracy [mail and wire fraud]); under Fraud, it lists 18 U.S.C. § 201 (Bribery of public officials and witnesses), 18 U.S.C. § 666 (Theft or bribery concerning programs receiving Federal funds), 18 U.S.C. § 1001 (Statements or entries generally [false statements]), 18 U.S.C. § 1341 (Frauds and swindles [mail fraud] Antitrust Division Manual, Fourth Edition II-9), 18 U.S.C. § 1343 (Fraud by wire, radio, or television [wire fraud]). Under Money Laundering, it lists 18 U.S.C. § 1952 (Interstate and foreign travel or transportation in aid of racketeering enterprise), 18 U.S.C. § 1956 (Laundering of monetary instruments), and 18 U.S.C. § 1957 (Engaging in monetary transactions in property derived from specified unlawful activity). Under Tax Offenses, it lists 26 U.S.C. § 7201 (Attempt to evade or defeat tax), 26 U.S.C. § 7206 (Fraud and false statements), It also lists statutes under Offenses Involving the Integrity of the Investigative Process falling into three categories, Obstruction, Perjury and False Statements, and Criminal Contempt. Under Obstruction, it lists 18 U.S.C. § 1503 (Influencing or injuring officer or juror generally Antitrust Division Manual, Fourth Edition II-10), 18 U.S.C. § 1505 (Obstruction of proceedings before departments, agencies, and committees. This statute is used when there is obstruction of proceedings under the Antitrust Civil Process Act), 18 U.S.C. § 1509 (Obstruction of court orders), 18 U.S.C. § 1510 (Obstruction of criminal investigations), 18 U.S.C. § 1512 (Tampering with a witness, victim, or an informant), and 18 U.S.C. § 1519 (Destruction, alteration, or falsification of records in Federal investigations and bankruptcy). Under Perjury and False Statements, it lists 18 U.S.C. § 1621 (Perjury generally),18 U.S.C. § 1622 (Subornation of perjury), and 18 U.S.C. § 1623 (False declarations before grand jury or court).Under Criminal Contempt, it lists 18 U.S.C. § 402 (Contempts constituting crimes, Antitrust Division Manual, Fourth Edition II-11), 18 U.S.C. § 3691 (Jury trial of criminal contempts), and Fed. R. Crim. P. 42 (Criminal contempt).

particularly stark example of the use of the criminal obstruction statutes is described by the Antitrust Division on its website:

> In 2004, a Federal Grand Jury indicted Ian P. Norris, the former CEO of U.K. corporation The Morgan Crucible Company, on one count of fixing prices of carbon brushes and other carbon products, one count of conspiring to obstruct justice, and two counts of obstructing justice in connection with the Division's investigation of price fixing in the carbon products industry. Norris, a citizen of the United Kingdom, was extradited to the United States in March 2010 to face trial on the three obstruction charges. On July 27, 2010, a Federal jury in Philadelphia returned a guilty verdict on the conspiracy to obstruct justice count and not guilty verdicts on the witness tampering count and the count of corruptly persuading others to destroy or conceal documents. On Dec. 10, 2010, Norris was sentenced to serve 18 months in prison for his role in a conspiracy to obstruct a Federal Grand Jury investigation into price fixing of carbon brushes and other carbon products.[300]

215. In 2006, Bristol-Meyers Squibb and one of its former corporate officers were prosecuted by the Antitrust Division under the false statement statute[301] for misleading the FTC.[302]

III. Role of Prosecutors

A. The Prosecutor's Role in the Most Common Cases

216. All criminal prosecutions are brought by the Antitrust Division of the Department of Justice. They may be prosecuted by the central office in Washington D.C. or by attorneys at the Antitrust Division's various regional offices. The procedures followed by the Antitrust Division are set out in considerable detail in the Division Manual.[303]

217. An investigation by the Antitrust Division can be initiated by staff, either upon receiving a complaint from the public or discovering grounds for investigation. The staff, following very preliminary review, then may either request permission to undertake a preliminary investigation or seek to convene a grand jury. Either request requires approval by the appropriate section and field office chief and the Director of Enforcement. A request to convene a grand jury must also be approved by the Director of Criminal Enforcement. Clearance is also obtained from the FTC in order to assure

---

300. Dep't of Justice, Antitrust Division, *Division Update Spring 2011: Criminal Program*, <www.justice.gov/atr/public/division-update/2011/criminal-program.html> (last visited Nov. 17, 2011).

301. 18 U.S.C. § 1001.

302. Criminal Complaint, *United States v. Bristol-Myers Squibb Co.*, Criminal No. 07-140, *available at* <www.justice.gov/atr/cases/f223800/223808.htm> (last visited Nov. 18, 2011).

303. Dep't of Justice, Antitrust Division, *Antitrust Division Manual*, *available at* </www.justice.gov/atr/public/divisionmanual/index.html> (last visited Nov. 18, 2011).

that both agencies are not investigating the same conduct. The Director of Criminal Enforcement will then make a recommendation to the Assistant Attorney General. If approved, letters of authority are issued for all attorneys who will participate in the grand jury investigation. This establishes who the prosecutors will be.

218. During the course of grand jury proceedings, the issue of whether a particular witness should be granted immunity often arises. Depending on the scope of immunity proposed, the recommendation by the prosecutor must be reviewed either by the Criminal Division itself, in the case of formal immunity, or by the section and field office chief, in the case of informal immunity.

219. Persons may be "targets" or "subjects" of grand jury proceedings. A target is defined as a person:

> as to whom the prosecutor or the grand jury has substantial evidence linking him or her [or it] to the commission of a crime and who, in the judgment of the prosecutor, is a putative defendant. An officer or employee of an organization which is a target is not automatically to be considered as a target even if such officer's or employee's conduct contributed to the commission of the crime by the target organization. The same lack of automatic target status holds true for organizations which employ, or employed, an officer or employee who is a target.[304]

A "subject" of an investigation, is a person or entity "whose conduct is within the scope of the grand jury's investigation."[305]

220. The prosecutor will generally advise a person as to his or her status. The Manual of the Antitrust Division explains that counsel for a potential defendant is generally given opportunity to meet with the prosecutors – at least at the staff level – before any formal action is taken:

> At an appropriate point in the course of the Division's deliberations, staff also will usually inform counsel that it will forward any request of counsel for an appointment to meet on the matter with senior Antitrust Division officials. In general, parties who may be sued or recommended for indictment are usually afforded an opportunity to meet with a senior Antitrust Division official prior to a decision whether or not to file suit or seek an indictment. However, counsel are not entitled to such a meeting as a matter of right. If it is a close question about whether a meeting would or would not be useful, the appropriate Deputy Assistant Attorney General will advise staff whether there is or is not interest in hearing a presentation on behalf of a particular party. As a general rule, any argument which counsel for a prospective party wishes to be considered by sensior officials should first be presented to staff.

---

304. Dep't of Justice, *United States Attorneys' Manual* § 9–11.151, *available at* <www.justice.gov/usao/eousa/foia_reading_room/usam/title9/11mcrm.htm#9-11.151>.

305. *Ibid.*

The Manual further explains that:

> Counsel do not have any absolute right to be heard by the Director of Criminal Enforcement or the Criminal DAAG [Deputy Assistant Attorney General] although the Director and the Criminal DAAG will ordinarily give counsel an opportunity to be heard before recommending an indictment to the Assistant Attorney General. Only in very unusual circumstances will counsel be granted a meeting with the Assistant Attorney General. The Criminal DAAG, in his or her discretion, will ordinarily consider the arguments of counsel in making a final recommendation, but only after counsel has already met and discussed the issues with staff.

221. An indictment or plea agreement must be approved by the Deputy Assistant Attorney General (DAAG). It is based on formal recommendations by staff:

> Once staff has made its submission and any meetings with counsel for prospective defendants have been conducted, the Division's reviewers assess the merits of the case with a view towards considering all matters consistently and fairly. At the conclusion of the review process, the Assistant Attorney General makes the final decision as to whether to bring the action or to decline prosecution. When a final decision is made by the Assistant Attorney General, staff will be informed immediately. If a case is to be filed, the matter will be returned to staff with the approval papers, signed pleadings, and any other information that will be required for filing. At that point, staff will commence litigation of the matter or make its presentment to the grand jury.

B. The Leniency Program

222. The Antitrust Division has a formal leniency policy under which the first (but only the first) violator to come forward may avoid prosecution, if six criteria are met:

(1) At the time the corporation comes forward, the Division has not received information about the illegal activity being reported from any other source.
(2) Upon the corporation's discovery of the conduct, the corporation took prompt and effective action to terminate its participation in the illegal activity.
(3) The corporation reports the wrongdoing with candor and completeness and provides full, continuing and complete cooperation to the Division throughout the investigation.
(4) The confession of wrongdoing is truly a corporate act, as opposed to isolated confessions of individual executives or officials.
(5) Where possible, the corporation makes restitution to injured parties.

(6) The corporation did not coerce another party to participate in the illegal activity and clearly was not the leader in, or the originator of, the activity.[306]

If the agency has already begun an investigation, a violator may be granted leniency if:

> (1) The corporation is the first to come forward and qualify for leniency with respect to the illegal activity being reported; [and] (2) The Division, at the time the corporation comes in, does not have evidence against the company that is likely to result in a sustainable conviction.[307]

223. The rules governing the leniency program are detailed and admission into the program is conditional until the overall prosecution is complete. Where companies have not complied with all the terms of the program, the government has prosecuted notwithstanding the voluntary disclosures already made.[308]

224. Because of the importance of being the initial informant, the government will grant applicants to the program a "marker" which will hold their place, as first in line, until their counsel is able to provide sufficient information to complete an initial application for amnesty.

225. A final determination as to whether a company is admitted into the leniency program is made by the Criminal DAAG based upon the recommendation of the staff. If the staff recommends against conditional leniency, the applicant's counsel may seek a meeting with the DAAG, who will generally grant requests for a meeting upon such a request.

IV. Competent Criminal Courts

226. Any criminal cases under federal antitrust law must be brought in a US District Court – the federal trial court of general jurisdiction. There are no relevant specialized courts – neither specialized criminal courts nor specialized antitrust courts – and judges are assigned to cases randomly. Defendants in an antitrust case have the right to trial before a jury made up of randomly chosen lay people.

227. The same applies to the appellate process. There is no special appellate process for antitrust cases. An appeal will follow the same procedure for any case within the federal system: the losing party has an appeal as of right to the appropriate Court of Appeals and the losing party in the Court of Appeals can appeal to the Supreme Court, which can hear the case at its discretion.

306. Dep't of Justice, Antitrust Division, *Corporate Leniency Policy* § A (Aug. 10, 199), *available at* <http://www.justice.gov/atr/public/guidelines/0091.htm>.

307. *Ibid.*, at § B.

308. *U.S. v. Andreas*, 39 F. Supp. 2d 1048 (N.D. Ill. 1998) (upholding jury conviction for price-fixing of three defendants including one, Mark Whitacre, who had served as an informant to the government about the price-fixing conspiracy before losing his immunity for violating additional laws).

Part II. The Application of the Prohibitions

Chapter 1. Restrictive Agreements

§1. Horizontal Agreements

228. While the general rule is that horizontal agreements among competitors are per se violations of the antitrust laws, a number of subsidiary questions exist that are discussed in the succeeding sections. Can the alleged violation be properly characterized as price-fixing or is it something else that should be considered under a rule of reason test? What is an agreement and how is its existence proved? How does American law deal with concepts of tacit collusion as opposed to overt agreement? Are there areas, notwithstanding the general per se rule, in which overt agreements relating to price are tested under a rule of reason?

229. The specific modes of analysis relating to different substantive conduct are discussed in the succeeding sections, but an initial question is, absent direct evidence of an overt agreement violating the antitrust laws, what is the quantum of evidence required to place the question of antitrust conspiracy or agreement to a jury?

230. Because section 1 of the Sherman Act is rooted in criminal law and has always held the threat of incarceration, American antitrust law demands a higher degree of proof of collusion than would otherwise be warranted for matters involving purely economic regulation. It is not often the case that there is a tape or document recording the conspirators' agreement to stabilize prices or restrict production. While certain general principles exist, their application to specific recent cases makes the decisions almost appear random. Take, for example, *Blomkest Fertilizer, Inc. v. Potash Corp. of Saskatchewan,*[309] a case relating to the cartelization by the producers of potash, a major fertilizer. The plaintiff had adduced evidence "of a market structure ripe for collusion, a sudden change from price war to supracompetitive pricing, price-fixing overtures from one competitor to another, voluntary disclosure of secret price concessions, an explicitly discussed cheater punishment program, and advance knowledge of other producers' price moves."[310] There was even evidence that the president of one defendant visited the new management of another with a flip chart and demonstrated how the company had stolen too much market share and threatened consequences if it continued. Five judges found this evidence more than adequate to put the issue of conspiracy to

309. 203 F.3d 1028 (8th Cir. 2000).
310. 203 F.3d at 1051.

a jury. Unfortunately for the plaintiffs, eleven judges were sitting en banc and six judges, blinded by a simplistic understanding of oligopoly economics, joined an opinion concluding, "the class's proffered evidence, far from overwhelming, fails to establish the elements of a prima facie case."[311] Eleven judges on a single court splitting six to five over whether the evidence sufficed to raise sufficient question of conspiracy to even put the question to a jury underscores the lack of clarity of any standard.

231. In a case covering a conspiracy roughly coextensive in time with that in *Blomkest*, the Seventh Circuit, finding very similar industry structure and facts to those in *Blomkest,* per Judge Richard Posner, held the plaintiff had produced more than sufficient evidence to put the issue of collusion to a jury in *In re High Fructose Corn Syrup Antitrust Litig.* [312]

232. None of these cases involved an explicit meeting at which the parties actually agreed to fix prices – though the evidence was often very close to that – the question is what must be shown, short of explicit, direct evidence, to establish the existence of a conspiracy.

233. There are certain general principles. Parallel conduct alone does not establish a conspiracy. Even "conscious parallelism" does not give rise to a cause of action standing alone. Conscious parallelism is the process "not in itself unlawful, by which firms in a concentrated market might in effect share monopoly power, setting their prices at a profit-maximizing, supracompetitive level by recognizing their shared economic interests."[313] There must be something more. The something more is often referred to as "plus factors." As one court has put it, "We have identified…at least three such plus factors: (1) evidence that the defendant had a motive to enter into a price-fixing conspiracy; (2) evidence that the defendant acted contrary to its interests; and (3) 'evidence implying a traditional conspiracy.'"[314] Judge Posner explains in *High Fructose Corn Syrup* how such cases are proven. Two forms of evidence relating to the market are usually introduced. First, there is proof that the market is susceptible to price collusion. Second, there is the evidence of non-competitive behavior in the market. Evidence that the market is susceptible to price collusion might include the presence of few sellers, which would facilitate coordination; a fungible product, which would reduce product differentiation and therefore require that the conspirators need only collude on price rather than also on such things as product standards and service terms; lack of substitutes, which allow conspirators to raise prices without losing customers; and high barriers to entry, which allow prices to be raised without attracting new competitors.

234. Evidence of non-competitive behavior can take many forms. In *High Fructose Corn Syrup*, all participants in the industry adopted a new form of pricing at roughly the same time and in the same manner. In *Blomkest*, no member of the industry took advantage of certain cost advantages that arose just as the conspiracy period began as the result of certain antidumping duties. Both of these examples

---

311. 203 F.3d at 1032.

312. 295 F.3d 651 (7th Cir. 2002). Compare also *In re Baby Food Antitrust Litig.*, 166 F.3d 112 (3d Cir. 1999) with *In re Flat Glass Antitrust Litig.*, 385 F.3d 350 (3d Cir. 2004).

313. *Brooke Group Ltd. v. Brown & Williamson Tobacco Corp.*, 509 U.S. 209, 227, 113 S.Ct. 2578, 125 L.Ed.2d 168 (1993).

314. *In re Flat Glass Antitrust Litig.*, 385 F.3d 350, 360 (3d Cir. 2004).

involved uniform conduct by participants raising prices. In both cases the participants engaged in parallel pricing.

235. This evidence would set the scene for evidence from which actual collusion could be inferred. In *High Fructose Corn Syrup* the participants in the industry spoke as though they had a common agreement using such phrases as "We have an understanding in the industry not to undercut each other's prices." They had a common attitude towards customers, one saying, "our competitors are our friends. Our customers are the enemy." And there were invocations of the Fifth Amendment's protection against self-incrimination by high ranking officials with pricing authority. In a civil case, as opposed to a criminal case, an adverse inference may be drawn from a person's invocation of the Fifth Amendment. In *Blomkest* there had been several unsuccessful efforts to raise prices before the conspiracy began and a memo stating that prices could only be raised through joint action. There were meetings among the competitors at which pricing was discussed and there were price verification calls which the dissenters properly recognized were the necessary component of the conspiracy in order to detect possible cheating. As the dissent put it, there was no legitimate reason for a competitor to reveal to a competitor its non-public price to a customer.

236. Such is the type of evidence that must be adduced. The standard that must be met is often skewed depending on the outcome the court wants to reach. Thus, the majority in *Blomkest* describe the standard, at the summary judgment phase, as, "evidence that 'tends to exclude the possibility of independent action' by the defendants. ... This means that conduct that is 'as consistent with permissible [activity] as with illegal conspiracy does not, standing alone, support an inference of antitrust conspiracy.'... the standard requires that if it is as reasonable to infer from the evidence a price-fixing conspiracy as it is to infer permissible activity, then the plaintiffs' claim, without more, fails on summary judgment."[315] The dissent phrased it somewhat differently. It "only required 'direct *or circumstantial* evidence that reasonably tends to prove... a conscious commitment to a common scheme designed to achieve an unlawful objective.'"[316]

237. The difficulty of applying this fuzzy language is made even more difficult by the unsettled approach the law has taken to oligopolies. Oligopolies are markets with few sellers. On the one hand, as Judge Posner explained in the case described above, the presence of few sellers should facilitate collusion. On the other hand, certain scholarly authority taken up by the courts have recognized that in markets with few sellers and high barriers to entry each seller is going to be acutely conscious of the likely response of its competitor to any change in its price.

238. If there are but a few firms in the market, firm A, when planning a price reduction, must consider what the other few firms in the market will do. If it recognizes, as is likely the case, that its competitors will simply drop their prices to avoid losing market share, then, proceeding logically, it will determine not to drop prices. Its move would only result in everybody obtaining lower profits. Rather, a rational market will, without any need for overt collusion, assume some form of price leadership in which one member might pre-announce a future price increase to test the waters and the remaining members of the industry would logically follow since then they all will reap the benefits of the higher prices. If they follow, they all reap the benefits of increased

315. *Blomkest Fertilizer, Inc. v. Potash Corp. of Saskatchewan*, 203 F.3d 1028, 1032 (8th Cir. 2000).
316. 203 F.3d at 1039.

prices. If one does not, they all fall back and nothing is lost.[317] The Third Circuit tried to explain why such conduct does not violate the antitrust laws:

> [T]here exists the notion that interdependent behavior is not an "agreement" within the term's meaning under the Sherman Act. See Turner, supra, at 663-65; but see Posner, Antitrust Law, supra, at 94-95. Second, Turner and Areeda argued that judicial remedies are incapable of addressing the anticompetitive effects of consciously parallel pricing. Turner, supra, at 669-71, Areeda, Antitrust Law, supra,¶¶ 1432d5-1432f, at 232-36; but see Posner, supra, at 98. Indeed, the Supreme Court has described conscious parallelism in dicta as "the process, not in itself unlawful, by which firms in a concentrated market might in effect share monopoly power, setting their prices at a profit-maximizing, supracompetitive level by recognizing their shared economic interests and their interdependence with respect to price and output decisions."Brooke Group Ltd. v. Brown & Williamson Tobacco Corp., 509 U.S. 209, 227, 113 S.Ct. 2578, 125 L.Ed.2d 168 (1993) (emphasis added).[318]

239. Such is the logic of oligopoly pricing. And in cases such as *Blomkest,* a misunderstanding of this rather opaque logic led the court to give a pass to an industry engaged in astonishing collusion based upon the mistaken assumption that because the court was dealing with an oligopoly prices necessarily would have risen in the absence of collusion. But if this logic is so inevitable, why then are there so many instances of the need for price exchanges among competitors in oligopolies as is evidenced in all of the cases cited in preceding paragraphs?

240. For one thing, external causes may force a spiral downward. The very same concern that raising prices in the absence of cooperation will gain an oligopolist no increase in market share can lead prices to remain ruinously low. *Blomkest* quoted a memo of one of the potash companies composed during the period of ruinously low prices before the alleged conspiracy: "It is not possible for a single producer to affect [sic] a turn-around; however, joint action by a group of producers or governments could achieve this."[319] The very existence of an oligopoly created the need for collusion.

241. Second, there is always the incentive to cheat and obtain a greater share of the market. Players do not always proceed with cool rationality of joint interest. In the absence of express agreements, oligopolists, "must rely on uncertain and ambiguous signals to achieve concerted action. The signals are subject to misinterpretation and are a blunt and imprecise means of ensuring smooth cooperation, especially in the context of changing or unprecedented market circumstances. This anticompetitive minuet is most difficult to compose and to perform, even for a disciplined oligopoly."[320]

242. In short, rather than excusing conduct based on the abstract rationality of oligopoly price conduct, the oligopoly structure should serve equally as a red flag in

317. *In re Flat Glass Antitrust Litig.,* 385 F.3d 350, 359 (3d Cir. 2004).
318. 385 F.3d at 360.
319. 203 F.3d at 1039.
320. *Brooke Group Ltd. v. Brown & Williamson Tobacco Corp.,* 509 U.S. 209, 227-28, 113 S.Ct. 2578, 125 L.Ed.2d 168 (1993).

the event of supracompetitive pricing. Richard Posner has written that if the concern is price behavior, then less emphasis should be placed on the technical law of conspiracy.[321]

I. Cartels

A. *Price-Fixing*

243. The general rule is that any agreement affecting price among horizontal competitors is a per se violation of section 1 of the Sherman Act. "A horizontal agreement to fix prices is the archetypal example of such a practice. It has long been settled that an agreement to fix prices is unlawful per se. It is no excuse that the prices fixed are themselves reasonable."[322]

244. No extenuating circumstance or justification for a price-fixing agreement will be heard by an American court. Price-fixing is a felony for which the perpetrators are likely to be jailed and may be sued civilly. The government need not prove that the agreement was effective, nor can the defendant introduce evidence that the agreement was doomed to fail. It is not a moral issue: there have been agreements to fix prices that were rational efforts by competitors to protect themselves from larger rivals that were nonetheless determined to be criminal conspiracies.

245. For example, in *United States v. Soc'y of Indep. Gasoline Marketers of Am. (SIGMA)*,[323] one of a series of decisions relating to an effort to fix retail prices for gasoline,[324] the perpetrators were regional, independent gasoline companies operating in the Baltimore, Maryland area. They sought to protect themselves from retaliation for low prices from major international oil companies. The major oil companies would allow a limited, usually two-cent, margin per gallon, between the prices at the gasoline pumps at secondary, regional marketers' gas stations and the prices at the major brand stations. If the price at a regional marketer's gas station dropped below the two-cent margin, the majors would retaliate by dropping prices throughout the regional marketer's territory. To protect themselves, the regional marketers – several of whom operated through independent gasoline stations which they did not own and whose pricing was difficult to control – formed an association, SIGMA, to stabilize their prices and avoid competition with one another so as not to face retaliation from the majors. Although it was a logical defensive measure, it was found to be a per se violation of the antitrust laws. Members of the conspiracy were criminally convicted.

246. In *United States v. Apple, Inc.*,[325] the Second Circuit affirmed a civil conspiracy judgment against Apple for its role in organizing a conspiracy between itself and the major book publishers. Because, the conspiracy was a horizontal conspiracy

---

321. Posner, Antitrust Law (2d Ed.) at 94.
322. *Catalano, Inc. v. Target Sales, Inc.*, 446 U.S. 643, 646, 100 S. Ct. 1925, 1927, 64 L.Ed.2d 580 (1980).
323. 624 F.2d 461 (4th Cir. 1979).
324. *See, e.g., Phillips v. Crown Cent. Petroleum Corp.*, 602 F.2d 616 (4th Cir. 1979); *In re Indep. Gasoline Antitrust Litig.*, 79 F.R.D. 552 (D. Md. 1978).
325. 791 F.3d 290 (2d Cir. 2015), *cert. denied*, 136 S. Ct. 1376, 194 L. Ed. 2d 360 (2016).

among publishers directed towards, among other things, increasing prices of electronic books, the court affirmed application of a per se rule and refused to entertain justifications advanced that the arrangement was a legitimate challenge to Amazon's dominance of the electronic books market which threatened the overall market for books.

247. As these cases indicate, agreements to fix prices can take forms other than the paradigm of a group of competitors agreeing on prices. In *SIGMA,* the defendants' primary violation was their agreement to punish renegade discounting to assure that their prices remained within the margin tolerated by the majors. *Apple* represented a complex conspiracy involving use of most favored nations clauses, suggested target prices and other efforts to force Amazon to accept the business practices advanced by the conspiracy which led to the successful inflation of electronic book prices.

248. Catalano, Inc. v. Target Sales, Inc. [326] held that an agreement among competitors to eliminate certain early payment discounts to customers was a per se violation. The Court explained that an agreement to eliminate a credit term was tantamount to an agreement to raise prices. *Catalano* gave examples of other cases in which price was indirectly the object of a conspiracy. In *Sugar Institute v. United States,*[327] the Court held unlawful an agreement by sugar refiners to adhere to previously announced prices and terms of sale, even though advance price announcements were perfectly lawful and even though the particular prices and terms were not themselves fixed by private agreement. *In re Plywood Antitrust Litig.* [328] affirmed a class action judgment against producers of plywood who conspired to use a single method of charging for "phantom" freight.

249. Catalano also cited *National Society of Professional Engineers v. United States* [329] where "an agreement among competing firms of professional engineers to refuse to discuss prices with potential customers until after negotiations had resulted in the initial selection of an engineer was held unlawful without requiring further inquiry."[330] Technically, *Professional Engineers* involved application of the rule of reason, but so basic a restraint, that the Court felt no need to weigh any pro-competitive factors since the restraint had been premised on the assumption that competition itself was bad.

250. Plywood and *National Society of Professional Engineers* both illustrate the complexity of applying the per se rule to price-fixing. *National Society of Professional Engineers* did not appear to apply a per se rule to the price-fixing conspiracy arising from the professional engineers' ethical rule that eliminated competition in bidding. While *Plywood* applied a per se analysis to the conspiracy to utilize phantom freight pricing, the case settled after the Supreme Court agreed to review it and after the Ninth Circuit found no violation when reviewing the same practice, albeit on an entirely different record, in a case brought by the FTC.[331]

326. 446 U.S. 643, 100 S. Ct. 1925, 64 L. Ed. 2d 580 (1980).
327. 297 U.S. 553, 601–602, 56 S.Ct. 629, 643, 80 L.Ed. 859 (1936).
328. 655 F.2d 627 (5th Cir. 1981).
329. 435 U.S. 679, 98 S. Ct. 1355, 55 L. Ed. 2d 637 (1978).
330. *Catalano,* 446 U.S. at 648, 100 S. Ct. 1928.
331. *See , Boise Cascade Corp. v. F.T.C.,* 637 F.2d 573 (9th Cir. 1980).

1. Exceptions from Per Se Treatment

251. The Supreme Court has held that in certain contexts, such as with professional associations, while conduct is not exempt from the antitrust laws, it may require a form of rule of reason analysis. In *Goldfarb v. Virginia State Bar*, the Court had held that a mandatory minimum fee schedule that fixed rates of lawyers was a violation of the antitrust laws but recognized that:

> The fact that a restraint operates upon a profession as distinguished from a business is, of course, relevant in determining whether that particular restraint violates the Sherman Act. It would be unrealistic to view the practice of professions as interchangeable with other business activities, and automatically to apply to the professions antitrust concepts which originated in other areas. The public service aspect, and other features of the professions, may require that a particular practice, which could properly be viewed as a violation of the Sherman Act in another context, be treated differently. We intimate no view on any other situation than the one with which we are confronted today.[332]

252. Both *Goldfarb* and *National Society of Professional Engineers* involved "naked" restraints on competition so that, though apparently applying a rule of reason analysis, the court found no significant cognizable pro-competitive justification for the restraints. So, in *Catalano*, the Court could say that *National Society of Professional Engineers* found the restriction on bidding "unlawful without requiring further inquiry."[333] In those cases, there was no significant distinction between a per se analysis and a rule of reason analysis except that the court was permitted to at least consider – and reject – the justifications advanced for the restraint.

253. In *National Collegiate Athletic Association v. Board of Regents of University of Oklahoma*,[334] the Court held that sports, like the learned professions, was an area in which restraints formerly considered subject to per se treatment were to be considered under the rule of reason. The Court reasoned that sports represented an area in which the product required some level of mutual cooperation among competitors. There had to be rules for the game and the league. Therefore, the rule of reason was to be applied. But the restraint in *NCAA*, like the restraints in *National Society of Professional Engineers* and *Goldfarb*, was a naked restraint on output. The Court explained that while the rule of reason applied, "[t]he essential point is that the rule of reason can sometimes be applied in the twinkling of an eye."[335]

---

332. 421 U.S. 773 n. 17, 775, 95 S. Ct. 2004, 2007, 44 L. Ed. 2d 572 (1975).
333. *Catalano,* 446 U.S. at 648, 100 S. Ct. 1928.
334. 468 U.S. 85, 104 S. Ct. 2948, 82 L. Ed. 2d 70 (1984).
335. *Ibid.*, at 110, 104 S. Ct. 2948, 2965, 82 L. Ed. 2d 70 (1984) (citation omitted); *See also, Am. Needle, Inc. v. Nat'l Football League*, 130 S. Ct. 2201, 2216–2217, 176 L. Ed. 2d 947 (2010).

2. The Rule of Reason and Quick Look Tests

254. A number of Supreme Court decisions have held that a rule of reason test had to be applied but it should be applied in a quick, perfunctory fashion to the conduct at issue. Subsequent cases concluded that there were different rule of reason tests: a full-blown rule of reason analysis and a truncated "quick look" rule of reason analysis. In *F.T.C. v. Indiana Federation of Dentists*, the Court explained the speed with which the rule of reason could be applied to certain cases:

> Application of the Rule of Reason to these facts is not a matter of any great difficulty. The Federation's policy takes the form of a horizontal agreement among the participating dentists to withhold from their customers a particular service that they desire – the forwarding of x rays to insurance companies along with claim forms. "While this is not price fixing as such, no elaborate industry analysis is required to demonstrate the anticompetitive character of such an agreement."[336]

These cases led courts to fashion a truncated version of the rule of reason referred to as the "quick look." In some cases, "an observer with even a rudimentary understanding of economics could conclude that the arrangements in question would have an anticompetitive effect on customers and markets."[337] In other words, "quick-look analysis carries the day when the great likelihood of anticompetitive effects can easily be ascertained."[338] Under "quick look" analysis, the competitive harm is presumed, and the defendant must advance "some competitive justification" for the restraint. If no legitimate justifications are set forth, adverse competitive impact is established. If cognizable pro-competitive justifications are presented, the court must proceed to weigh the overall reasonableness of the restraint using a full-scale rule of reason analysis.[339]

255. The Supreme Court explained that the full rule of reason and "quick look" tests often run together:

> [T]here is generally no categorical line to be drawn between restraints that give rise to an intuitively obvious inference of anticompetitive effect and those that call for more detailed treatment. What is required, rather, is an enquiry meet for the case, looking to the circumstances, details, and logic of a restraint. The object is to see whether the experience of the market has been so clear, or necessarily will be, that a confident conclusion about the principal tendency of a restriction

---

336. 476 U.S. 447, 459, 106 S. Ct. 2009, 2018, 90 L. Ed. 2d 445 (1986) (quoting. *National Society of Professional Engineers, supra,* 435 U.S. at 692, 98 S.Ct., at 1365).
337. *Cal. Dental Ass'n v. FTC,* 526 U.S. 756, 770, 119 S.Ct. 1604, 143 L.Ed.2d 935 (1999).
338. *Ibid.*
339. *See Deutscher Tennis Bund v. ATP Tour, Inc.*, 610 F.3d 820, 830–831 (3d Cir. 2010) *cert. denied,* 131 S. Ct. 658, 178 L. Ed. 2d 482 (U.S. 2010).

will follow from a quick (or at least quicker) look, in place of a more sedulous one.[340]

256. Courts have shied away from employing a "quick look" analysis. In *California Dental*, the Supreme Court was split, with a majority holding that the Court of Appeals erred in approving the application of a "quick look" analysis to an ethical rule promulgated by an association of dentists limiting forms of advertising. The Court held that the proposed justification based on the need for accuracy in professional advertising required a full rule of reason analysis.

257. By contrast, other cases involving pure, naked restraints among professionals or in sports have applied a "quick look." In *Law v. National Collegiate Athletic Association*, the court applied a "quick look" to condemn a collegiate athletic association rule that limited the amounts teams would pay assistant athletic coaches, explaining:

> Under a quick look rule of reason analysis, anticompetitive effect is established, even without a determination of the relevant market, where the plaintiff shows that a horizontal agreement to fix prices exists, that the agreement is effective, and that the price set by such an agreement is more favorable to the defendant than otherwise would have resulted from the operation of market forces.[341]

In *North Texas Specialty Physicians v. F.T.C.*, a Court of Appeals found that an arrangement under which independent specialists provided rates they would accept to a central firm that represented them in negotiations with insurers was properly subject to a "quick look" because "the net anticompetitive effects of certain of [the central firm]'s practices were obvious. The pro-competitive justifications do not plausibly result in a net pro-competitive effect or in no effect at all on competition."[342]

258. These cases underscore the advantages to a plaintiff of a "quick look" analysis compared to a full rule of reason analysis. *Law v. National Collegiate Athletic Association* pointed to two immediate benefits. A "quick look" eliminates the need to prove the relevant market, and it shifts the burdens. "[T]he plaintiff only has the burden of establishing the anticompetitive effect of the restraint at issue. Once the plaintiff meets that burden, the burden shifts to the defendant to justify the restraint as a 'reasonable' one."[343]

3. Characterization: Is It Price-Fixing?

259. *National Collegiate Athletic Association v. Board of Regents of University of Oklahoma* and *National Society of Professional Engineers* created broad exceptions from per se treatment for cases involving particular segments of commerce: sports and the professions. In 1979, the Supreme Court more radically upset the traditional dichotomy between per se and rule of reason analyses. In *Broadcast Music, Inc. v.*

340. *Cal. Dental*, 526 U.S. at 780–781.
341. 134 F.3d 1010, 1020 (10th Cir. 1998).
342. 528 F.3d 346, 362–363 (5th Cir. 2008).
343. *Law v. Nat'l Collegiate Athletic Ass'n*, 134 F.3d 1010, 1021 (10th Cir. 1998).

Columbia Broadcasting Systems, Inc.[344] (*BMI*), the Court faced what appeared to be a naked price-fixing conspiracy among composers. Composers had banded together into one of two organizations to enforce the copyrights to their music. The organizations, BMI and the American Society of Composers, Authors and Publishers (ASCAP), each provided only blanket licenses to broadcast rights of all their respective composers' works. They did not offer licenses to particular works or to works of particular composers. The charge for the blanket license was based on the advertising revenue of the broadcaster. Composers retained the right to license their own works, but the record established that this virtually never occurred.

260. The Court of Appeals held that the agreement was a price-fixing arrangement – a per se violation of section 1 of the Sherman Act. The Supreme Court conceded that the agreement was a price-fixing agreement, but that it was not price-fixing in the classic sense because it involved a unique confluence of copyright and antitrust law. The blanket license did not appear to the Court to be the "naked restraint of trade with no purpose except stifling of competition."[345] Rather, it seemed to result from demand in a market where there were thousands of users, thousands of copyright owners, and millions of compositions, and most users wanted "unplanned, rapid and indemnified access to any and all of the repertory... and the owners want[ed] a reliable method of collecting for the use of their copyrights."[346] Viewed in this light, the blanket license arguably increased output by decreasing both transaction costs and enforcement costs. The Court concluded that the blanket license was itself a new product different from anything any individual composer could have offered and could not be "wholly equated with a simple horizontal arrangement among competitors."[347] It held that the complexities of the arrangement required that a court judge it under a rule of reason analysis.

261. The effect of *BMI* is to create a new defense raising the question of whether an agreement is actually price-fixing or, instead, some variant warranting rule of reason consideration. After *BMI*, courts have been more apt to use the rule of reason analysis in cases that formerly would have been subject to per se treatment.[348]

B. Market/Client Allocation

262. Horizontal competitors' agreements to allocate markets and customers among themselves are also per se violations of section 1 of the Sherman Act. Among the earliest articulations of the per se rule occurred in the customer allocation context in *United States v. Addyston Pipe & Steel Co.*[349] That case involved a common form of customer allocation, bid-rigging. In bid-rigging, competitors agree which of them

---

344. 441 U.S. 1, 99 S. Ct. 1551, 60 L.Ed.2d 1 (1979).
345. *Ibid.*, at 20 (citation omitted).
346. *Ibid.*
347. *Ibid.*, at 23.
348. Compare, for example, *Rothery Storage & Van Co. v. Atlas Van Lines, Inc.*, 792 F.2d 210 (D.C. Cir. 1986) (Bork, J.) applying *BMI* to approve a contractual restriction under the rule of reason with *Gen. Leaseways, Inc. v. Nat'l Truck Leasing Ass'n*, 744 F.2d 588, 589 (7th Cir. 1984) (Posner, J.) distinguishing *BMI*, finding the restriction to be a per se violation and, alternatively, finding it a violation under a "quick look" rule of reason analysis.
349. 85 F. 271 (6th Cir. 1898) *aff'd as modified*, 175 U.S. 211, 20 S. Ct. 96, 44 L. Ed. 136 (1899).

is to win the bid. The remaining competitors either do not bid or intentionally bid a higher amount than the amount they know is to be bid by the competitor to whom they have allocated the contract.

263. Customer and territorial allocation schemes are arguably more pernicious than price-fixing because, while price-fixing leaves open the possibility of competition for service, territorial and customer allocation schemes eliminate all competition. Territorial and customer allocation cases often occur in industries that have high initial costs for new customers. For example, in the uniform service industry, where there is a high cost of cutting and sizing uniforms for a new customer's employees, or in the linen supply industry, which has similar high initial costs, industry members do not to want to lose a customer after the initial contract term and may be tempted to agree not to pursue other competitors' existing customers.[350] Air gas firms, which have high initial costs of installing equipment, face similar temptations.[351]

264. In *United States v. Cadillac Overall Supply Co.*, a uniform supplier argued that the dynamics in its industry justified a customer allocation scheme:

> Cadillac urges that the District Court should have applied the "rule of reason" analysis in determining whether or not the actions of Cadillac violated section 1. Cadillac argues that its conduct was justified as a reasonable restraint of trade. The non-solicitation of each other's customers was simply a method of assuring non-interference with the service contracts existing between the customer and the other particular company. Cadillac points out that the customers were originally acquired through free and open competition and that it makes a substantial capital investment in purchasing garments to supply each new customer. Cadillac asserts that free and open competition would result in the raiding of accounts which would result in the loss of this capital investment. To litigate against the customer breaching a service contract or against the raiding competitors, Cadillac contends, is too expensive a course of action. The "balancing of accounts" was simply a method of keeping records "to make sure that one competitor was not tortiously interfering or raiding one's accounts to the point where retaliatory raiding or court action was in order to protect or rectify violations of their proprietary rights."[352]

The court refused to consider these arguments because allocation of customers is a per se violation for which no justification can be considered.

---

350. *See, e.g.*, *United States v. Cadillac Overall Supply Co.*, 568 F.2d 1078 (5th Cir. 1978); *United States v. Consol. Laundries Corp.*, 291 F.2d 563 (2d Cir. 1961); *United States v. Am. Linen Supply Co.*, 141 F. Supp. 105, 108 (N.D. Ill. 1956).

351. *In re Carbon Dioxide Antitrust Litig.*, 149 F.R.D. 229 (M.D. Fla. 1993); *In re Indus. Gas Antitrust Litig.*, 100 F.R.D. 280, 286 (N.D. Ill. 1983) ("Plaintiffs also assert that defendants conspired to allocate customers, mainly through an agreement not to offer competitive bids to 'historical' accounts of rivals.").

352. 568 F.2d 1078, 1087–1088 (5th Cir. 1978) (citations omitted).

265. Many Supreme Court cases have reiterated that the per se rule applies to customer and territorial allocation. In *United States v. Topco Associates, Inc.*,[353] the Court held it was a per se violation of the antitrust laws for a cooperative that supplied supermarkets to allow a member-supermarket a veto over the acceptance into the cooperative of a competing company in its territory. The Court held that this effectively allocated markets among members. It so held even though the members of the cooperative were regional supermarkets that faced significant competition in their markets from large national supermarket chains. In *Palmer v. BRG of Georgia, Inc.*,[354] the Court held that an agreement between vendors of bar review courses to law students not to seek business in the other's territory was a per se violation even though one of the parties to the agreement had not historically done business in the territory it had agreed not to enter.

C. Production/Innovation Limitation

266. Because price is a function of the quantity of supply, any agreement among manufacturers to limit supply is necessarily an agreement to raise prices. Conversely, any *effective* agreement to fix prices must necessarily involve an implicit agreement to curtail supply. Therefore, any agreement among competitors to curtail production is no different than price-fixing and is a per se violation of the antitrust laws. As Judge Posner explained in *General Leaseways, Inc. v. National Truck Leasing Association*:

> An agreement on output also equates to a price-fixing agreement. If firms raise price, the market's demand for their product will fall, so the amount supplied will fall too – in other words, output will be restricted. If instead the firms restrict output directly, price will as mentioned rise in order to limit demand to the reduced supply. Thus, with exceptions not relevant here, raising price, reducing output, and dividing markets have the same anticompetitive effects.[355]

The Third Circuit, in *In re Linerboard Antitrust Litigation*, applied this same analysis where the defendants sought to distinguish a case involving limitation on production from price-fixing:

> (1) Prices in the marketplace are controlled by the economic laws of supply and demand, to wit, if a product is in short supply, the price will increase. During the period in question, linerboard was in short supply. Therefore, during this period, the price of linerboard increased. (2) Closing down production will create a shortage in supply and a corresponding price increase. The linerboard manufacturers closed down production. Therefore, the linerboard manufacturers created a shortage in supply and a price increase.[356]

---

353. 405 U.S. 596, 92 S. Ct. 1126, 31 L. Ed. 2d 515 (1972).
354. 498 U.S. 46, 49, 111 S. Ct. 401, 402, 112 L. Ed. 2d 349 (1990).
355. 744 F.2d 588, 594–595 (7th Cir. 1984).
356. 305 F.3d 145, 151 (3d Cir. 2002).

267. United States v. Socony-Vacuum Oil Co.,[357] generally considered the seminal case creating the modern per se rule, involved a conspiracy to stabilize prices by limiting supply. *Socony-Vacuum* was a criminal action brought against the largest oil companies. During the Depression, at the outset of the New Deal, the Roosevelt administration sought to ameliorate chronic overproduction of petroleum. The overproduction was in part the result of the limited technology of the time, which required that the majority of oil wells either be in production or else be shut down permanently, without any intermediate stage. Under the National Industrial Recovery Act, the government encouraged major oil companies with adequate storage facilities to enter into an arrangement with independent oil producers, who did not have storage, to purchase their overproduction or "overhang," and prevent it from being dumped onto the "spot" market. The effect of the arrangement – known as the "dancing partner" scheme – was that prices in fact stabilized, and even rose. Unfortunately for the "dancing partners," the National Industrial Recovery Act was invalidated by the Supreme Court. A new antitrust regime arose within the Roosevelt administration that vigorously attacked the elaborate price stabilization scheme, which, even though previously encouraged by the government, had no antitrust immunity. The government charged all the participants criminally for participating in a conspiracy to stabilize the price of gasoline. In *Socony-Vacuum*, the Court held that the scheme was a per se violation. The Court would not entertain arguments attempting to justify it as necessary under the circumstances:

> The elimination of so-called competitive evils is no legal justification for such buying programs. The elimination of such conditions was sought primarily for its effect on the price structures. Fairer competitive prices, it is claimed, resulted when distress gasoline was removed from the market. But such defense is typical of the protestations usually made in price-fixing cases. Ruinous competition, financial disaster, evils of price cutting and the like appear throughout our history as ostensible justifications for price-fixing. If the so-called competitive abuses were to be appraised here, the reasonableness of prices would necessarily become an issue in every price-fixing case. In that event the Sherman Act would soon be emasculated; its philosophy would be supplanted by one which is wholly alien to a system of free competition; it would not be the charter of freedom which its framers intended.[358]

268. Socony-Vacuum makes clear that the issue of per se violations is not so much a matter of morality as one of economic and judicial policy.

269. Just as customer allocation schemes are more likely to occur in certain industries responding to a particular market structure and conditions, production restriction schemes also are often responses to a particular industry characteristic. Industries that must make high capital investments in operating equipment, and cannot easily adjust those investments to fit changes in the economic cycle are prone to production restriction conspiracies. That was the case in *Socony-Vacuum* and also is

357. 310 U.S. 150, 60 S. Ct. 811, 84 L. Ed. 1129 (1940).
358. *Ibid.*, at 220–221, 60 S. Ct. 811 at 843.

a recurring issue in the paper and box industries. The corrugated box industry, for example, requires huge mills to make the material for boxes from pulp which cannot be temporarily shut down, except at great cost. It has repeatedly been the subject of antitrust enforcement cases alleging collusion to stabilize prices or limit production.[359]

270. Cases involving limitations on innovation are less common. They arise most often with standard-setting organizations, which competitors can use to set industry standards to exclude an innovating new entrant. In the classic case of *Radiant Burners, Inc. v. Peoples Gas Light & Coke Co.*,[360] competitors of a manufacturer of a new ceramic gas burner attempted to preclude its entry into the market by assuring that it was denied a necessary certification by the American Gas Association. In *Allied Tube & Conduit Corp. v. Indian Head, Inc.*,[361] manufacturers of steel conduit who were members of the National Fire Protection Association used that organization's standard setting to exclude a new entrant that manufactured an innovative plastic conduit. In both cases, the Supreme Court found that the plaintiffs stated causes of action, but in neither case did the Court reach the issue of whether using an industry standard to prevent entry of a competitor was a per se violation or merited rule of reason analysis.

271. Subsequent cases have applied a rule of reason in a standard-setting context.[362] In *United States v. National Association of Realtors*,[363] the government specifically charged a conspiracy to enjoin innovation. The government sought to enjoin enforcement of a realtor association's rules intended to thwart the threat to their real estate listing services from the on-line listings of properties. The court applied a rule of reason. There have been similar cases in other contexts, but they are uncommon. In *U. S. v. Auto. Mfrs. Ass'n*,[364] the government alleged a conspiracy by automobile manufacturers to stifle innovation in auto emission technology. The case was settled pursuant to a consent decree.

272. The FTC and the Antitrust Division may sue to prevent a merger that would harm innovation.[365] The agencies also "consider whether a merger may lessen competition by eliminating a 'maverick' firm," that is, a firm that "plays a disruptive role in the market to the benefit of consumers." For example …"[it may] threaten[] to disrupt market conditions with a new technology or business model …."[366] The agencies have worked to protect innovation in other contexts. For example, the FTC has considered regulations to prevent companies from making patented technology the basis for an

359. *See, e.g.*, *United States v. Container Corp. of Am.*, 393 U.S. 333, 89 S. Ct. 510, 21 L. Ed. 2d 526 (1969); *In re Corrugated Container Antitrust Litig.*, 643 F.2d 195, 202 (5th Cir. 1981); *In re Linerboard Antitrust Litig.*, 305 F.3d 145, 151 (3d Cir. 2002).

360. 364 U.S. 656, 81 S. Ct. 365, 5 L. Ed. 2d 358 (1961).

361. 486 U.S. 492108 S. Ct. 1931100 L. Ed. 2d 497 (1988).

362. *See, e.g.*, *Eliason Corp. v. Nat'l Sanitation Found.*, 614 F.2d 126 (6th Cir. 1980); *Structural Laminates, Inc. v. Douglas Fir Plywood Ass'n*, 261 F. Supp. 154 (D. Or. 1966) *aff'd* 399 F.2d 155 (9th Cir. 1968); *Consol. Metal Products, Inc. v. Am. Petroleum Inst.*, 846 F.2d 284 (5th Cir. 1988).

363. 05 C 5140, 2006 WL 3434263 (N.D. Ill. Nov. 27, 2006).

364. 307 F. Supp. 617 (C.D. Cal. 1969).

365. Dep't of Justice and the Fed. Trade Comm'n, *Horizontal Merger Guidelines*§ 6.4 (Aug. 19, 2010).

366. *Ibid.*, at § 2.1.5.

industry standard.[367] Otherwise, the owner of the patent incorporated into the industry standard could extract "excessive royalty payments from other firms," creating "an antitrust risk known as a patent hold-up" that can stifle innovation.[368]

D. Group Boycott

273. Group boycotts historically were considered per se violations of section 1 of the Sherman Act.[369] Naked boycotts among competitors to affect price remain per se violations.[370] It is generally accepted, however, that in most contexts, boycotts are governed by a modified per se analysis – neither the per se rule nor standard rule of reason analysis. The threshold question is *how* the competitors are wielding their boycott.

274. F.T.C. v. Superior Court Trial Lawyers Ass'n,[371] involved a classic boycott to raise prices, albeit in an unusual context. The lawyers who took criminal case assignments from the District of Columbia courts collectively refused to accept any assignments until the courts raised the lawyers' compensation rates. Although the lawyers raised a perceived clash between First Amendment speech rights and the Sherman Act, the Court had little problem finding that the boycott was a per se violation. The Court took the opportunity to emphasize the importance of per se treatment even where there were arguably very important competing considerations, such as freedom of speech:

> The administrative efficiency interests in antitrust regulation are unusually compelling. The per se rules avoid the necessity for an incredibly complicated and prolonged economic investigation into the entire history of the industry involved, as well as related industries, in an effort to determine at large whether a particular restraint has been unreasonable. If small parties were allowed to prove lack of market power, all parties would have that right, thus introducing the enormous complexities of market definition into every price-fixing case.[372]

---

367. Abigail Slater, *FTC Holds Workshop on Preventing Patent Hold-Ups*, *RegBlog* (Jul. 27, 2011), <www.law.upenn.edu/blogs/regblog/2011/07/ftc-holds-workshop-on-preventing-patent-hold-ups.html>.
368. *Ibid.*
369. *Fashion Originators' Guild of Am. v. Fed. Trade Comm'n*, 312 U.S. 457, 61 S. Ct. 703, 85 L. Ed. 949 (1941).
370. *FTC v. Superior Court Trial Lawyers Ass'n*, 493 U.S. 411 110 S. Ct. 768, 107 L. Ed. 2d 851 (1990).
371. 493 U.S. 411, 110 S. Ct. 768, 107 L. Ed. 2d 851 (1990).
372. *Ibid.*, at 430–431, 110 S. Ct. 768 at 779 (citations omitted). The Court distinguished the situation before it, where the object of the boycott was to obtain higher compensation – i.e., the goal was economic, from its prior decision in *N.A.A.C.P. v. Claiborne Hardware Co.*, 458 U.S. 886, 102 S. Ct. 3409, 73 L. Ed. 2d 1215 (1982). In *N.A.A.C.P.*, the Court had held that boycotts by African-Americans during the civil rights era directed at integrating public facilities were insulated by the First Amendment from the Sherman Act because the goal of the boycott was primarily political rather than economic.

275. The most common boycott is when horizontal competitors pressure suppliers to cut off supply to a price-cutting competitor. This was the case in *United States v. Gen. Motors Corp.*,[373] where the Court found that such action was an illegal group boycott.

276. In *Northwest Wholesale Stationers, Inc. v. Pac. Stationery & Printing Co.*,[374] a company expelled from a buyer's cooperative claimed that its exclusion constituted a "group boycott" by its competitors who remained members of the cooperative. The Supreme Court reaffirmed that *certain* group boycotts were subject to the per se rule, but held that others were not. Classic boycotts, "[t]o which this Court has applied the per se approach have generally involved joint efforts by a firm or firms to disadvantage competitors by either directly denying or persuading or coercing suppliers or customers to deny relationships the competitors need in the competitive struggle."[375] The Court found that the situation before it did not fit that description. It held that, at least in the context of a buyers' cooperative, to be subject to per se treatment, a party would have to demonstrate that, "[t]he cooperative possesses market power or exclusive access to an element essential to effective competition."[376] In the case before it, that showing had not been made. In fact, the cooperative was willing to sell to the plaintiff, just not on the same terms as it did to members of the cooperative.[377]

277. *Northwest Wholesale Stationers* involved a buyers' cooperative which, the Court recognized, was not a form of concerted activity likely to result in predominantly anticompetitive effects. Cooperatives were designed to increase economic efficiency. A cooperative necessarily had to have rules for membership. For these reasons, the Court held that in the absence of a showing of "market power or exclusive access to an element essential to effective competition,"[378] a rule of reason analysis applied.

278. *Superior Court Trial Lawyers* was decided after *Northwest Wholesale Stationers* and mentions it. Appellate courts have reviewed allegations of boycott with an eye towards *Northwest Wholesale Stationers*, even in egregious circumstances. What emerges is a per se test requiring a threshold showing of certain harms. But this threshold showing is far less onerous than what would have to be proven under a rule of reason analysis. Two examples make this clear.

279. In *Rossi v. Standard Roofing, Inc.*,[379] a new roofing company alleged that its competitors pressured manufacturers of essential roofing material to withhold product from it. Following *Northwest Wholesale Stationers,* the court determined that the withheld material was "necessary for him to compete in the marketplace."[380] It found that the boycott fit precisely the conduct the per se rule was intended to prohibit:

373. 384 U.S. 127, 86 S. Ct. 1321, 16 L. Ed. 2d 415 (1966).

374. 472 U.S. 284, 105 S. Ct. 2613, 86 L. Ed. 2d 202 (1985).

375. *Ibid.*, at 294, 105 S. Ct. at 2619 (citation omitted).

376. *Ibid.*, at 296, 105 S. Ct. at 2620–2621.

377. Moreover, in the case before it, the cooperative had annual sales of USD 5.8 million, while the expelled member had annual sales greater than that of the entire cooperative: USD 7.6 million.

378. *Nw. Wholesale Stationers*,472 U.S. at 294, 105 S. Ct. at 2619.

379. 156 F.3d 452 (3d Cir. 1998).

380. *Ibid.*, at 464.

> Further, the gravamen of his complaint fits snugly within the Court's Northwest Wholesale Stationers description of per se concerted refusals to deal – namely,... horizontal competitors...conspired with manufacturers...and suppliers...to deny Rossi access to...product as well as to coerce other suppliers not to sell any products to him. Importantly, all of this activity was done against the backdrop of [the horizontal competitors'] dissatisfaction with Rossi's price-cutting proclivities, and thus an inference can be drawn that the conspiracy was at least partially conceived as a price restraint.[381]

The court explained that because the per se rule was appropriate, far less was left to be proven than would have been necessary under a rule of reason analysis:

> In the usual rule of reason case, to establish a violation of § 1, plaintiffs must prove:
>
> (1) that the defendants contracted, combined or conspired among each other; (2) that the combination or conspiracy produced adverse, anti-competitive effects within the relevant product and geographic markets; (3) that the objects of and the conduct pursuant to that contract or conspiracy were illegal; and (4) that the plaintiffs were injured as a proximate result of that conspiracy.
>
> Here, because per se analysis applies, prongs two and three are conclusively presumed satisfied and need not be addressed.[382]

280. Toys "R" Us, Inc. ("TRU") v. FTC.[383] involved a more complicated boycott but an equally elegant application of a modified per se analysis. There, "TRU," the leading toy retailer, was incensed at warehouse stores' deep discounting of the best-selling toys. It pressured toy manufacturers to cease selling these best-selling toys to warehouse clubs unless they carried the toy manufacturers' full-line of toys. It let each manufacturer know that the others had agreed to the terms and assured all of them that TRU would monitor compliance. The court found that TRU's actions created a horizontal conspiracy among the toy manufacturers to boycott the warehouse stores. It purported to follow the criteria established in Northwest Wholesale Stationers to find that the action was a per se violation:

> (1) the boycotting firm has cut off access to a supply, facility or market necessary for the boycotted firm (i.e. the clubs) to compete; (2) the boycotting firm possesses a "dominant" position in the market (where "dominant" is an undefined term, but plainly chosen to stand for something different from antitrust's term of art

381. *Ibid.*
382. *Ibid.*, at 464–465 (citations omitted).
383. 221 F.3d 928 (7th Cir. 2000).

> "monopoly"); and (3) the boycott, as we explain further below, cannot be justified by plausible arguments that it was designed to enhance overall efficiency.[384]

It is questionable whether the latter two criteria were relevant to the analysis in *Northwest Wholesale Stationers* once it was established that access had been blocked to an item necessary for a competitor to compete.

281. Thus, modern boycott analysis involves two steps: first, does the boycott involve cutting a competitor's access to a necessary product? Alternatively, do the boycotting firms possess a dominant position in the marketplace? If so, a per se rule applies. These recent cases suggest that this analysis may be informed by a determination of whether the boycott is of a kind that has been traditionally considered harmful to economic efficiency.[385]

E. *Collusion on Other Objects*

282. The above sections describe the primary forms of collusion.

II. Information Exchange Practices

283. Information exchange practices involve two considerations. First, what kind of information can a trade association disseminate without running afoul of the antitrust laws? Second, to what degree will the otherwise permissible information exchange through the trade association serve as evidence of a conspiracy when the trade association is charged with some form of price stabilization?

284. Information exchange practices themselves are governed by a rule of reason analysis. The Supreme Court explained in *United States v. U.S. Gypsum Co.*[386] that: "the exchange of price data and other information among competitors does not invariably have anticompetitive effects; indeed such practices can in certain circumstances increase economic efficiency and render markets more, rather than less, competitive. For this reason, we have held that such exchanges of information do not constitute a *per se* violation of the Sherman Act."[387]

But in certain circumstances, particularly where there has been an exchange of current price information, courts have invariably found the behavior to violate the Sherman Act, even though it was not a per se violation. The Court explained:

---

384. *Ibid.*, at 936. While the court went on to discuss issues of market power, it made clear this was only done in the alternative and that its primary holding was that the violation was to be condemned per se and there was no need for a market power analysis.

385. An entirely different and separate boycott issue arises in the context of the statutory exemption of the insurance industry from the antitrust laws. Under the McCarran-Ferguson Act, the business of insurance is exempted from the antitrust laws except for certain violations, including boycott. However, in that limited context, the Supreme Court has defined boycott distinctly and narrowly. *Hartford Fire Ins. Co. v. California*, 509 U.S. 764, 800, 113 S. Ct. 2891, 2911, 125 L. Ed. 2d 612 (1993).

386. 438 U.S. 422, 443, 98 S. Ct. 2864, 2876, 57 L. Ed. 2d 854 (1978).

387. *Ibid.*, at 443 n. 16.

> A number of factors including most prominently the structure of the industry involved and the nature of the information exchanged are generally considered in divining the procompetitive or anticompetitive effects of this type of interseller communication. Exchanges of current price information, of course, have the greatest potential for generating anticompetitive effects and although not per se unlawful have consistently been held to violate the Sherman Act.[388]

285. In *Gypsum*, the defendants had argued that price verification among competitors was necessary to assure they were complying with the "meeting competition defense" to the price discrimination statute.[389] The Court rejected this defense, finding that the risk of price stabilization arising from the exchange of price information by competitors in an oligopolistic market outweighed the concern raised by the defendants.

286. *Gypsum* explained that the Court's prior decision in *United States v. Container Corporation of America* [390] had held that reciprocal exchange of price information, together with proof of an anticompetitive effect, was sufficient to establish liability. No further proof of a purpose to restrain trade was needed.

287. In *Gypsum* and *Container Corp.*, the Court was concerned that exchange of current price information would lead to high, oligopolistic pricing. However, the initial Supreme Court decision on price exchange, *American Column & Lumber Co. v. United States*,[391] involved what was, at least at the time, a diffuse industry involving hundreds of sellers in which barely 30% of the producers were participants in the price exchange. The association members circulated detailed weekly reports of their sales, including prices, quantities, and customers. The exchange of information also included detailed monthly inventory and production reports. The association's director also recommended future conduct.

288. On these facts, but without evidence of price effect, the Court held that the extensive exchange of price and production information was "simply an expansion of the gentlemen's agreement of former days and was therefore illegal."[392]

289. Justice Brandeis, in his dissent, explained his concern that restricting the exchange of information would lead to economic inefficiency:

> The co-operation which is incident to this plan does not suppress competition. On the contrary, it tends to promote all in competition which is desirable. By substituting knowledge for ignorance, rumor, guess, and suspicion, it tends also to substitute research and reasoning for gambling and piracy, without closing the door to adventure, or lessening the value of prophetic wisdom. In making such knowledge available to the smallest concern, it creates among producers equality of opportunity. In making it available, also, to purchasers and the general

388. *Ibid.* (citations omitted).
389. 15 U.S.C. § 13(a).
390. 393 U.S. 333, 89 S. Ct. 510, 21 L. Ed. 2d 526 (1969).
391. 257 U.S. 377, 42 S. Ct. 114, 66 L. Ed. 284 (1921).
392. *Ibid.*, at 410, 42 S. Ct. at 121.

> public, it does all that can actually be done to protect the community from extortion. If, as is alleged, the Plan tends to substitute stability in prices for violent fluctuations, its influence, in this respect, is not against the public interest. The evidence in this case, far from establishing an illegal restraint of trade, presents, in my opinion, an instance of commendable effort by concerns engaged in a chaotic industry to make possible its intelligent conduct under competitive conditions.[393]

Brandeis looked to the actual prices and competition in the industry and saw no evidence of restraint. To the extent that the exchange of information led to "rational" competition and curbed overproduction, he was willing to accept that "harm" in return for the increased efficiency, especially in a market like that before the Court which included, quite literally, many backwoods lumber mills without the sources of information available to large purchasers. Brandeis was also concerned that prohibitions on the exchange of information necessary to compete rationally would lead to consolidations and mergers, which the law could not reach.

290. Subsequent cases have sought to distinguish *American Column & Lumber*, and to provide guidance as to what information exchanges would be considered reasonable. Aggregated, anonymous data, whether relating to sales, costs, inventory, production or capacity is deemed reasonable so long as the information is generally available on fair terms to all participants in the market. For example, in *Maple Flooring Manufacturers Association v. U. S.*,[394] the data that was circulated involved past transactions, and the data on prices and inventories was aggregated without identifying any specific company data. The Court held that any limitation on production that would result from the circulation of such information was simply the result of informed management. It underscored that the information gathered by the association was submitted to the federal government and publicly available. The Court emphasized what information was not disseminated:

> [T]he statistics gathered and disseminated do not include current price quotations; information as to employment conditions; geographical distribution of shipments; the names of customers or distribution by classes of purchasers; the details with respect to new orders booked, such as names of customers, geographical origin of orders; or details with respect to unfilled orders, such as names of customers, their geographical location; the names of members having surplus stocks on hand; the amount of rough lumber on hand; or information as to cancellation of orders. Nor do they differ in any essential respect from trade or business statistics which are freely gathered and publicly disseminated in numerous branches of industry producing a standardized product such as grain, cotton, coal oil, and

393. 257 U.S. at 418, 42 S. Ct. at 123 (Brandeis, J., dissenting).
394. 268 U.S. 563, 45 S. Ct. 578, 69 L. Ed. 1093 (1925).

involving interstate commerce whose statistics disclose volume and material elements affecting costs of production, sales price, and stock on hand.[395]

291. An issue that has arisen in subsequent conspiracy cases – and that courts often misunderstand – is the use of trade association reporting requirements, especially in oligopolistic markets, to avoid cheating and hidden discounts. In *Sugar Institute, Inc. v. U. S.*,[396] the industry practice was to announce price increases publicly in advance and then to allow customers a grace period in which they could place orders before the price increased. The problem was that members of the industry cheated. They secretly extended discounts below the quoted price, increased the time for placing orders, and allowed for other means of deviating from the publicly announced price. To combat these "unethical" practices, sugar refiners created the Sugar Institute which promulgated what was known as the "basic agreement." "The distinctive feature of the 'basic agreement' was a requirement of adherence, without deviation, to the prices and terms publicly announced."[397] The agreement enforced this adherence through penalties not only upon cheating refiners, but upon customers as well. As a result, the various forms of cheating were abolished.

292. While there was no evidence of collusion in setting of prices, the Court found the structure put in place to assure no deviation from the published price unreasonable.[398] The Court also found that the circulation of production and inventory data, among only the Institute's members was unreasonable. The Court required that the information be made available to buyers and distributors.

293. A risk in entering into information exchange agreements is that, while standing alone, they may pass rule of reason review, they often do not stand alone. Instead, they are cited as evidence of collusion where broader conspiracies are alleged. The Court made it clear in *Gypsum* that the exchange of price information, together with an effect on prices, created a permissible inference of intent. Attendance at trade

395. *Ibid.*, at 574, 45 S. Ct. at 581–582. In a companion case decided the same day, the Court held that a cross-reporting system by cement manufacturers, in which they disclosed to each other their pending contracts, was justified to prevent fraud that had been prevalent in the previous, complicated market system that had led buyers intentionally to over-book supplies of cement and then play the market against the sellers. *Cement Mfrs.' Protective Ass'n v. United States*, 268 U.S. 588, 45 S. Ct. 586, 69 L.Ed. 1104 (1925).

396. 297 U.S. 553, 56 S.Ct. 629, 80 L. Ed. 859 (1936).

397. 297 U.S. at 582, 56 S.Ct. at 635.

398. *Ibid.* Later decisions, concentrating solely on the issue of price collusion, have failed to recognize the key importance of mechanisms to check cheating to assure effective oligopoly pricing. For example, the majority in *Blomkest Fertilizer, Inc. v. Potash Corp. of Saskatchewan*, 203 F.3d 1028 (8th Cir. 2000), failed to realize that the purpose of price exchanges was simply to serve as a check on cheating. The majority focused on the relative infrequency of pricing contacts among competitors during the alleged conspiracy period and the fact that many related to already prevailing prices. It completely missed the fact that the frequency and timing were irrelevant because the purpose of the contacts was not so much to fix future prices as to check cheating from the announced prices.

association meetings, and the opportunities for collusion they provide, have been coupled with other evidence to support allegations of price-fixing.[399]

III. Cooperation Agreements

294. Cooperation agreements can take different forms. They may involve a formal joint venture in which independent entities form a third entity, or they may involve a contractual relationship between two entities to act jointly in some fashion. Recent authority treats genuine joint ventures with a high degree of deference under a rule of reason analysis.[400] However, a joint venture, even created as a separate entity, may be viewed as vehicle for collusion among competitors.[401] Where a joint venture, even an independent entity, appears to be a sham created solely to restrain output or price competition, it may even be judged under a per se standard.

295. Many cooperation agreements fall under two separate antitrust statutes, the National Cooperative Research Act of 1984 and the National Cooperative Research and Production Act of 1993.[402] The acts cover joint ventures created to engage in research and development and joint ventures for "production of a product, process, or service."[403] The acts provide that certain joint ventures are to be tested under a rule of reason rather than a per se test. Also, they limit damages in cases in which the defendants have followed the acts' requirements and threaten the unsuccessful plaintiff with an assessment of attorneys' fees and costs if the plaintiff is found to have brought a frivolous suit or one in bad faith.

296. To obtain the act's protection, a party to a joint venture must formally notify the Attorney General and the FTC of the joint venture within ninety days after entering into a written agreement to form the venture.[404] The party must provide the names of the parties to the joint venture, the nature and objectives of the venture and, if it is a production venture, the nationalities of the venture partners. Parties have an ongoing requirement to report changes in the venture membership.[405]

A. Research and Development

297. Genuine research and development agreements are looked upon favorably because, in theory, they should increase efficiency. To the extent such agreements are challenged, it is where they are cosmetic, i.e. where the ultimate goal of the arrangement is not research and development but, rather, to shield what is effectively a horizontal

399. *See, e.g., In re Flat Glass Antitrust Litigation*, which explained that "a finder of fact could reasonably infer that the flat glass producers used the information to implement collusive price increases; that is, the exchanges of information had an impact on pricing decisions." 385 F.3d 350, 369 (3d Cir. 2004) (citation omitted).
400. *Texaco Inc. v. Dagher*, 547U.S. 1, 126 S. Ct. 1276, 164 L. Ed. 2d 1 (2006).
401. *Am. Needle, Inc. v. Nat'l Football League*,.130 S. Ct. 2201, 176 L. Ed. 2d 947 (2010).
402. These statutes are currently codified together at 15 U.S.C. §§ 4301–4306.
403. 15 U.S.C. § 4301(a)(6)(D).
404. 15 U.S.C. § 4305.
405. 15 U.S.C. § 4303.

agreement among competitors to restrict output, or the arrangement contains ancillary provisions deemed to be excessively restrictive.

298. The law recognizes that research and development agreements require a degree of restriction to avoid free riding. Those who have participated in a collaborative research and development project are entitled to the fruits of the project and those who have not participated should not be permitted to "free ride," i.e., reap the fruits of a project to which they did not contribute.

299. Research and development agreements are judged under a rule of reason. The analysis involves the concept of innovation markets. "An innovation market consists of the research and development directed to particular new or improved goods or processes and the close substitutes for that research and development."[406] There are several concerns raised by research and development collaborations but most of those concerns are directed to the ancillary aspects of an agreement rather than to the concept of joint research and development itself. The primary concern is limiting independent decision-making or stifling competition by providing certain market participants dominant control, either in the product market or the innovation market. The benefits of collaboration, i.e., that the participants can more quickly develop new or improved products, must be weighed against several risks. The collaboration may reduce the number of independent competitors. By reducing innovators, the agreement may reduce the number of competitors in the market for the goods derived from the research and development collaboration, leading to higher prices or reduced output, quality or service. Similarly, the research and development collaboration may further entrench dominant participants in a market.

300. The government has established "safety zones" for parties contemplating research and development collaborations. It will not challenge collaboration among competitors where three or more independently controlled competitors exist in the innovation market in addition to the collaborative effort, provided all have the assets and incentive to engage in research and development that is a close substitute to that which is the subject of the collaborative effort. The safety zone will not insulate a collaboration agreement that is, in fact, otherwise a per se violation of the antitrust laws.

301. Two examples demonstrate the framework for analyzing research and development collaboration agreements. If two software manufacturers with worldwide marketing departments, but each with less than a 10% market share each in the market for word-processors, form a joint venture to develop a new word-processing program, the government will not object, provided each contributes software developers and the expenses and profits of the joint venture are split evenly.

302. However, if the endeavor prohibits each of the co-venturers from selling their existing word-processing software once the new software hits the markets, that output-restricting provision would require justification. In an example the government provides, the venturers attempted to justify the restriction based on the past experience of another joint venture that failed because a co-venturer appropriated know-how developed by the joint venture. In such a circumstance, the government would examine whether less-restrictive alternatives exist than the absolute bar on sales.

406. Antitrust Guidelines for Collaborations among Competitors, Federal Trade Commission and U.S. Department of Justice, April 2000.

303. Of course, had the collaboration agreement provisions contained a provision setting the price at which the existing word-processing software of the two firms could be sold following introduction of the new software, it would likely be challenged as a per se violation.

B. Specialization

304. Specialization is not a concept dealt with under American antitrust law.

C. Standardization

305. Litigation over standard has setting arisen in a variety of contexts including standards for particular products,[407] proposed codes,[408] to standards for accrediting law schools.[409]

306. Standard-setting can be beneficial. It allows for easy comparison of products by consumers. It allows for reduced informational costs since a common standard avoids the need to research the products of varying manufacturers. Purchasers can rely on certifying organizations for quality assurance. It can provide for more competitive markets where a particular standard will allow multiple vendors to offer comparable products. For example, a common standard for recordings such as CDs and DVDs allows multiple sellers to sell competing devices on which all CDs or DVDs can be played.

307. There are risks associated with these benefits. Standardization allows for highly transparent pricing which can facilitate collusion by allowing easy detection of deviation from price-fixing agreements. Standards can be set by competitors to eliminate or reduce competition. The standard-setting process can be used to stifle competition or innovation.

308. In *Radiant Burners, Inc. v. Peoples Gas Light & Coke Co.*,[410] the Supreme Court held that an allegation that a certifying organization made up of certain gas burner manufacturers arbitrarily denied a certification for the plaintiff's new gas burner in order to exclude plaintiff from the market stated a per se violation of the antitrust laws, citing to earlier boycott cases.

309. Later cases, however, have generally upheld legitimate standard-setting under rule of reason analysis. *Structural Laminates, Inc. v. Douglas Fir Plywood Ass'n,* [411] held that denial of certification for a plywood manufactured by the plaintiff that did not conform to the industry standard did not violate the antitrust laws even though the plaintiff's plywood was of equal quality to that provided in the standard. Similarly, *Eliason Corp. v. Nat'l Sanitation Found.* [412] held that independently established standards

407. *See, e.g., Structural Laminates, Inc. v. Douglas Fir Plywood Association*, 261 F. Supp. 154 (D. Or. 1966) aff'd, 399 F.2d 155 (9th Cir. 1968).

408. *See , e.g., Allied Tube & Conduit Corp. v. Indian Head, Inc.*, 486 U.S. 492 (1988).

409. *See, Massachusetts school of Law at Andover v. American Bar Ass'n*, 107 F.3d 1026 (3d Cir. 1997)

410. 364 U.S. 656, 81 S. Ct. 365, 5 L. Ed. 2d 358 (1961).

411. 261 F. Supp. 154, 155 (D. Or. 1966) *aff'd,* 399 F.2d 155 (9th Cir. 1968).

412. 614 F.2d 126, 129 (6th Cir. 1980).

served a valuable purpose and refusal to certify a product would not state a cause of action without an allegation of corruption of the process:

> The District Court expressly found that NSF standards were developed to promote uniformity in the health requirements that products are required to meet in different jurisdictions. This uniformity helps promote nationwide competition and enables manufacturers who elect to comply with NSF standards to be reasonably sure that they will not have to modify their product in order to meet the different requirements of many jurisdictions....
>
> The practice of treating NSFTL approval of a product as Prima Facie evidence of compliance with local standards avoids waste of time and money for duplicative testing in many different jurisdictions. NSF standards are periodically revised so that no product of adequate sanitary quality is excluded from qualifying for the seal of approval. NSF and NSFTL have never disparaged the quality of products which they have not tested. NSF and NSFTL are independent organizations and are not dominated or controlled by manufacturers of any one product. They are not in direct competition with the plaintiff and have no intent to exclude plaintiff from competition.

310. Where, however, the standard-setting process is corrupted to exclude a competitor, there is unquestionably a cause of action under the antitrust laws. For example, *Allied Tube & Conduit Corp. v. Indian Head, Inc.*,[413] involved efforts by members of the steel conduit industry to block approval of polyvinyl conduit under the National Electrical Code. The steel conduit producers "collectively agreed to exclude respondent's product from the 1981 Code by packing the upcoming annual meeting with new Association members whose only function would be to vote against the polyvinyl chloride proposal." The Court stated, "What petitioner may not do (without exposing itself to possible antitrust liability for direct injuries) is bias the process by, as in this case, stacking the private standard-setting body with decision-makers sharing their economic interest in restraining competition."[414]

311. Standard-setting organizations and the relationship of standards to intellectual property has become increasingly important. Cases have grappled with the use of standards to augment patents. Corruption of the standard-setting process has led to divergent views. Two recent cases have come to conflicting results highlighting the complex issues relating to standard-setting in high technology. In *Rambus Inc. v. FTC*,[415] the FTC charged a patent holder with monopolization. The FTC found that the patent holder had violated the antitrust laws when, in the course of petitioning for adoption of a particular standard, it had failed to disclose to a standard-setting body that it held a key patent covering the proposed standard. The D.C. Circuit reversed the FTC, holding that any deception did not give rise to an antitrust violation because

413. 486 U.S. 492, 108 S. Ct. 1931, 100 L. Ed. 2d 497 (1988).
414. 486 U.S. at 511, 108 S. Ct. at 1942.
415. 522 F.3d 456 (D.C.Cir. 2008).

there was no injury to competition. The FTC conceded that it could not prove that the standard-setting body would not have adopted the technology as the standard even if the patent holder's patent position had been disclosed. It argued that there would have been one of two outcomes had there been disclosure. The same technology would have been standardized or the standard-setting organization would have been able to extract more favorable licensing terms from the petitioner. The D.C. Circuit held that there was no competitive harm in an otherwise legal monopolist's end run around price constraints though deception. Even had the standard-setting organization been able to extract better terms, the fact that that opportunity was lost through deception did not amount to competitive injury since there was no difference in the number of actual participants in the market.

312. The D.C. Circuit acknowledged that a very different view was taken by the Third Circuit in *Broadcom Corp. v. Qualcomm Inc.*[416] The Third Circuit cited extensively to the FTC opinion in *Rambus* and endorsed its reasoning as well as the reasoning in a number of other FTC decisions critical of misrepresentations to standard-setting organizations. Following *Indian Head,* the Third Circuit held that misleading a standard-setting organization can give rise to an antitrust claim:

> We hold that (1) in a consensus-oriented private standard-setting environment, (2) a patent holder's intentionally false promise to license essential proprietary technology on [fair, reasonable, and non-discriminatory]terms, (3) coupled with an [Standard Determining Organization's] reliance on that promise when including the technology in a standard, and (4) the patent holder's subsequent breach of that promise, is actionable anticompetitive conduct. This holding follows directly from established principles of antitrust law and represents the emerging view of enforcement authorities and commentators, alike. Deception in a consensus-driven private standard-setting environment harms the competitive process by obscuring the costs of including proprietary technology in a standard and increasing the likelihood that patent rights will confer monopoly power on the patent holder.

416. 501 F.3d 297, 314 (3d Cir. 2007).

Subsequent authority has read *Rambus* to involve a failure of proof rather than a finding that no cause of action existed.[417]

D. *Joint Production*

313. The further one moves from a pure research joint venture to a marketing joint venture the more strict the antitrust scrutiny becomes. Except for a naked restraint on output or price, a production joint venture will be governed by a rule of reason. However, there is a risk that some aspect of the venture will include a more naked restraint that will subject it to per se analysis.

314. Such was the case in *United States v. Topco Associates, Inc.*,[418] where a joint venture among regional supermarkets to produce private-label foods to compete against the private-label products of national chains was condemned because the joint-venture agreement effectively allocated geographic markets among the participants. The geographic restriction was not necessary to achieve the joint-production aims of the venture.[419] If the venture had been structured without the territorial limitations, it would have been found to be a legitimate venture that allowed the smaller, regional supermarkets to compete with national supermarket chains.[420]

315. *Topco* demonstrates the pro-competitive efficiencies that can be gained through a production joint venture. The Court discussed the ability such joint venture provided to small regional supermarkets to develop store-branded products and how this ability increased competition with major national chains. The individual regional chains could not have undertaken this absent the cooperative venture. Subsequent

---

417. *See, e.g.*, *Apple Inc. v. Samsung Electronics Co., Ltd.*, 11-CV-01846-LHK, 2011 WL 4948567 (N.D. Cal. Oct. 18, 2011)("The Commission failed to show that but for Rambus's failure to disclose its intellectual property rights, the SSO would not have adopted the standard at issue. The court held that in order to establish anticompetitive conduct, the plaintiff must show that the patent holder's failure to disclose its intellectual property rights induced the SSO to set the standard incorporating the essential patent. In other words, Apple must allege that there was an alternative technology that the SSO was considering during the standard-setting process and that the SSO would have adopted an alternative standard had it known of the patent holder's intellectual property rights."); *Research In Motion Ltd. v. Motorola, Inc.*, 644 F. Supp. 2d 788, 796 (N.D. Tex. 2008) ("RIM has sufficiently alleged harm to competition. Both the Third Circuit, in *Broadcom,* and the Supreme Court, in *Allied Tube,* have stated that standards, without the proper safeguards, are inherently anticompetitive. It follows that when an entity side-steps these safeguards in an effort to return the standard to its natural anticompetitive state, anticompetitive effects are inevitable.").

418. 405 U.S. 596, 92 S. Ct. 1126, 31 L. Ed. 2d 515 (1972).

419. *See* , Peter C. Cartensen & Harry First, "Rambling Through Economic Theory: Topco's Closer Look," in *Antitrust Stories* (Foundation Press, 2007).

420. Similarly, in *Gen. Leaseways, Inc. v. Nat'l Truck Leasing Ass'n,* 744 F.2d 588, 589 (7th Cir. 1984), the court struck down, as a per se violation of s. 1, a territorial allocation clause that was part of by-laws of a truck leasing association that otherwise facilitated creation of a national auto leasing association among small, local companies to compete against national leasing companies. But *see, Rothery Storage & Van Co. v. Atlas Van Lines, Inc.*, 792 F.2d 210 (D.C. Cir. 1986) which upheld under a rule of reason analysis applied to joint ventures certain association rules limiting behavior of participants in an association of national movers.

studies showed that when the *Topco* venture continued, without the market-allocation provisions, it significantly increased competition.[421]

316. In a rule of reason analysis, the court will weigh the reduction of actual and potential competition among the production co-venturers against the increased efficiencies created by the venture. It will weigh the potential that each venturer would have engaged in the production individually with similar efficiency and determine the degree to which the joint venture may facilitate other forms of collaboration or collusion among the competitors. For example, while each production joint-venture participant may retain discretion over its downstream pricing, high transfer pricing by the joint venture to the participants may be an effective means of illegal price stabilization. In some cases, joint-venture arrangements of this kind had been found to be price-fixing.[422]

317. Certain joint-production ventures have passed scrutiny for surprising reasons. Thus, a joint auto plant to be operated by General Motors and Toyota was justified to the FTC on the basis that it would allow General Motors to learn Japanese production techniques and would increase the availability of low-cost automobiles in the US.[423] The FTC approved the joint venture with restrictions curtailing the scope of information exchange between the parties and limiting its duration. These restrictions were later lifted.[424]

318. Where the joint-production venture becomes essential to participate in the industry, cases require that membership be open to anyone on equal terms. For example, in *Associated Press v. United States*,[425] the Court was persuaded that membership in the Associated Press, a news service encompassing all of the major newspapers, was essential to enter the news market. The Court struck down by-laws that precluded membership by new entrants in cities in which members were already present. Similarly, in *United States v. St. Louis Terminal Railroad Association*,[426] a group of competing railroads formed a terminal association that acquired all available means of access across the Mississippi River at St. Louis. Other railroads were allowed to use these facilities only with the unanimous consent of all the owners and payment of a fee. While the Court found this combination of competing railroads to be an unreasonable restraint of trade, it found that the joint venture served a number of useful, pro-competitive purposes through its unification of the terminal systems. Therefore, rather than ordering the association to dissolve, the Court required it to allow all competing railroads to use its facilities on equal terms.[427]

E. Joint Purchasing

319. Historically, joint purchasing has not been an object of antitrust scrutiny even though it raises many of the concerns of joint activity by competitors. The Supreme

421. *See, supra* n. 408.
422. *See, Freeman v. San Diego Ass'n of Realtors*, 322 F.3d 1133, 1147 (9th Cir. 2003)("The associations purposely fixed the support fee they charged …at a supracompetitive level.").
423. *See , Matter of Gen. Motors Corp.*, 103 F.T.C. 374 (1984).
424. *In the Matter of Gen. Motors Corp.*, et al., 116 F.T.C. 1276 (1993).
425. 326 U.S. 1, 65 S. Ct. 1416, 89 L. Ed. 2013 (1945).
426. 224 U.S. 383, 32 S.Ct. 507, 56 L.Ed. 810 (1912).
427. *See also, United States v. Realty Multi-List, Inc.*, 629 F.2d 1351 (5th Cir. 1980).

Court has explained that significant efficiencies are commonly achieved through joint purchasing arrangements:

> The arrangement permits the participating retailers to achieve economies of scale in both the purchase and warehousing of wholesale supplies, and also ensures ready access to a stock of goods that might otherwise be unavailable on short notice. The cost savings and order-filling guarantees enable smaller retailers to reduce prices and maintain their retail stock so as to compete more effectively with larger retailers.[428]

The sole restriction has been that a buying cooperative cannot arbitrarily exclude a member where "the cooperative possesses market power or exclusive access to an element essential to effective competition."[429]

F. Joint Selling

320. Joint-selling arrangements are common but run greater risk of violating the antitrust laws than do the forms of joint activity discussed previously. They are not covered by the National Cooperative Research Act of 1984 and the National Cooperative Research and Production Act of 1993, which provides limited protection to those other arrangements. When joint-selling agreements provide for multiple producers to confer price authority on a joint-vendor, they run a high risk of being deemed a per se violation of section 1. Where manufacturers created a single joint-seller that determined price such arrangements have been held to be per se price-fixing.[430] However, there would be no violation if each producer chose a common sales agent but retained independence in pricing, production and other such decisions.[431]

321. In *United States v. Sealy, Inc.*,[432] the Court condemned an arrangement under which mattress manufacturers created a joint marketing organization as a per se violation of section 1. The marketing organization developed and licensed to its members a trademark and set both price and territories for the sale of the trademarked mattresses.

322. The *Antitrust Guidelines for Collaborations Among Competitors*, which is issued by the FTC and the Department of Justice, distinguishes between two kinds of ventures. In one, two start-up firms developing competing software form a partnership

428. *Nw. Wholesale Stationers, Inc. v. Pac. Stationery & Printing Co.*, 472 U.S. 284, 295, 105 S. Ct. 2613, 2620, 86 L. Ed. 2d 202 (1985).

429. *Ibid.*, at 296.

430. *See , e.g., Virginia Excelsior Mills, Inc v. FTC*, 256 F.2d 538, 540 (4th Cir. 1958)("the obligatory delegation of all discretion in fixing prices to the Board of Directors of Mills was a violation, per se, of § 1 of the Sherman Act.").

431. *Ibid.*, 256 F.2d 538, 541 (4th Cir. 1958)("in some businesses, it is common practice for several producers to utilize the services of one sales agency, and there is nothing unlawful in such an arrangement when each producer reserves, and exercises, independence in pricing, acceptance of orders, production and other material matters.").

432. 388 U.S. 350, 87 S. Ct. 1847, 18 L. Ed. 2d 1238 (1967).

to market their software. The two firms will agree on the price at which the partnership will sell the software and will divide the revenue based on the proportion of each company's software sold by the partnership. This venture is identified as a per se violation, i.e., an agreement not to compete on price.[433] However, the *Guidelines* approve the same structure under a rule of reason analysis if the two companies independently set the prices at which their software will be sold by the partnership, so long as there is a provision to prevent information specific to one company in the partnership from being disclosed to the other.[434]

323. In the joint-selling arrangement at issue in *Am. Needle, Inc. v. Nat'l Football League*,[435] all of the independent member teams of NFL conferred the right to sell their separately owned intellectual property – i.e. trademarks and logos – to a new entity, NFLP, which then marketed the rights jointly. The Court considered whether such an enterprise involved the requisite multiplicity of actors to conspire under section 1 or whether NFLP was a single entity. The Court concluded, following *Sealy*, that NFLP represented a concerted effort by the thirty-two member teams and therefore represented a multiplicity of actors under section 1:

> Directly relevant to this case, the teams compete in the market for intellectual property. To a firm making hats, the Saints and the Colts are two potentially competing suppliers of valuable trademarks. When each NFL team licenses its intellectual property, it is not pursuing the "common interests of the whole" league but is instead pursuing interests of each "corporation itself,"Copperweld, 467 U.S., at 770, 104 S.Ct. 2731; teams are acting as "separate economic actors pursuing separate economic interests," and each team therefore is a potential "independent cente[r] of decisionmaking."[436]

While the Court applied a rule of reason analysis, that may have been based on its prior rulings relating to the area of sports, in which some degree of concerted activity is necessary for there to be a product at all, rather than its prior joint-venture decisions.

§2. Vertical Agreements

324. Vertical agreements are analyzed under a rule of reason. American antitrust law in this area differs from that of the European Community, which takes a more rigorous view of vertical restrictions. This is in part because the European Community is, at this juncture, more vigilant in removing barriers, particularly territorial barriers, to trade within Europe – a political/economic concern less present in the already more integrated economy of the US. And it is, in part, because the European Community takes more seriously the risks posed by vertical price-fixing.

433. *Antitrust Guidelines for Collaborations among Competitors* issued by the Federal Trade Commission and the U.S. Department of Justice (April 2000).

434. *Ibid.*, at 32.

435. 130 S. Ct. 2201, 176 L. Ed. 2d 947 (2010).

436. 130 S. Ct. at 2213.

325. American cases have slowly shifted analysis of vertical relationships from the per se doctrine to the rule of reason, believing that interbrand competition will more likely discipline the market than court intervention. The per se ban on territorial allocation by a manufacturer was revised to bring it within the rule of reason in *Cont'l T. V., Inc. v. GTE Sylvania Inc.* [437] The Court concluded that the benefits that would accrue from more aggressive interbrand competition outweighed any harms that might arise from curtailment of intrabrand competition that would result from allowing a manufacturer to allocate territories among distributors. By allocating territories, a manufacturer could encourage promotion of the product by distributors within the exclusive territory. It curtailed the free-rider problem where a discounter, providing little in the way of promotion or service, could take advantage of the advertising and services provided by a higher-priced distributor within the same territory.

326. If a manufacturer abused its position by allocating territories in a manner that harmed promotion of its product, the manufacturer would be penalized through lost sales to other manufacturers of similar products that were more astute in their distribution and pricing. The risk of reduced competition in the vertical relationship was much less than the risk in horizontal agreements. The latter necessarily impinges upon interbrand, and thus overall, competition. Where the manufacturer has sufficient market power for its distribution scheme to significantly impinge upon competition in the overall product market, the rule of reason provides a means of seeking relief.

327. Having adopted this position with regard to exclusive territories, it was not a huge step for the Court to lift the per se restriction on vertical price maintenance, or "vertical price-fixing," the ability of a manufacturer to set the downstream price at which its product is sold. The Court did that in *Leegin Creative Leather Products, Inc. v. PSKS, Inc.*, [438] which held that vertical price maintenance would also be analyzed under a rule of reason. In *Leegin*, the Court weighed the risk that allowing such vertical relationships would facilitate horizontal price-fixing – and the dissent cited to the studies showing that vertical price maintenance led to higher prices – but the Court believed interbrand competition provided sufficient discipline to ameliorate such risks. It held that the application of the rule of reason would allow court intervention where such market forces did not function.

328. The opinion of the Court of Appeals upon remand in *Leegin* demonstrates the degree to which that decision eviscerated any claim for vertical price-fixing. Fundamental to any rule of reason analysis is a demonstration of market power in a relevant market. *Leegin* involved distribution of a brand of luxury leather goods. The plaintiff sought to define the relevant market as the market in the defendant's particular leather goods. The court was not persuaded:

> In rare circumstances, a single brand of a product or service can constitute a relevant market for antitrust purposes. ... But that possibility is limited to situations in which consumers are "locked in" to a specific brand by the nature of the product. There is no structural barrier to the interchangeability of Brighton

437. 433 U.S. 36, 97 S. Ct. 2549, 53 L. Ed. 2d 568 (1977).
438. 551 U.S. 877, 127 S. Ct. 2705, 168 L. Ed. 2d 623 (2007).

> products with goods produced by competing manufacturers, nor has PSKS alleged any such structural barriers.[439]

An effort to define the market as women's accessories at the wholesale level was also rejected: "women's accessories' is too broad and vague a definition to constitute a market. Indeed, it is impossible to imagine that Leegin could have power over such a market. ... even anticompetitive uses of R[esale] P[rice]M[aintenance] do not create concern unless the relevant entity has market power."[440]

329. The decision neatly summarized the prevailing view on vertical restraints under which the sections below need to be read:

> PSKS also alleged that the R[esale]P[rice]M[aintenance] policy deprived consumers of "free and open competition in the purchase of Brighton-brand products," because RPM limits price competition among retailers. One problem with that argument is that it ignores interbrand competition, which forces Brighton retailers to offer a combination of price and service that attracts consumers away from competing products. It also fails to recognize that retailers will cease carrying Brighton goods if Leegin imposes onerous requirements that make Brighton products difficult to sell. Moreover, robust competition can exist even in the absence of price competition. ... Retailers may seek to attract customers with better service, more knowledgeable staff, more appealing stores, and other nonprice-oriented strategies.[441]

I. Distribution

A. Exclusive Distributorship

330. Exclusive *distribution* involves a manufacturer or distributor assigning exclusive rights to *sell* a product – usually within a particular territory. Exclusive *dealing*, is where a distributor, or retailer, agrees to *purchase* only the products of a particular manufacturer or vendor. The two have very different economic effects and are treated differently under the law.

331. Exclusive distribution is governed under a rule of reason analysis and is generally permitted so long as it arises in a vertical relationship. A manufacturer may assign its distributors exclusive territories.[442] However, agreements among horizontal

439. 615 F.3d 412, at 418 (5th Cir. 2010) *cert. denied,* 131 S. Ct. 1476, 179 L. Ed. 2d 301 (U.S. 2011).

440. *Ibid.*, at 418–419.

441. *Ibid.*, at 419.

442. *Cont'l T. V., Inc. v. GTE Sylvania Inc.*, 433 U.S. 36, 97 S. Ct. 2549, 53 L. Ed. 2d 568 (1977); *Leegin Creative Leather Products, Inc. v. PSKS, Inc.*, 551 U.S. 877, 903, 127 S. Ct. 2705, 2723, 168 L. Ed. 2d 623 (2007) ("A manufacturer can impose territorial restrictions on distributors and allow only one distributor to sell its goods in a given region.").

competitors assigning territories is a per se violation of the antitrust laws.[443] This is because each involves an entirely different economic analysis.

332. Territorial allocation among horizontal competitors involves the most pernicious form of collusion. Where successful, it results in the stifling of competition – both as to price and service – since it involves complete elimination of active competitors from the assigned market. Even where the elimination of competition is less than complete, competition is nonetheless reduced by the agreement of potential competitors to stay out of the market. In *Topco*, the regional supermarket chains that were members of the Topco cooperative had effectively assigned exclusive territories to the members. There was, nonetheless, active competition within the allocated markets from national supermarket chains as well as regional vendors that were not members of the Topco cooperative. However, after the territorial restriction clause was struck down, major regional chains that were members of the Topco cooperative expanded into surrounding markets increasing the competitive offerings and Topco's sales increased dramatically, indicating a sharp increase in competition and output.[444]

333. However, vertical allocation of markets by a manufacturer among its distributors or retailers does not carry the same risk and there are countervailing benefits that warrant taking a more tolerant approach. A manufacturer, other than a monopolist or one with substantial market power, faces significant interbrand competition and has every incentive to assure maximum sales revenue from distribution of its products. It has little motive to restrain trade by limiting distributors of its products through a territorial allocation scheme unless there are efficiencies or benefits obtained that will increase the attractiveness of its products in the market. Territorial allocation may increase incentives for distributor investment by protecting the distributor and avoiding "free riding" by discounters not making similar investment in service and distribution. A full-line distributor may carry a wide array of products, provide full warranty service, and engage in extensive advertising. All of this investment would be compromised if a discount store opened next door selling only the best-selling of the manufacturer's products at steep discount with no service. If the manufacturer errs significantly in the restrictions it places on its distributors, absent considerable market power and high barriers to entry, the manufacturer will be disciplined by interbrand competition.

334. That is the theory and the Supreme Court in *Leegin Creative Leather Products, Inc. v. PSKS, Inc.*,[445]analyzed the competing economic interests supporting and opposing significant vertical restraints.

335. Where a vertical restriction by a manufacturer is merely subterfuge for a horizontal restraint by distributors, such cases should fall under the per se rule. But proof and characterization in such cases is difficult. *Monsanto Co. v. Spray-Rite Serv. Corp.* [446]was a leading case on vertical price-fixing conspiracies before *Leegin.* There, a distributor alleged that a manufacturer successfully colluded with other distributors to impose a vertical price-fixing scheme. Could the case have been characterized as a horizontal price-fixing scheme among distributors into which the manufacturer, which

443. *United States v. Topco Associates, Inc.*, 405 U.S. 596, 92 S. Ct. 1126, 31 L. Ed. 2d 515 (1972).

444. *See* , Peter C. Cartensen & Harry First, "Rambling Through Economic Theory: Topco's Closer Look," in *Antitrust Stories* (Foundation Press, 2007).

445. 551 U.S. 877, 127 S. Ct. 2705, 168 L. Ed. 2d 623 (2007).

446. 465 U.S. 752, 104 S. Ct. 1464, 79 L. Ed. 2d 775 (1984).

had its own retail outlets, was co-opted? Such was the case in *United States v. Gen. Motors Corp.*,[447] where General Motors, at the behest of dealers and a dealers association, began cutting off dealers who sold cars through discounters. The Court seemed to find this a horizontal conspiracy among competitors that was per se unlawful. It stated: "Nor do we propose to construe the Sherman Act to prohibit conspiracies to fix prices at which competitors may sell, but to allow conspiracies or combinations to put competitors out of business entirely."*Leegin* itself left the door open to such claims. The majority explained:

> A group of retailers might collude to fix prices to consumers and then compel a manufacturer to aid the unlawful arrangement with resale price maintenance. In that instance the manufacturer does not establish the practice to stimulate services or to promote its brand but to give inefficient retailers higher profits. Retailers with better distribution systems and lower cost structures would be prevented from charging lower prices by the agreement. ... Historical examples suggest this possibility is a legitimate concern. ...
>
> A horizontal cartel among competing manufacturers or competing retailers that decreases output or reduces competition in order to increase price is, and ought to be, per se unlawful. ... To the extent a vertical agreement setting minimum resale prices is entered upon to facilitate either type of cartel, it, too, would need to be held unlawful under the rule of reason. This type of agreement may also be useful evidence for a plaintiff attempting to prove the existence of a horizontal cartel.[448]

336. *Leegin* also outlined the circumstances in which the rule of reason could properly be applied to abuses in vertical distribution. It provided examples:

> Resale price maintenance, furthermore, can be abused by a powerful manufacturer or retailer. A dominant retailer, for example, might request resale price maintenance to forestall innovation in distribution that decreases costs. A manufacturer might consider it has little choice but to accommodate the retailer's demands for vertical price restraints if the manufacturer believes it needs access to the retailer's.... A manufacturer with market power, by comparison, might use resale price maintenance to give retailers an incentive not to sell the products of smaller rivals or new entrants. ...As should be evident, the potential anticompetitive consequences of vertical price restraints must not be ignored or underestimated.[449]

337. While not the subject of the present treatise, there is a significant body of state law governing distribution which, in certain states, accords a distributor considerable

---

447. 384 U.S. 127, 148, 86 S. Ct. 1321, 1332, 16 L. Ed. 2d 415 (1966).
448. 551 U.S. 877, 893, 127 S. Ct. 2705, 2717, 168 L. Ed. 2d 623 (2007).
449. 551 U.S. 877, 893–894, 127 S. Ct. 2705, 2717, 168 L. Ed. 2d 623 (2007).

rights limiting termination and oppressive business practices. For example, in *Beilowitz v. Gen. Motors Corp.*,[450] a court, ruling under the New Jersey Franchise Practices Act, enjoined General Motors from imposing a territorial distributorship system on its auto parts distributors that would have cut out 40% of an existing distributor's market. In *Builder's World, Inc. v. Marvin Lumber & Cedar, Inc.*,[451] *modified sub nom Builders World, Inc. v. Marvin Lumber & Cedar, Inc.*, [452] a court acting under the Wisconsin Fair Dealership Law, enjoined a new distribution program by a window manufacturer because it would have harmed the business of an existing distributor. These state statutes generally limit the ability to terminate a distributor or to impose unreasonable standards of performance.

338. Not all distributors fall within the protections of these statutes, and the statutes themselves vary considerably from state to state. They generally require a high degree of identity between the distributor's business and that of the manufacturer or supplier, including significant "franchise" specific investment, i.e., investment that would be lost absent the particular distribution arrangement.

B. Exclusive Dealing

339. Exclusive dealing involves the requirement that the distributor only carry the manufacturer's product. Exclusive dealing is subject to challenge under sections 1 and 2 of the Sherman Act and is addressed specifically by section 3 of the Clayton Act. Section 3 of the Clayton Act provides:

> § 14. Sale, etc., on agreement not to use goods of competitor
>
> It shall be unlawful for any person engaged in commerce, in the course of such commerce, to lease or make a sale or contract for sale of goods, wares, merchandise, machinery, supplies, or other commodities, whether patented or unpatented, for use, consumption, or resale within the United States or any Territory thereof or the District of Columbia or any insular possession or other place under the jurisdiction of the United States, or fix a price charged therefor, or discount from, or rebate upon, such price, on the condition, agreement, or understanding that the lessee or purchaser thereof shall not use or deal in the goods, wares, merchandise, machinery, supplies, or other commodities of a competitor or competitors of the lessor or seller, where the effect of such lease, sale, or contract for sale or such condition, agreement, or understanding may be to substantially lessen competition or tend to create a monopoly in any line of commerce.[453]

450. 233 F. Supp. 2d 631 (D.N.J. 2002).
451. 482 F. Supp. 2d 1065, 1069 (E.D. Wis. 2007).
452. 06C0555, 2007 WL 2138760 (E.D. Wis. Jul. 23, 2007).
453. 15 U.S.C.A. § 14.

In contrast to the provisions of the Sherman Act, section 3 of the Clayton Act only applies to goods or commodities. It does not apply to services.

340. The law of exclusive dealing is considerably less settled than that of exclusive distributing. This is partly because exclusive dealing presents a greater risk of market foreclosure than does exclusive distributing. Historically, a major manufacturer, at least theoretically, had the potential of foreclosing entry to rivals by requiring exclusive dealing by distributors or retailers. Whereas exclusive distribution most likely forecloses *intrabrand* competition while potentially increasing *interbrand* competition, exclusive dealing forecloses *interbrand* competition, the very competition that serves to protect the market in the exclusive distribution context. A requirement that a distributor carry only one manufacturer's products forecloses that distributor from carrying the products of a competitor and thereby restrains interbrand competition. Exclusive distribution is known as a foreclosure restraint because it eliminates outlets for distribution.

341. However, exclusive dealing is also sometimes termed a "requirements contract." From that perspective, there are significant advantages that parties may achieve. For one thing, it assures a source of product within a price range for an extended period of time and may encourage investment. Assurance of supply may also reduce the need for warehousing. Justice Frankfurter recognized several of these advantages in *Standard Oil Co. of California v. United States*:

> Requirements contracts, on the other hand, may well be of economic advantage to buyers as well as to sellers, and thus indirectly of advantage to the consuming public. In the case of the buyer, they may assure supply, afford protection against rises in price, enable long-term planning on the basis of known costs, and obviate the expense and risk of storage in the quantity necessary for a commodity having a fluctuating demand. From the seller's point of view, requirements contracts may make possible the substantial reduction of selling expenses, give protection against price fluctuations, and-of particular advantage to a newcomer to the field to whom it is important to know what capital expenditures are justified-offer the possibility of a predictable market. ... They may be useful, moreover, to a seller trying to establish a foothold against the counterattacks of entrenched competitors.[454]

342. *Standard Oil* grappled with determining a test to establish that a requirements contract "substantially lessened competition" under section 3. *Standard Oil* focused on the absolute size of the potential foreclosure in a market without analysis of the actual competitive conditions and the actual relative foreclosure. This became known as the "quantitative substantiality rule."

343. A more sophisticated approach was used in *Tampa Elec. Co. v. Nashville Coal Co.*[455] There, an electric utility entered into a twenty-year contract with a coal company to supply all the needs of its plant. The coal company challenged agreement as a violation of the antitrust laws. The contract was for USD 128 million and the district court, applying the quantitative substantiality rule, found this to be a sufficient

454. 337 U.S. 293, 306–307, 69 S. Ct. 1051, 1058–1059, 93 L. Ed. 1371 (1949).
455. 365 U.S. 320, 81 S. Ct. 623, 5 L.Ed. 2d 580 (1961).

amount of commerce foreclosed to violate section 3. The Supreme Court reversed, modifying the rule, to make the substantiality of the commerce involved just one of several factors:

> It is necessary to weigh the probable effect of the contract on the relevant area of effective competition, taking into account the relative strength of the parties, the proportionate volume of commerce involved in relation to the total volume of commerce in the relevant market area, and the probable immediate and future effects which pre-emption of that share of the market might have on effective competition therein. It follows that a mere showing that the contract itself involves a substantial number of dollars is ordinarily of little consequence.[456]

344. The Court found that less than 1% of the market was foreclosed by the agreement and that there was ample justification for a long-term agreement to secure coal at stable prices for the utility. It therefore found no violation.

345. Subsequent cases have found exclusive dealing to be a violation where it was used to obtain or preserve large market shares. In *United States v. Dentsply Int'l, Inc.,*[457] an exclusive dealership requirement by a company with a 75%–80% market share, enforced through contracts terminable at will, was found to be a violation of section 2. Its practice effectively foreclosed a large number of distributors from taking on competing products. By contrast, the same circuit had earlier held in, *Barr Laboratories, Inc. v. Abbott Laboratories,*[458] that a company with a 15% market share did not violate section 3 by entering into a series of exclusive dealing arrangements where its market share increased by less than 2%, the level of concentration in the market had increased by less than 1%, new manufacturers and related products had emerged, and prices had remained stable. However, in the monopolization context, where the manufacturer has a large market share, courts have found exclusive dealing contracts to be strong evidence of monopolization.[459]

C. Selective Distribution

346. Selective distribution is not a concept dealt with under American antitrust law.

---

456. *Tampa Elec. Co. v. Nashville Coal Co.* 365 U.S. 320, 329, 81 S. Ct. 623, 629, 5 L.Ed. 2d 580 (1961).

457. 399 F.3d 181, 184 (3d Cir. 2005).

458. 978 F.2d 98 (3d Cir. 1992).

459. *See, e.g., LePage's Inc. v. 3M,* 324 F.3d 141, 159 (3d Cir. 2003) ("Only by dealing exclusively with 3M in as many product lines as possible could customers enjoy the substantial discounts. Accordingly, the jury could reasonably find that 3M's exclusionary conduct violated § 2."); *United States v. Microsoft Corp.,* 253 F.3d 34, 70 (D.C. Cir. 2001)("a monopolist's use of exclusive contracts, in certain circumstances, may give rise to a § 2 violation even though the contracts foreclose less than the roughly 40% or 50% share usually required in order to establish a § 1 violation."). In *United States v. Microsoft Corp.,* 253 F.3d 34, 71 (D.C. Cir. 2001) the court found that Microsoft's exclusive dealing contracts with internet access providers foreclosed a significant market to rivals and violated § 2 of the Sherman Act.

D. *Franchising*

347. While franchising is very common and generally comports with American antitrust law, the overall concept raises basic questions relating to product tying and requirements contracts, among other things, that leave the relationship vulnerable to antitrust challenges where a franchisor abuses the relationship.

348. Aside from regulation under federal antitrust law, franchises are required to meet disclosure requirements under the FTC's Franchise Rules,16 C.F.R. §§ 436.1 et seq., and a variety of state franchise practices acts. Certain franchises, such as gasoline stations and auto dealerships, are also governed by separate federal statutes.

349. In the typical franchise relationship, a franchisor licenses a trademark together with a business model that requires the franchisee to maintain a level of quality, whether in product, service, or both, consonant with the trademark. Often this includes a requirement that the franchisee purchase products of a particular quality. It is not uncommon for the franchisor to designate specifically the vendors from which the products must be purchased – often the franchisor itself. Once the relationship is established and the franchisee had made its investment, its sunk costs often confer what has been termed "relational market power" upon the franchisor. The franchisee is bound to the relationship. For example, a recent opinion described how non-compete clauses in a franchise agreement rendered the franchisee's restaurant properties virtually worthless outside the franchise relationship with the particular franchisor.[460] It is the imbalance created by that relationship and the power it confers to coerce or force purchases by the franchisee that has given rise to litigation.

350. Franchise related antitrust litigation generally involves claims of tying or requirements contracts. They may be raised under sections 1 and 2 of the Sherman Act or under section 3 of the Clayton Act. In any case, they require some proof of market power either as part of proof of the tying claim or to establish the market being affected by the violation.

351. All of these issues arose in *Queen City Pizza, Inc. v. Domino's Pizza, Inc.*[461] *Queen City Pizza, Inc.*, the most recent appellate authority, was decided by a divided panel of the Court of Appeals. Five judges on the court – just short of the required majority – voted for reconsideration. Judge Edward Becker, among the most respected jurists on the court and the author of an earlier learned opinion in the area of franchising, departed from usual practice and filed an opinion describing why he thought en banc reconsideration was appropriate.[462] The franchisees alleged that Domino's, the second largest pizza chain in the US, forced them to purchase products from Domino's at supracompetitive prices by making it effectively impossible to purchase products from competing suppliers. They claimed that Domino's used its power over the pizza dough purchase requirements to force franchisees to buy other products and entered into

460. *Burda v. Wendy's Int'l, Inc.*, 659 F. Supp. 2d 928, 931 (S.D. Ohio 2009)("though he owned the real estate on which his stores were located, he was bound by an agreement with Wendy's that the locations could only be used for Wendy's stores. If he no longer was a Wendy's franchisee, the stores could not be converted to another use. Instead, Burda would have to sell the properties to a Wendy's approved operator or to one of Wendy's corporate entities.").

461. 124 F.3d 430 (3d Cir. 1997).

462. 129 F.3d 724 (3d Cir. 1997).

exclusive dealing arrangements with its franchisees in order to foreclose the market to other potential competitors who could have sold their products of equal quality more cheaply.

352. The majority resolved the case with its definition of the relevant market. It held that contractual terms alone – such as those that established the franchise arrangement – could not create a relevant market. If pizza dough used by Domino's franchisees was interchangeable with other pizza dough, a fact the plaintiffs were forced to concede since it was central to their claim that they could buy equally good dough more cheaply elsewhere, then the fact that a Domino's franchisee was contractually bound to purchase pizza dough only from Domino's could not establish a relevant market. Having reached that conclusion, the court rejected all of the plaintiffs' antitrust claims on the basis that Domino's hardly held monopoly power in the pizza dough market.

353. The court feared that if it recognized relevant markets and market power based upon the franchise contract it would render all franchise agreements vulnerable to antitrust claims. The court focused upon the knowledge of the franchisee upon entering the agreement and the disclosure to the franchisee at the time of contract. The contract had specified that Domino's could require the franchisee to purchase from a limited number of suppliers or even just from Domino's.

354. But the court had to distinguish the Supreme Court's decision in *Eastman Kodak Co. v. Image Technical Services, Inc.*,[463] which had found a market limited to services and parts for Kodak copiers. *Kodak* had found such a relevant market because owners of the expensive Kodak copiers were "locked in" to the copiers and the aftermarket for services and parts. Their sunk cost in buying the copiers and the information and switching costs precluded easy switching. The franchisee of Domino's was in much the same position. The *Queen City Pizza* majority's effort to distinguish *Kodak* is weak. The majority focused on the "uniqueness" of the Kodak replacement parts, yet that was hardly the distinction recognized by the Supreme Court. Indeed, a later opinion showed that the "unique" parts for the Kodak copiers were patented so they would hardly have formed a basis for the antitrust analysis.[464] The majority also distinguished Kodak because it involved a change in policy regarding parts and service that could not have been foreseen by purchasers at the time they purchased the copiers. They contrasted that circumstance with the circumstances of the Domino's franchisees whose contracts had provision allowing Domino's to designate a narrow range of sources for product. But, as the dissent pointed out, this too was a weak distinction because the disclosure materials provided to the franchisees at the time they entered the contract stressed the policy of providing alternative sources of supply – and it was the change in *that* policy that gave rise to the suit.

355. The *Queen City* decision has been criticized for ignoring the serious abuses that antitrust law could remedy within the franchise relationship.[465] Judge Becker's dissent from the denial of en banc review highlighted the flaws in the majority's reasoning and strongly supports what it characterizes as the "splendid dissenting

---

463. 504 U.S. 451, 112 S. Ct. 2072, 119 L. Ed. 2d 265 (1992).

464. *See* , *Image Technical Services, Inc. v. Eastman Kodak Co.*, 125 F.3d 1195 (9th Cir. 1997).

465. *See* , *e.g.*, Sullivan and Grimes, The Law of Antitrust: An Integrated Handbook (Thompson West 2006) at 516 et seq.

opinion."[466] There are basic questions that arise with its analysis that would effectively remove almost all antitrust protection from the franchise relationship. It focuses upon a definition of a relevant market that does not really exist for the litigants in an analysis that may be beside the point. As the Supreme Court explained:

> Since the purpose of the inquiries into market definition and market power is to determine whether an arrangement has the potential for genuine adverse effects on competition, 'proof of actual detrimental effects, such as a reduction of output,' can obviate the need for an inquiry into market power, which is but a 'surrogate for detrimental effects.'[467]

356. While the majority opinion in *Queen City Pizza* has been influential, certain succeeding opinions have distinguished it. *Burda v. Wendy's Int'l, Inc.*,[468] for example, denied a motion to dismiss antitrust claims brought by Wendy's franchisees when the hamburger chain sought to change its policy to require franchisees to purchase buns from the franchisor. There the court found no basis in the contract for allowing the change, a fact that distinguished it from *Queen City*. The court found *Kodak* controlling.[469]

357. State franchise protection laws remedy certain of the market power imbalances created by the franchise relationship. Certain of these statutes, such as those in New Jersey and Wisconsin, prohibit a franchisor from imposing unreasonable standards of performance upon a franchisee[470] and prohibit termination absent "good cause." New Jersey, for example, takes a narrow view of what constitutes "good cause" for termination. "It is a violation of the NJFPA [New Jersey Franchise Practices Act] to cancel a franchise for any reason other than the franchisee's substantial breach, even if the franchisor acts in good-faith and for a bona fide reason."*Beilowitz v. Gen. Motors Corp.*[471] These protections go far in protecting the franchisee from abuses that otherwise would be remedied by antitrust law. These statutes vary from state to state and some states lack any such statutes at all. The New Jersey statute is among the more comprehensive and protective statutes.

---

466. 129 F.3d at 724.
467. *F.T.C. v. Indiana Fed'n of Dentists*, 476 U.S. 447, 460–461, 106 S. Ct. 2009, 2019, 90 L. Ed. 2d 445 (1986) quoting 7 P. Areeda, Antitrust Law ¶ 1511, 429 (1986).
468. 659 F. Supp. 2d 928 (S.D. Ohio 2009).
469. *See also, Collins v. Int'l Dairy Queen, Inc.*, 980 F. Supp. 1252 (M.D. Ga. 1997); *See also,* B. Klein, *Market Power in Franchise Cases in the Wake of Kodak: Applying Post Contract Hold Up Analysis to Vertical Relationships,* 67 Antitrust L.J. 283 (1999); W. Grimes, *"Market Definition in Franchise Antitrust Claims: Relational Market Power and the Franchisor's Conflict of Interest,"* Antitrust L.J. 67 (1999): 243. Contra *George Lussier Enterprises, Inc. v. Subaru of New England, Inc.*, 286 F. Supp. 2d 86 (D.N.H. 2003) *aff'd*, 393 F.3d 36 (1st Cir. 2004); *Arnold v. Petland, Inc.*, 2:07-CV-01307, 2009 WL 816327 (S.D. Ohio Mar. 26, 2009).

In *Shamrock Mktg., Inc. v. Bridgestone Bandag, LLC*, 775 F. Supp. 2d 972 (W.D. Ky. 2011), the court allowed claims to proceed brought by a competitor that was foreclosed from a significant part of the market because of an alleged tie imposed by a franchisor on its franchisees to proceed.

470. N.J.S.A. § 56:10-7(e).
471. 233 F. Supp. 2d 631, 644 (D.N.J. 2002).

II. Technology Licensing

A. Patent Licensing

358. The DOJ and FTC have issued *Antitrust Guidelines for the Licensing of Intellectual Property*.[472] These *Guidelines* take the view that intellectual property, is, like other property, subject to traditional antitrust analysis, but emphasize the particular traits of patents, copyrights and trade secrets which must be considered in such an analysis. They recognize that the patent grant is itself a monopoly and that a degree of sharing of the monopoly through licensing is necessary to promote economic efficiency. For example, cross-licensing or patent "pooling," is often necessary, particularly in high technology industries, in order to exploit any individual patent. Manufacture of an appropriate microchip may require licenses to many patents owned by different persons. The Guidelines provide that almost all licensing agreements – save those that are merely a cover for cartelization or other naked restraints – will be judged under a rule of reason.

359. An example of an agreement that is merely a cover, cited by the Guidelines, would be a license for a relatively valueless patent for a particular means of manufacture of a product, call it X, that can be produced by many methods. The owner of the patent licenses it to all members of the industry, none of whom actually manufacture under the process. The license gives to each member a right to manufacture X under the patent within an exclusive territory in return for their agreement to market all their output of X, regardless of how manufactured, solely within the exclusive territory. In this case, the license of an effectively valueless patent is a cover for a naked territorial allocation scheme and would be prosecuted as a per se horizontal agreement.

360. But few agreements are so extreme. Certain basic rules apply. A license may not exceed the scope of the patent itself, i.e. it may not seek to obtain royalties on products not covered by the patent[473] or beyond the term of the patent[474] (though it may obtain royalties based on sales of the product manufactured under a process

---

472. *Available at*, <www.justice.gov/atr/public/guidelines/0558.pdf>.

473. *Zenith Radio Corp. v. Hazeltine Research, Inc.*, 395 U.S. 100, 136, 89 S. Ct. 1562, 1583, 23 L. Ed. 2d 129 (1969)("just as the patent's leverage may not be used to extract from the licensee a commitment to purchase, use, or sell other products according to the desires of the patentee, neither can that leverage be used to garner as royalties a percentage share of the licensee's receipts from sales of other products; in either case, the patentee seeks to extend the monopoly of his patent to derive a benefit not attributable to use of the patent's teachings.").

474. *Brulotte v. Thys Co.*, 379 U.S. 29, 85 S. Ct. 176, 13 L. Ed. 2d 99 (1964).

patent).[475] On the other hand, a license may impose both price and output restrictions[476] and may restrict the license to specific geographic territories[477] or "fields of use."[478]

361. Patent pools, in which patent holders agree to license one another's patents to each other, are generally found legal under a rule of reason analysis.[479] They can have the positive effect of integrating complementary technologies and avoiding blocking situations where one patent may preclude development of another. The Guidelines warn against adding further restrictions as part of the pool that would jointly restrain output or result in collusion on price. The Guidelines reserve the government's option to move against such restrictions as a per se violation.

362. In weighing a claim against a patent pool under the rule of reason, a court would likely weigh the degree to which participation in the pool restrains competition in the development of new technology. Will the terms of the pool limit the incentives of individual participants to further their research and development? If so, is the restraint outweighed by the benefits it provides? Are there sufficient competitors with the ability to pursue research and development that limits the effects the pool may have?

363. The analysis relating to patent pools would apply to cross-licensing agreements and what are known as grantbacks, where a licensee agrees to license back to the licensor any improvements it makes in the patent. All of these devices – cross-licenses, patent pools, grantbacks and even allocation of territories and fields of use – can provide significant pro-competitive benefits in the context of the overall patent grant. They can provide incentives for the licensees to develop the patent without the fear of free riding within the territory, be it geographic or a field of use. They can provide for development of products and patents that would otherwise be blocked by related and necessary patents.

364. For many years, licenses requiring a licensee to purchase products from the licensor as a condition for obtaining the license were considered per se tying. However, in *Illinois Tool Works Inc. v. Indep. Ink, Inc.*,[480] the Court held that there was no presumption that a patent conferred market power on the patentee, and that there was no longer a presumption of per se tying.

365. A particularly controversial area of patent licensing arises in the pharmaceutical industry in conjunction with settlements of patent cases brought under the Hatch-Waxman Act governing the interplay of food and drug law and patent law relating to generic pharmaceuticals. Under the act, a patent holder may list a patent for a drug in the "Orange Book" of the Food and Drug Administration, thereby obtaining certain additional rights. A generic drug company may thereafter file what is known as an

475. *Automatic Radio Mfg. Co. v. Hazeltine Research*, 339 U.S. 827, 70 S. Ct. 894, 94 L. Ed. 1312 (1950).

476. For many years there were many questions over whether a patent holder could in fact impose resale price restrictions on a licensee. However, since resale price maintenance was held to be subject to a rule of reason analysis in *Leegin Creative Leather Products, Inc. v. PSKS, Inc.*, 551 U.S. 877, 127 S. Ct. 2705, 168 L. Ed. 2d 623 (2007), the issue of whether *United States v. Gen. Elec. Co.*, 272 U.S. 476, 47 S. Ct. 192, 71 L. Ed. 362 (1926)(allowing price restrictions by licensor) remained good law may have been rendered academic.

477. *Ethyl Gasoline Corp. v. United States*, 309 U.S. 436, 60 S. Ct. 618, 84 L. Ed. 852 (1940).

478. *Gen. Talking Pictures Corp. v. W. Elec. Co.*, 305 U.S. 124, 59 S. Ct. 116, 83 L. Ed. 81 (1938).

479. A "field of use" license is a license for a particular purpose or use of the patent.

480. 547 U.S. 28, 126 S. Ct. 1281, 164 L. Ed. 2d 26 (2006).

abbreviated new drug application with the Food and Drug Administration. The first generic drug company to file such an application is entitled to 180 days of market exclusivity for generic sales beginning from the time the generic drug can first be sold, whether through invalidating the patent through litigation or otherwise. The company filing an abbreviated new drug application must, at the same time, give notice to the patent holder that it has filed such an application. The filing of the abbreviated new drug application is deemed a technical act of infringement and the patent holder has forty-five days in which to sue the filer for infringement. If it files suit within forty-five days, the Food and Drug Administration is precluded from approving the abbreviated new drug application for thirty months, the time the statute optimistically anticipated it would take for the litigation to conclude.

366. This scheme gives great incentive for the patent holder to pay-off the first filing generic to drop the patent litigation, usually with a large cash payment and a license to enter the market at some long-deferred date a few months before the patent expires. These payments are known as "reverse payments," because it is a situation where the plaintiff in the lawsuit is paying the defendant. By paying off the first filer to settle its case and to discontinue its challenge to the patent, the patent holder can effectively insulate the patent from challenge since there is generally little incentive for a later filer to challenge the patent. That is because the first filer retains the 180 exclusivity even after settling. This "exclusivity" precludes the Food and Drug Administration from approving any later-filed abbreviated new drug application until after the first filer actually begins delivering drugs into the market.

367. The issue divided the courts of appeal for a decade and was finally reached by Supreme Court in *F.T.C. v. Actavis, Inc.*[481] The Court decided that the issue was to be determined under a rule or reason analysis but rejected the rule of reason analysis performed by several courts of appeal which had adopted a "scope of the patent" test which effectively had created a virtual per se rule approving such arrangements.

The Sixth Circuit Court of Appeals had held a variant of such an agreement to be a per se violation because it constituted a market division between the patent holders and the generic manufacturer accepting the payments.[482] In *In re K-Dur Antitrust Litigation,*[483] the Third Circuit had held such agreements to be prima facie illegal and required application of a "quick look" under the rule of reason. A series of decisions decided between *Cardizen* and *K-Dur* had fashioned a "scope of the patent" test which had held that the interest of the patent laws and the policy of encouraging settlements trump the antitrust laws so long as the only claims settled fall within the scope of the claims in the patent.[484] But these later decisions had proven highly controversial since, as the Third Circuit noted in *K-Dur*, they almost invariably resulted in sustaining the agreements and really did not apply "the rule of reason" test as commonly understood.

481. __U.S.__, 133 S. Ct. 2223 (2013).

482. *In re Cardizem CD Antitrust Litigation*, 332 F.3d 896 (6th Cir. 2003).

483. 10-2077, 2012 WL 2877662 (3d Cir. Jul. 16, 2012).

484. See, e.g., *Arkansas Carpenters Health & Welfare Fund v. Bayer AG*, 604 F.3d 98 (2d Cir. 2010), as corrected (Jun. 17, 2010), *cert. denied*, 131 S. Ct. 1606, 179 L. Ed. 2d 517 (U.S. 2011); *In re Ciprofloxacin Hydrochloride Antitrust Litig.*, 544 F.3d 1323 (Fed. Cir. 2008); *In re Tamoxifen Citrate Antitrust Litig.*, 466 F.3d 187 (2d Cir. 2006); but *see* , *In re Terazosin Hydrochloride Antitrust Litig.*, 352 F.Supp.2d 1279 (S.D.Fla.2005).

368. In *Actavis,* the Supreme Court rejected the "scope of the patent" test recognizing its manifest weaknesses and held that a full "rule of reason"analysis was to be applied without any presumption that patent law trumped antitrust law. The Court considered it incongruous to analyze the situation based on an underlying assumption that the patent was valid and the patent holder was merely exercising its exclusionary power in reaching the settlement. After all, the validity of the patent was the very issue placed in question by the underlying litigation. How, under those circumstances, could one ignore the fundamental policies of antitrust law. The facts of *Actavis* underscored this concern because the patent holder had agreed as part of the settlement to pay three generic manufacturers millions of dollars annually which the FTC alleged was paid in return for staying off the market.

The Court articulated five reasons for rejecting the scope of the patent case and was equally clear that it was rejecting the Third Circuit's prima facie, "quick look" standard. While holding that traditional rule of reason analysis was to be applied, the Court was not clear on how. Certainly the basic restraint arising from the market allocation created by the reverse payment would represent the first step in such an analysis, however the Court did not follow through on how the analysis was to be completed leaving the issue to be resolved by the district courts in subsequent cases and succeeding decisions have raised many questions

Need a payment be in cash? Courts that have considered the question have answered "no". For example, a common form of a non-cash payment is an agreement by the patent holder to withhold its own generic form of the drug, yielding higher sales and profits for the generic. This type payment has been held sufficient to state a claim under *Actavis.*[485] What did *Actavis* mean when it said the payment must be "large"? *Actavis* suggested a payment is "large" if it induces a generic manufacturer to forego its patent challenge or agree to delayed generic entry.[486] Other metrics have also been suggested, such as the amount of the litigation costs that the brand companies saved by settling.[487]

In a typical rule of reason case, the plaintiff bears the burden of establishing that the alleged restraint caused anticompetitive effects and the defendants then bear the burden of proving that the restraint (here, the payment) is justified by legitimate, pro-competitive reasons.[488] How is this applied in an *Actavis* setting? One court held the plaintiffs' initial burden is to show the payment was "large," because "a large payment

485. *In re Loestrin 24 Fe Antitrust Litig.*, 814 F.3d 538 (1st Cir. 2016); *King Drug Co. of Florence, Inc. v. Smithkline Beecham Corp.*, 791 F.3d 388, 406 (3d Cir. 2015) ("*Lamictal*"); *In re Nexium (Esomeprazole) Antitrust Litig.*, 968 F.Supp.2d 367, 392 (D. Mass. 2013); *United Food & Commercial Workers v. Teikoku Pharma USA*, 74 F.Supp.3d 1052, 1070-71 (N.D. Cal. 2014); *See also, In re Effexor XR Antitrust Litig.*, No. 11-5479(PGS)(LHG), 2014 WL 4988410, at *19 (D.N.J. Oct. 6, 2014); *Time Ins. Co. v. Astrazeneca AB*, 52 F. Supp. 3d 705, 710 (E.D. Pa. 2014); *In re Lipitor Antitrust Litig.*, 46 F.Supp.3d 523, 543 (D.N.J. 2014).

486. *Actavis*, 133 S. Ct. at 2235

487. *See, King Drug Co. of Florence v. Cephalon, Inc.*, 88 F. Supp. 3d 402, 417 (E.D. Pa. 2015); *In re Solodyn (Minocycline Hydrochloride) Antitrust Litig.*, No. 14-MD-02503-DJC, 2015 WL 5458570, at *7 (D. Mass. Sept. 16, 2015)

488. *See, e.g., Lamictal*, 791 F.3d at 412 quoting *United States v. Brown Univ. in Providence in State of R.I.*, 5 F.3d 658, 668-69 (3d Cir. 1993); *In re Aggrenox Antitrust Litig.*, 94 F. Supp. 3d 224, 245 (D. Conn. 2015), No. 3:14-MD-2516 SRU, 2015 WL 4459607 (D. Conn. July 21, 2015).

can provide strong evidence of the relevant anticompetitive harm – 'that the patentee seeks to induce the generic challenger to abandon its claim with a share of its monopoly profits that would otherwise be lost in the competitive market.'"[489] Other courts have required more. One court assigned plaintiffs "the initial burden of proof" that the payment delayed generic entry, that the brand company paid the generic consideration "of some kind," "and that the consideration exchanged in the settlement exceeded the estimated cost of litigation and the costs of other services and products, in order to establish a prima facie case."[490] That initial burden appears to remain light, because the court assigned to defendants the "burden of production" of presenting evidence regarding the value of the products, services, and estimated litigation costs saved by the settlement reasoning that defendants are more likely to have access to information on point.[491]

Once pro-competitive justifications have been properly presented, a plaintiff may "rebut the defendant's explanation"[492] by showing the anticompetitive harms outweighed any procompetitive benefits.[493] The plaintiff may also show that any procompetitive benefits could have been achieved through less restriction on competition.[494] *Actavis* delineated two possible procompetitive justifications: that the payment "amount[s] to no more than a rough approximation of the litigation expenses saved through the settlement" or "reflect[s] compensation for other services that the generic has promised to perform[.]"[495] Other justifications have been proffered.[496]

Finally, the role of the patent in the antitrust case continues to invite debate. Some defendants have asserted the patent's relevance to causation and injury, arguing that private plaintiffs must prove not only that the payments were anticompetitive under *Actavis*, but must also prove the patent would not have kept the generic out of the market. Courts are divided on the issue.[497]

---

489. *King Drug*, 88 F. Supp. 3d at 415 (quoting *Actavis*, 133 S. Ct. at 2235). .

490. *In re K-Dur Antitrust Litig.*, No. 01-CV-1652-SRC/CLW, 2016 WL 755623, at *12 (D.N.J. Feb. 25, 2016).

491. *Id. See also, In re Nexium (Esomeprazole) Antitrust Litigation*, 42 F. Supp. 3d 231, 262 (D. Mass. 2014) .

492. *Lamictal*, 791 F.3d at 412.

493. *King Drug*, 88 F. Supp. 3d at 411.

494. *King Drug*, 88 F. Supp. 3d at 416

495. *Actavis*, 133 S. Ct. at 2236. *See also Lamictal*, 791 F.3d at 412 (noting these two defenses and reserving judgment as to whether other justifications are available).

496. *King Drug Co. of Florence, Inc. v. Cephalon, Inc.*, No. 2:06-CV-1797, 2015 WL 5783603, at *8 (E.D. Pa. Oct. 5, 2015). *See also Actavis*, 133 S. Ct. at 2236 ("[t]he owner of a particularly valuable patent might contend, of course, that even a small risk of invalidity justifies a large payment. But, be that as it may, the payment (if otherwise unexplained) likely seeks to prevent the risk of competition. And...that consequence constitutes the relevant anticompetitive harm."). However, the *King Drug* court declined to preclude the generic companies from arguing the agreement removed their risk from the litigation. *See id.* at *9.

497. *In re Aggrenox Antitrust Litig.*, No. 3:14-MD-2516 SRU, 2015 WL 4459607, at *9 (D. Conn. July 21, 2015); *In re Wellbutrin XL Antitrust Litig.*, 133 F. Supp. 3d 734, 764-65 (E.D. Pa. 2015) (appeal pending).

B. Trademark Licensing

369. Because the Lanham Act governing trademarks mentions an antitrust defense, a number of cases have sought to advance the defense. They have been universally unsuccessful. Section 33(b)(7) of the Lanham Act, 15 U.S.C. § 1115(b)(7), provides in pertinent part:

> The certificate (of trademark registration) shall be conclusive evidence of the registrant's exclusive right to use... except when one of the following defenses or defects is established:
>
> (7) That the mark has been or is being used to violate the antitrust laws of the United States.

However, "in almost every reported instance where the antitrust misuse of a trademark has been raised as a defense, it has been rejected."[498] The reason for this was explained in the often cited opinion in *Carl Zeiss Stiftung v. V. E. B. Carl Zeiss, Jena,*[499] which distinguished patents from trademarks:

> although misuse of a patent almost inevitably is accompanied by unlawful restraints, the opportunity for effective antitrust misuse of a trademark, as distinguished from collateral anti-competitive activities on the part of the manufacturer or seller of the goods bearing the mark, is so limited that it poses a far less serious threat to the economic health of the nation. As a result, it has been recognized that a sharp distinction must be drawn between the antitrust misuse defense in patent infringement suits, on the one hand, and its use in trademark suits, on the other. ... Although we do not accept the view that the defense should be unavailable as a matter of law, ... it is significant that in almost every reported instance where the antitrust misuse of a trademark has been raised as a defense, it has been rejected. In the great majority of such cases the evidence revealed the antitrust activities to be collateral and did not demonstrate that the trademark, as distinguished from collateral activities with respect to goods bearing the trademark, was itself being used as the prime and effective instrument to effectuate the antitrust activity.

498. *Adidas-Am., Inc. v. Payless Shoesource, Inc.*, 546 F. Supp. 2d 1029, 1078–1079 (D. Or. 2008).
499. 298 F. Supp. 1309, 1314 (S.D.N.Y. 1969) *modified sub nom. Carl Zeiss Stiftung v. VEB Carl Zeiss Jena,* 433 F.2d 686 (2d Cir. 1970).

C. Know-How and Trade Secret Licensing

370. "Like the holders of other intellectual property rights, possessors of trade secrets are entitled to assert their rights against would be infringers and to defend their rights in court."[500] Trade secrets licensure is similar to that of patents:

> [T]he critical question in an antitrust context is whether the restriction may fairly be said to be ancillary to a commercially supportable licensing arrangement, or whether the licensing scheme is a sham set up for the purpose of controlling competition while avoiding the consequences of the antitrust laws.[501]

Similarly, a license agreement that purports to cover trade secrets that do not genuinely exist, but merely seeks to restrain competition, will also give rise to an antitrust claim.[502]

371. In a series of early cases, complicated worldwide networks of cross-licensing agreements were struck down as subterfuges enabling the participants to divide markets and fix prices while avoiding antitrust laws. The courts found a lack of any true trade secrets or that whatever secrets existed were not sufficiently substantial to support restraints of such magnitude. The parties' intent, principally to restrain competition, was regarded as a critical factor.[503]

372. Similarly, assertion of trade secret licenses in litigation in bad faith, i.e. where no genuine trade secret exists, will give rise to an antitrust claim. [504]

373. In a sense, trade secret agreements run greater risk of running afoul the antitrust laws than do patent licenses because they lack the umbrella of patent protection. A patent holder receives a state granted monopoly of limited duration in return for fully disclosing its invention. That is not the case with an entity seeking to control a trade secret that has not made disclosure and has not received any monopoly grant.

---

500. *A. & E. Plastik Pak Co. v. Monsanto Co.*, 396 F.2d 710, 715 (9th Cir. 1968). It is worth noting that the cases cited in *A&E Plastik Pak* for this proposition are cases involving enforcement of patent rights.
501. *Ibid.*
502. *CVD, Inc. v. Raytheon Co.*, 769 F.2d 842, 851 (1st Cir.1985) ("[I]t is well established that an agreement which purports to license trade secrets, but in reality, is no more than a sham, or device designed to restrict competition, may violate antitrust laws.").
503. *United States v. Imperial Chemical Industries*, 100 F.Supp. 504 (S.D.N.Y.1951); *United States v. Timken Roller Bearing Co.*, 83 F.Supp. 284 (N.D.Ohio 1949), aff'd, 341 U.S. 593, 71 S.Ct. 971, 95 L.Ed. 1199 (1951); *United States v. General Electric Co.*, 82 F.Supp. 753 (D.N.J.1949).
504. *CVD, Inc. v. Raytheon Co.*, 769 F.2d 842, 850–851 (1st Cir. 1985)("the assertion in bad faith of trade secret claims, that is, with the knowledge that no trade secrets exist, for the purpose of restraining competition does not further the policies of either the antitrust or the trade secrets laws.... Thus, it seems clear that the assertion of a trade secret claim in bad faith, in an attempt to monopolize, can be a violation of the antitrust laws.").

Chapter 2. Monopolization (Dominant Undertakings' Prohibited Practices)

374. As discussed earlier, the concept of "dominant undertakings" does not exist under American antitrust law. The area covered by the European laws relating to dominant undertakings is covered in American law primarily by the laws relating to monopolization under section 2 of the Sherman Act, while certain specific practices such as price discrimination, tying and refusals to deal, are also covered by specific statutes and case law under section 1 of the Sherman Act. Because EU laws relating to dominant undertakings were, in part, a reaction to perceived gaps and failures under the Sherman Act, the two may differ significantly in certain areas. A significant area of departure is the analysis of monopoly leveraging. The European Commission takes a very different view of "monopoly leveraging" than do American courts. The Commission views the use by a party of a dominant position in one market to gain advantage in another market in which it does not have a dominant position as an abuse, unless the dominant firm can show a legitimate business justification for its conduct. American courts, by contrast, do not condemn such monopoly leveraging unless it can be shown that such leveraging either serves to maintain the existing monopoly or creates a risk of creating a monopoly in the second market. This treatise covers only American antitrust law.

375. The American law of monopolization was originally passed to curb excesses and abuses of enterprises that had come to dominate markets. The issue was size and the abusive use of the power that size conferred. The offense of monopolization has two elements: (1) the possession of monopoly power in a relevant market; and (2) the willful acquisition, maintenance, or use of that power by anticompetitive or exclusionary means or for anticompetitive or exclusionary purposes.[505] For this reason, many practices, when coupled with a dominant position in the market, may be found to be evidence of monopolization, though such practices would be deemed competitive had they been undertaken by an entity lacking monopoly power. These have included certain common forms of behavior such as product tying, exclusive dealing contracts, and secret rebates, as well as less conventional forms of behavior such as physically sabotaging competitors and product bundling. In most instances, the illegality of the behavior – and its restraint on competition – derived almost entirely from the exercise of monopoly power.

376. It is difficult to adduce general principles. However, one can distill from the cases a general sense that courts will approve behavior by a monopolist that can be justified as genuine efforts to improve a product or its distribution and will find a violation where the behavior is directed solely at excluding or impeding rivals through means other than upon the merits of the product, its price, or means of distribution. "A monopolist willfully acquires or maintains monopoly power when it competes on some basis other than the merits."[506]

505. *Aspen Skiing Co. v. Aspen Highlands Skiing Corp.*, 472 U.S. 585, 595–596, 105 S. Ct. 2847, 2854, 86 L. Ed. 2d 467 (1985).

506. *LePage's Inc. v. 3M*, 324 F.3d 141, 147 (3d Cir.2003).

§1. Exploitive Practices

I. Excessive/Unfair Pricing

377. There is no such concept under American antitrust law. A monopolist may charge whatever the market will bear and excessive price alone is not a violation of American antitrust laws. The Supreme Court recently put it bluntly: "Simply possessing monopoly power and charging monopoly prices does not violate § 2."[507]

378. The concept has been taken to extremes at times. For example, pharmaceutical companies having patent monopolies on certain life-giving drugs have been able to exact huge margins, often many, many times the cost of product even when research and development costs are factored in. The very life-saving nature of the drug can vastly increase the value of the patent monopoly to be exploited. Because, under American antitrust law, price is left to the marketplace and the rewards of legally obtained monopolies are monopolistic prices, there is no basis for intervention based upon excessive or unfair pricing.

II. Price Discrimination

379. The ability to discriminate in price may be an indication of monopoly power, and was historically used by classic monopolists as part of predatory schemes to assure their monopoly. It was a tool of the Rockefeller oil trust in assembling the oil trust broken up by the government in *Standard Oil Co. of New Jersey v. United States,*[508] and a similar discriminatory pricing scheme was described as part of the conduct condemned in *United States v. Grinnell Corp.*[509] However, price discrimination is generally governed by its own statute, the Robinson-Patman Act.[510] While encompassing a detailed scheme governing the area, one treatise has described the efforts to govern price discrimination as "an almost unrelieved policy failure."[511] This is because claims relating to price discrimination usually claim that a price was too low and low prices are the general goal of the antitrust laws.

380. The Robinson-Patman Act is complex. It prohibits price discrimination. It applies to goods, but not to services. The commodities must be of like grade and quality. The discrimination must be between the same "class of purchaser," though distinctions between classes of purchaser must be legitimate. Unlike the Sherman Act, it only reaches transactions that themselves cross state lines. There are several basic

507. *Pac. Bell Tel. Co. v. Linkline Communications, Inc.*,555 U.S. 438, 447–448, 129 S. Ct. 1109, 1118, 172 L. Ed. 2d 836 (2009).

508. 221 U.S. 1, 31 S. Ct. 502, 55 L. Ed. 619 (1911).

509. 384 U.S. 563, 570, 86 S. Ct. 1698, 1703, 16 L. Ed. 2d 778 (1966)("ADT over the years reduced its minimum basic rates to meet competition and renewed contracts at substantially increased rates in cities where it had a monopoly of accredited central station service.")

510. 15 U.S.C. § 13(a) et seq.

511. Gellhorn, Kovacic & Calkins, *Antitrust Law and Economics,* 5th ed. (West 2004), 506.

defenses specified in the statute, the most important of which are a price to meet competition and a genuine cost justification.

381. Cases under the act are divided into two groups: those which injure competitors of the discriminating seller and those which injure competitors of the buyer receiving the favored price. Primary-line cases are those where a seller charges different prices in different markets. The *Grinnell* case cited above is an example of primary-line discrimination: a sale at a low price into one market where the potential monopolist still faced competition while retaining a high price in a market in which the seller held a monopoly. A once-leading case in the field underscored the costs of a blanket rule in primary-line cases. In *Utah Pie Co. v. Cont'l Baking Co.,*[512] a local frozen pie manufacturer dominated its local market in Utah. A large national manufacturer of frozen pies entered the Utah market with frozen pies priced well below the prices it charged in adjoining states. The Court found in favor of the local pie company even though an effect of the its holding may have been to decrease competition since it effectively eliminated major national sellers from attacking markets dominated by local firms. However, the purpose of the act was to protect the local firm in such a position.

382. While not technically overruled, *Utah Pie* was severely circumscribed by *Brooke Group Ltd. v. Brown & Williamson Tobacco Corp.* [513] There, the Court held that a party alleging claims under section 2(a) of the Robinson Patman-Act had to demonstrate that the prices charged in its market were below cost *and* that the entity charging the below cost price had a reasonable likelihood of recouping the losses incurred from the below cost sales after eliminating the rival. This, as discussed in the predatory pricing section below, is a formidable hurdle.

383. Secondary-line cases are brought by a purchaser injured because its competitor has received a more favorable discriminatory price from the same seller and as a result, the purchaser lost business to its competitor. For example, in *Texaco Inc. v. Hasbrouck,* [514]the Court upheld damages awarded to independent Texaco gasoline dealers that had lost business because of lower prices that Texaco had charged a competing distributor/dealer. The plaintiff established that it sold into the same market as the favored dealer and had lost significant sales as a result of the lower prices the favored competitor was able to charge. However, a victim's damages are not the mere difference between the price it paid and the price paid by its competitors. Rather, the victim must prove actual competitive harm. For example, it may need to prove that its competitors passed on the discriminatory low price to their customers and thereby took away the victim's sales or that the discrimination provided the favored firm with other competitive advantages.[515]

384. But courts have been unwilling to extend the requirements of *Brooke Group* to secondary-line cases because, unlike the other antitrust laws, which are directed

512. 386 U.S. 685, 87 S. Ct. 1326, 18 L. Ed. 2d 406 (1967).

513. 509 U.S. 209, 113 S. Ct. 2578, 125 L. Ed. 2d 168 (1993).

514. 496 U.S. 543, 110 S. Ct. 2535, 110 L. Ed. 2d 492 (1990).

515. *See* , *J. Truett Payne Co., Inc. v. Chrysler Motors Corp.,* 451 U.S. 557, 564, 101 S. Ct. 1923, 1928, 68 L. Ed. 2d 442 (1981)("Although Payne asserted that his salesmen and customers told him that the dealership was being undersold … he admitted he did not know if his competitors did in fact pass on their lower costs to their customers").

toward consumer welfare, the Robinson-Patman Act was passed to protect small sellers from discriminatory disadvantage and is not directed at the consumer level. In *FTC v. Morton Salt Co.*,[516] a secondary-line price discrimination case, the Supreme Court had held that because the Robinson-Patman Act was "especially concerned with protecting small businesses" section 2(a) competitive injury may be inferred from evidence demonstrating injury to an individual competitor.[517] "More specifically, *Morton Salt* permits an inference of injury to competition from evidence of a substantial price difference over time, because such a price difference may harm the competitive opportunities of purchasers, and thus create a 'reasonable possibility' that competition itself may be harmed."[518] This distinguishes the Robinson Patman-Act from other antitrust laws where a plaintiff must prove injury to competition rather than just to a competitor.

385. In *Volvo Trucks N. Am., Inc. v. Reeder-Simco GMC, Inc.*,[519] the most recent pronouncement by the Supreme Court in the area, a Volvo truck dealer alleged that other dealers received more favorable price concessions from Volvo and that it had lost business as a result. Ultimately, its claims failed as a matter of proof. The Court required that the discriminatory price lead to a loss of business in competition for the same customer, i.e., a showing that another Volvo dealer had won the business after receiving a more favorable price from Volvo than had the plaintiff. The plaintiff was unable to adduce such proof. It had demonstrated that it had lost business to other non-Volvo truck dealers allegedly because Volvo had not provided it the same incentives that it provided to other Volvo dealers. The Court found this insufficient, influenced perhaps by the fact that in those instances in which the plaintiff had bid against other Volvo dealers for the same customer and had lost to the other Volvo dealers, it was unable to show any discrimination in the incentives provided by Volvo.

386. There are two basic defenses to a price discrimination claim: (1) that the alleged discriminatory price was provided to meet competition, (2) that the lower price was cost justified.

387. The meeting-competition defense is intended to assure that the price discrimination laws do not stifle competition. A seller may meet, or beat, a price offered by a competitor. "A good-faith belief, rather than absolute certainty, that a price concession is being offered to meet an equally low price offered by a competitor is sufficient to satisfy the § 2(b) defense."[520] *U.S. Gypsum* held that price verification from a competitor that it had offered the lower price was unnecessary and could not justify price discussions among competitors that would otherwise violate the Sherman Act.

516. 334 U.S. 37, 49, 68 S.Ct. 822, 92 L.Ed. 1196 (1948).

517. 334 U.S. at 46–47, 68 S.Ct. 822.

518. *George Haug Co., Inc. v. Rolls Royce Motor Cars Inc.*148 F.3d 136, 142 (2d Cir. 1998); *See also, Stelwagon Mfg. Co. v. Tarmac Roofing Sys., Inc.*, 63 F.3d 1267 (3d Cir. 1995); *Chroma Lighting v. GTE Products Corp.*, 111 F.3d 653, 654 (9th Cir. 1997).

519. 546 U.S. 164, 179, 126 S. Ct. 860, 872, 163 L. Ed. 2d 663 (2006).

520. *United States v. U.S. Gypsum Co.* 438 U.S. 422, 453, 98 S. Ct. 2864, 2881, 57 L. Ed. 2d 854 (1978).

388. Cost justification allows for recognition of genuine differences in cost to service different classes of customer. Volume discounts, if they can be cost justified, would represent a strong cost justification, but it is not always easy to establish.

§2. Exclusionary Practices

I. Predation

389. Predation is a general term applied to efforts by companies possessing significant market power to eliminate rivals. Price predation involves the use of low prices to eliminate competitors. Other forms of predation may involve such things as pre-announcement of products not genuinely developed in order to foreclose efforts at entry by a rival and creation of unnecessary obstacles to entry such as use of lease-only policies. Forms of predation are only limited by the imagination of the predator.

A. Predatory Pricing

390. Predatory pricing, particularly geographically targeted discriminatory pricing, is a well-recognized tool of monopolists.[521] Until recent decades, courts accepted the common sense analysis that a well-financed monopolist could temporarily lower prices below cost to target a competitor and then raise prices once the competitor was either driven from the market or adequately disciplined. Nonetheless, in recent years, out of a zeal to create bright-line rules, the Supreme Court has tightly circumscribed the instances in which a claim can be advanced based upon predatory pricing.

391. Adopting a simplistic analysis based upon Chicago School economics, the Court in *Brooke Group Ltd. v. Brown & Williamson Tobacco Corp.* [522] limited predatory pricing claims to instances where the prices are below its rival's costs *and* where the competitor has a reasonable prospect or dangerous probability of recouping its investment in below-cost prices. As the Court now concedes, "[t]hese prerequisites to recovery are not easy to establish."[523] The concern is with "false positives," i.e., instances in which low prices are mistakenly labeled predatory behavior. Under this test, a court may disregard documentary evidence of predatory intent if either of the prongs of the test are not met.

392. The Supreme Court has not yet reached the issue of the appropriate measure of cost. An influential article has suggested that the appropriate measure is marginal cost – the cost of producing an additional increment of output – for which average variable cost has been suggested as a proxy because of the difficulties of measuring

521. *See , e.g., Standard Oil Co. of New Jersey v. United States,* 221 U.S. 1, 31 S. Ct. 502, 55 L. Ed. 619 (1911) and *United States v. Grinnell Corp.,* 384 U.S. 563, 570, 86 S. Ct. 1698, 1703, 16 L. Ed. 2d 778 (1966)("ADT over the years reduced its minimum basic rates to meet competition and renewed contracts at substantially increased rates in cities where it had a monopoly of accredited central station service.").

522. 509 U.S. 209, 113 S. Ct. 2578, 125 L. Ed. 2d 168 (1993).

523. *Id* at 509 U.S. 226, 113 S. Ct. 2589.

marginal cost.[524] The issue of appropriate cost is described in *United States v. AMR Corp.*[525] The court struggled to come up with an appropriate measure of cost to address a scheme where a major airline made deep price cuts and added capacity to drive out a regional price cutter and thereafter raise its own prices. The decision underscores the weakness of excessive literalism in focusing upon a definition of cost while blinding oneself to the clear predatory activity undertaken. A later decision by the Sixth Circuit, involving similar conduct by an airline to protect a hub market that it dominated, described a more nuanced approach:

> [W]e hold that to establish predatory pricing a plaintiff must prove that the anticipated benefits of defendant's price depended on its tendency to discipline or eliminate competition and thereby enhance the firm's long-term ability to reap the benefits of monopoly power. If the defendant's prices were below average total cost but above average variable cost, the plaintiff bears the burden of showing defendant's pricing was predatory. If, however, the plaintiff proves that the defendant's prices were below average variable cost, the plaintiff has established a prima facie case of predatory pricing and the burden shifts to the defendant to prove that the prices were justified without regard to any anticipated destructive effect they might have on competitors.[526]

393. This standard differs markedly from that of the European Union, which takes a much more aggressive view of predatory pricing. The EU does not require proof of possible future recoupment. Rather, that is only a factor to be considered in determining if a price cut is predatory.[527] The EU views any price below average variable cost to be abusive and will consider prices above variable cost but below total cost to be abusive if an intention to eliminate competition can be shown.[528]

394. The current standard in the US, in contrast to that of the EU, exalts the abstract hypothetical, often based on myopic views tainted by Chicago School economics, above the concrete evidence courts historically reviewed in antitrust cases. *Brooke Group,* built upon *Matsushita Elec. Indus. Co., Ltd. v. Zenith Radio Corp.*[529] In *Matsushita,* despite ample evidence cited by the dissent, the Court found implausible allegations of a conspiracy extending over ten years by Japanese television manufacturers to drive out American manufacturers by selling televisions below cost in the US, while subsidizing those sales with profits achieved in Japan. There, as in *Brooke Group,* the Court relied upon abstract academic analysis in concluding that, "predatory pricing schemes are rarely tried, and even more rarely successful."[530] The Court reasoned that

524. *See,* Phillip Areeda & Donald F. Turner, "Predatory Pricing and Practices Under Section 2 of the Sherman Act," Harv.L.Rev. 88 (1975): 697.
525. 335 F.3d 1109, 1115 (10th Cir. 2003).
526. *Spirit Airlines, Inc. v. Nw. Airlines, Inc.*, 431 F.3d 917, 937–938 (6th Cir. 2005), quoting *D.E. Rogers Associates, Inc.v. Gardner-Denver Co.*, 718 F.2d 1431 (6th Cir.1983).
527. *See, France Telecom SA v. Commission*, Case C-202/07 (Apr. 2, 2009).
528. *Tetra Pak International SA v. Commission*, Case T-83/91 [1994] ECR II-755.
529. 475 U.S. 574, 106 S. Ct. 1348, 89 L. Ed. 2d 538 (1986).
530. *Id* at 475 U.S. 589, 106 S. Ct. 1357.

this followed from the fact that the short-term losses to a company engaged in predatory pricing are certain, while the ability to recoup them in the future is speculative. In *Matsushita*, the predatory activity was alleged to have extended over ten years by over twenty Japanese firms. This the Court found particularly implausible. But, as the dissent pointed out:

> The Court, in discussing the unlikelihood of a predatory conspiracy, also consistently assumes that petitioners valued profit-maximization over growth. ... In light of the evidence that petitioners sold their goods in this country at substantial losses over a long period of time,... I believe that this is an assumption that should be argued to the fact finder, not decided by the Court.[531]

Subsequent research has added to that evidence[532] and subsequent commentators have been scathing in reviewing the analysis of the cartel behavior.[533]

395. *Brooke Group* itself illustrates a Court's view of economic theory trumping a concrete record that showed that the opposite of what abstract academic theory had predicted had in fact, occurred.[534]

396. Academic research has questioned the theory underlying *Brooke Group*.[535] More recent decisions have questioned the extreme skepticism with which courts viewed predatory pricing cases. As the Tenth Circuit explained:

> Recent scholarship has challenged the notion that predatory pricing schemes are implausible and irrational. See, e.g., Patrick Bolton et al., Predatory Pricing: Strategic Theory and Legal Policy, 88 Geo. L.J. 2239, 2241 (2000) ("Modern economic analysis has developed coherent theories of predation that contravene earlier economic writing claiming that predatory pricing conduct is irrational."). Post-Chicago economists have theorized that price predation is not only plausible, but profitable, especially in a multi-market context where predation can occur in one market and recoupment can occur rapidly in other markets. ...
>
> Although this court approaches the matter with caution, we do not do so with the incredulity that once prevailed.[536]

531. 475 U.S. 604, 106 S. Ct. 1365.
532. *See* , First, "An Antitrust Remedy for International Predation: Lessons from Zenith v. Matsushita," Pac. Rim. L. & Pol'y J. 4 (1995), 211.
533. *See,* particularly, Lawrence A. Sullivan & Warren Grimes, *The Law of Antitrust: An Integrated Handbook,* 2d ed. (2006), 180–181.
534. Sullivan and Grimes provide extended discussion of the weaknesses of the present test and the economically inefficient and competitively harmful conduct it permits.
535. This literature is discussed in Ernest Gellhorn, William E. Kovacic & Stephen Calkins, *Antitrust Law and Economics,* 5th ed. (2004), 171.
536. *United States v. AMR Corp.,* 335 F.3d 1109, 1114–1115 (10th Cir. 2003).

B. *Other Forms of Predation*

397. Predation can take a wide variety of forms. As discussed earlier, a court found evidence of illegal monopolization in perhaps its crudest form, where, in conjunction with other conduct, a monopolist systematically sabotaged its competitors' display racks in convenience stores.[537] Microsoft's efforts to deceive developers into believing that its Java developments materials were compatible with other Java materials was held to violate section 2.[538] The variety of conduct is endless, but courts are generally reluctant to find a violation absent significant evidence of predatory intent.

398. For example, a common allegation of predation involves false product "pre-announcement" by a monopolist. By pre-announcing a product it has not yet fully developed, a monopolist may foreclose a market to an incipient competitor by deterring customers from switching to the new competitor's product.[539] While courts have recognized that willful deception may give rise to a cause of action, such claims have not met with great success.[540] Similarly, lease-only policies by a monopolist involving long-term leases effectively foreclose markets to competitors and have been found to be exclusionary conduct under section 2.[541] However, subsequent decisions have been reluctant to impose liability under section 2 based solely upon a lease-only policy.[542]

399. The succeeding sections discuss forms of conduct that have been the object of more recent discussion by the courts.

---

537. *Conwood Co., L.P. v. U.S. Tobacco Co.*, 290 F.3d 768, 778 (6th Cir. 2002) ("when USTC sales representatives restocked or rearranged their own displays, they would routinely discard hundreds of thousands of Conwood racks").

538. *United States v. Microsoft Corp.*, 253 F.3d 34, 76 (D.C. Cir. 2001) ("Microsoft intended to deceive Java developers, and predicted that the effect of its actions would be to generate Windows-dependent Java applications that their developers believed would be cross-platform; these documents also indicate that Microsoft's ultimate objective was to thwart Java's threat to Microsoft's monopoly in the market for operating systems.").

539. *See, e.g.*, *United States v. Am. Tel. & Tel. Co.*, 524 F. Supp. 1336, 1356 (D.D.C. 1981).

540. *See, e.g.*, *MCI Communications Corp. v. Am. Tel. & Tel. Co.*, 708 F.2d 1081, 1129 (7th Cir. 1983); *Berkey Photo, Inc. v. Eastman Kodak Co.*, 603 F.2d 263, 287-88 (2d Cir.1979), *cert. denied,* 444 U.S. 1093, 100 S.Ct. 1061, 62 L.Ed.2d 783 (1980) (absent actual deception, a monopolist's vigorous and even one-sided advertising of a new product or service not violative of the Sherman Act); *ILC Peripherals Leasing Corp. v. IBM Corp.*, 458 F.Supp. 423, 442 (N.D.Cal.1978), *aff'd per curiam sub nom. Memorex Corp. v. IBM Corp.*, 636 F.2d 1188 (9th Cir.1980), *cert. denied,* 452 U.S. 972, 101 S.Ct. 3126, 69 L.Ed.2d 983 (1981) (defendant's premature announcement of new product not actionable absent evidence of knowing falsehood); *Solargen Electric Motor Car Corp. v. American Motors Corp.*, 530 F.Supp. 22, 26 n. 3 (S.D.N.Y.1981), *aff'd,* 697 F.2d 297 (2d Cir.1982) (competitor's allegations that dominant car company "knowingly exaggerated" success of its experimental battery do not support antitrust liability).

541. *United Shoe Mach. Corp. v. United States*, 347 U.S. 521, 74 S. Ct. 699, 98 L. Ed. 910 (1954).

542. *ILC Peripherals Leasing Corp. v. Int'l Bus. Machines Corp.*, 458 F. Supp. 423, 438 (N.D. Cal. 1978*) aff'd, sub nom. Memorex Corp. v. Int'l Bus. Machines*, 636 F.2d 1188 (9th Cir. 1980) ("Memorex also asserts that the one and two year leases locked out IBM's competitors during the term of the lease. In addition to the fact that these competitors offered even longer term leases and the fact that IBM still offered customers the option of a 30-day lease, the FTP lease terms were not so long as to have any significant lock-out effect.").

II. Tying

400. Tying conditions the sale of one product or service on the purchase of another product or service. Tying is prohibited under both section 1 and section 2 of the Sherman Act and under section 3 of the Clayton Act. It is generally subject to a modified per se analysis.[543] This analysis requires a showing that the seller has sufficient market power in the tying product to coerce a purchaser into buying the unwanted tied product and that a substantial volume of commerce is foreclosed.[544] Tying is sometimes referred to as a foreclosure violation because the existence of a tie not only may require a purchaser to purchase an unwanted product, but it forecloses others from selling into the market for the tied product. It allows a seller with market power in one market – the market for the tying product – to restrain competition in a second market – the market for the tied product – in which it does not have market power. For example, a classic case, *International Salt*, involved a seller of an important patented canning machine that would only license the machine on the condition that the licensee also purchase from it the salt tablets used in the machine. The seller used its market power in the canning machine market to force purchasers to purchase the salt – a market in which it lacked market power.[545] Ties can take many different forms and are sometimes referred to as bundling. They can be achieved through a discount structure in which the only rational means of purchasing requires the purchase of multiple products.[546]

401. The initial question is whether separate products are actually involved. Many products are sold together because consumers prefer such bundles out of convenience. Right and left shoes are sold together, as are shoes and their laces. Cars are sold with tires. In *Jefferson Parish Hosp. Dist. No. 2 v. Hyde,* [547] the Court established a "consumer demand" test to determine whether the products are separate: "the answer to the question whether one or two products are involved turns not on the functional relation between them, but rather on the character of the demand for the two items."[548] Applying the consumer demand test in *Jefferson Parish,* the Court reached the somewhat counterintuitive conclusion that anesthesiological services were distinct from other hospital services. Surgeons typically specified specific anesthesiologists for their patients and anesthesiological services were billed separately from hospital services.

402. Once separate markets are established, the plaintiff must prove that the seller has market power in the tying product sufficient to force the purchaser to buy the tied product. For example, in *Town Sound & Custom Tops, Inc. v. Chrysler Motors*

543. As discussed below, there is a split among the circuits as to whether it may, in circumstances in which the per se test does not apply, be proven through a rule of reason analysis.

544. *Jefferson Parish Hosp. Dist. No. 2 v. Hyde*, 466 U.S. 2, 104 S. Ct. 1551, 80 L. Ed. 2d 2 (1984); *Illinois Tool Works Inc. v. Indep. Ink, Inc.*, 547 U.S. 28, 126 S. Ct. 1281, 164 L. Ed. 2d 26 (2006).

545. *See, Int'l Salt Co. v. United States*, 332 U.S. 392, 68 S. Ct. 12, 92 L. Ed. 20 (1947) and *Morton Salt Co. v. G. S. Suppiger Co.*, 314 U.S. 488, 489, 62 S. Ct. 402, 403, 86 L. Ed. 363 (1942) both of which were abrogated in part by *Illinois Tool Works Inc. v. Indep. Ink, Inc.* 547 U.S. 28, 126 S. Ct. 1281, 164 L. Ed. 2d 26 (2006) (holding patent alone, absent other evidence, did not establish market power in the tying product).

546. *See , e.g. SmithKline Corp. v. Eli Lilly & Co.*, 575 F.2d 1056 (3d Cir. 1978).

547. 466 U.S. 2, 104 S. Ct. 1551, 80 L. Ed. 2d 2 (1984).

548. 466 U.S. at 19, 104 S. Ct. at 1562.

Corp.,[549] the plaintiffs, independent auto sound system sellers, sued Chrysler alleging that its decision to include radio systems as part of the overall car package tied the radio to the car. The parties conceded that the radio and car represented separate products. However, the court found that Chrysler lacked market power in the relevant tying product market: automobiles. Therefore, the claim of a per se tying violation failed. In *Jefferson Parish,* as in *Town Sound & Custom Tops,* the plaintiffs were given the benefit of the assumption that there were distinct markets, but failed to prove market power in the tying market – there, hospital services – when it was shown that the defendant hospital had only 30% of the relevant market, which was held insufficient to force the anesthesiological services on the patients. A patient wishing to use a particular anesthesiologist could choose a competing hospital.

403. The issue of the relevant market – and the required market power – was central in *Eastman Kodak Co. v. Image Technical Services, Inc.*,[550] which also is an example of how tying law may apply to what at first glance may not have seemed an obvious tie. There, independent service organizations had provided repair services for Kodak copy equipment and had purchased the required replacement parts from Kodak. They claimed that a new Kodak policy under which it refused to sell parts to independent service providers effectively tied the market for repair services to the market for parts, since, absent the necessary parts, independent service organizations could no longer provide repair services. Owners of the Kodak copiers were forced to purchase both the parts and service from Kodak. The Court found that replacement parts and repair services could constitute separate markets. But the significance of the opinion was in its finding that the relevant market could be limited to repair parts for Kodak copiers. It found that these copiers had unique characteristics and were very expensive, so that once they were purchased, purchasers were effectively locked in to them because of high switching costs. Once the market was limited to repair parts for Kodak copiers, Kodak then had sufficient market power with which to force the tie on Kodak copier owners who could not effectively obtain repair services from anyone other than Kodak since the others lacked access to the required parts.

404. Jefferson Parish left open the possibility that where a plaintiff could not prove market power in the tying product – and therefore could not avail itself of the per se rule – it might still prove its claim under a rule of reason analysis that demonstrated that the market in the tied product was unduly restrained or foreclosed by the tying arrangement. The Court did not reach the issue because:

> [t]he record shed[] little light on how this arrangement affected consumer demand for separate arrangements with a specific anesthesiologist ...[T]here is no evidence that any patient who was sophisticated enough to know the difference between two anesthesiologists was not also able to go to a hospital that would provide him with the anesthesiologist of his choice.[551]

549. 959 F.2d 468 (3d Cir. 1992).
550. 504 U.S. 451, 464, 112 S. Ct. 2072, 2080, 119 L. Ed. 2d 265 (1992).
551. 466 U.S. at 30, 104 S. Ct. at 1567 (footnotes omitted).

If the plaintiff had been able to establish a prevalence of exclusive dealing relationships between hospitals and anesthesiologists such that there was a significant restraint upon consumer choice, the plaintiff may have established a rule of reason claim.

405. An important issue related to tying is known as product integration, where two formerly separate products are combined into a single new product. This issue arose in *United States v. Microsoft Corp.,*[552] where it was alleged that integration of the Internet Explorer browser in the Windows operating system constituted an illegal tie. The court found that certain aspects of Microsoft's integration were acts of monopolization to the extent those acts of integration posed obstacles to installation or access to competing browsers. However, with regard to pure tying claims under section 1, the court was concerned that in the distinct area of software platform design the "consumer demand" test broke down. It accepted Microsoft's argument that per se treatment was inappropriate. The consumer demand test was backward looking in focusing upon what consumers had purchased in the past. Microsoft urged that its integration would improve functionality for third-party applications and that the backward-looking consumer demand test would stifle innovation. The court accepted this argument and held that such bundling or tying would be subject to a rule of reason analysis. However, it carefully circumscribed its holding to the issue before the court relating to software platform development that affected third-party applications.[553]

406. A second very important area related to tying is known as bundling, where certain discounts are effectively tied to purchases of multiple products. Since such discounts are typically provided in the form of rebates, bundling is discussed below.

III. Rebates and Bundling

407. Rebates as a form of wholesale discounting are sometimes disfavored under the antitrust law because they are generally retained at the distribution level and not passed on to the consumer. This is because they do not represent a price reduction on a particular product but generally are provided in a lump sum after certain purchase goals are achieved, and those goals may be achieved by purchases spread among many different products. But bundled discounts are not uncommon. Courts currently differ over how bundled rebates are to be treated. Bundled rebates have been condemned as a violation of section 2 in certain contexts where they reinforce the market position of a monopolist.

The question posed by bundled discounts was put as follows by the Ninth Circuit:

> It is evident that bundled discounts, while potentially procompetitive by offering bargains to consumers, can also pose the threat of anticompetitive impact by excluding less diversified but more efficient producers. These considerations put into focus this problem: How are we to discern where antitrust law draws the

552. 253 F.3d 34 (D.C. Cir. 2001).
553. By contrast, the European Commission found that the bundling of the Windows Media Player with the Windows operation system was a violation of Art. 82. *See Sun Microsystems v. Microsoft Corp.*, EC Comm 1(Comp/C-3-37/37.792) (Mar. 24, 2004).

> line between bundled discounts that are procompetitive and part of the normal rough-and-tumble of our competitive economy and bundled discounts, offered by firms holding or on the verge of gaining monopoly power in the relevant market, that harm competition and are thus proscribed by § 2 of the Sherman Act?[554]

408. The earliest and most pristine case of bundled discounts is *SmithKline Corp. v. Eli Lilly & Co.*[555] In that case, the defendant, Eli Lilly & Co., held strong patent positions on certain drugs known as cephalosporins. It held the patents on the dominant forms of cephalosporins. It faced significant competition from SmithKline on only one form of cephalosporin. To counter this competition, Eli Lilly offered major rebates to hospitals on all cephalosporin purchases, provided that a hospital purchased at least three forms of cephalosporin from it. Thus, to get a discount on the necessary patented cephalosporins, a hospital had, as a practical matter, to purchase the one cephalosporin that faced competition, Kefzol, from Eli Lilly as well:

> The district court determined that the effect of the [plan] was to combine for purposes of pricing hospital purchases of Keflex and Keflin [which were subject to defendant's patents] with those of Kefzol [which faced competition]. An examination of the working of the [plan] makes this conclusion inescapable. Although eligibility for the 3% bonus rebate was based on the purchase of specified quantities of any three of Lilly's cephalosporins, in reality it meant the combined purchases of Kefzol and the leading sellers, Keflin and Keflex. In 1974 these two market leaders accounted for 75% of all hospital cephalosporin purchases. Although hospitals were free to purchase SmithKline's [competiting] Ancef with their Keflin and Keflex orders with Lilly, thus avoiding the penalties of a tie-in sale, the practical effect of that decision would be to deny the Ancef purchaser the 3% bonus rebate on all its cephalosporin purchases.

As a result, the competitor, SmithKline, seeking to meet Eli Lilly's discount had to offer a discount on the one cephalosporin it could sell equal in amount to the discount that Eli Lilly was providing across all three drugs, including the rebate on the much

554. *Cascade Health Solutions v. PeaceHealth*, 515 F.3d 883, 897 (9th Cir. 2008).
555. 575 F.2d 1056, 1061-62 (3d Cir. 1978).

higher-priced and better-selling patented drugs.[556] The Court found this bundled rebate to be a form of monopolization that allowed Eli Lilly to exclude competitors from the entire cephalosporin market.

409. A similar bundled rebate plan was condemned, again by the Third Circuit, in *LePage's Inc. v. 3M*.[557] The market at issue was for transparent tape, commonly known as "Scotch tape" the very brand name used by 3M. It was conceded that 3M had a monopoly in the transparent tape market. 3M was a major consumer conglomerate that sold a wide variety of different consumer goods aside from stationery, such as cleaning supplies and automotive products. LePage had made inroads in the secondary-brand market for transparent tape – manufacturing tape sold under such store brands as Staples and K-Mart. It claimed that, among other things, 3M had instituted a policy of rebates that only could be achieved if a customer purchased products and reached sales goals among multiple product lines:

> 3M offered many of LePage's major customers substantial rebates to induce them to eliminate or reduce their purchases of tape from LePage's. Rather than competing by offering volume discounts which are concededly legal and often reflect cost savings, 3M's rebate programs offered discounts to certain customers conditioned on purchases spanning six of 3M's diverse product lines. The product lines covered by the rebate program were: Health Care Products, Home Care Products, Home Improvement Products, Stationery Products (including transparent tape), Retail Auto Products, and Leisure Time. In addition to bundling the rebates, both of 3M's rebate programs set customer-specific target growth rates in each product line. The size of the rebate was linked to the number of product lines in which targets were met, and the number of targets met by the buyer determined the rebate it would receive on all of its purchases. If a customer failed to meet the target for any one product, its failure would cause it to lose the rebate across the line. This created a substantial incentive for each customer to meet the targets across all product lines to maximize its rebates.[558]

The court held that such rebates constituted monopolization. It explained:

---

556. The court explained:

In understanding the effects of Lilly's Revised CSP, the importance of cephalosporins in hospital pharmacies cannot be understated. They are carried in stock by virtually every general hospital in the country. To meet the bonus discounts offered by Lilly, a competitor was forced to more than meet the competition on the one product, cefazolin; it had to match the bonus rebate awarded to the hospital purchaser based on total purchases of three cephalosporins, including the leading sellers, Keflin and Keflex. In SmithKline's case, this meant it had to compete "three-on-one." (Brief for Appellee at 36.) In computing its percentage of rebate on the one product, Ancef, SmithKline was forced to meet the total dollar discounts available to purchasers of Lilly's three high volume cephalosporins. Although the Revised CSP only gave a 3% bonus rebate, because of Lilly's volume advantage, in order to offer a rebate of the same net dollar amount as Lilly's, SmithKline had to offer purchasers of Ancef rebates of some 16% to hospitals of average size, and 35% to larger volume hospitals.

557. 324 F.3d 141 (3d Cir. 2003).

558. 324 F.3d at 154.

> [T]he principal anticompetitive effect of bundled rebates as offered by 3M is that when offered by a monopolist they may foreclose portions of the market to a potential competitor who does not manufacture an equally diverse group of products and who therefore cannot make a comparable offer.[559]

It provided stark illustrations showing that 3M's total rebates to certain customers it had taken from LePage actually equaled as much as half the customer's total purchases of transparent tape. Under the circumstances, the Third Circuit refused to extend the holding in *Brooke Group Ltd. v. Brown & Williamson Tobacco Corp.,*[560] to require that the bundled discount be shown to be below cost.

410. The Ninth Circuit, concerned that bundled discounts were pervasive within the economy and that the Third Circuit's view might reward less efficient competitors, adopted a modified cost-based rule that it termed the "discount-attribution test." It held that:

> [t]o prove that a bundled discount was exclusionary or predatory for the purposes of a monopolization or attempted monopolization claim under § 2 of the Sherman Act, the plaintiff must establish that, after allocating the discount given by the defendant on the entire bundle of products to the competitive product or products, the defendant sold the competitive product or products below its average variable cost of producing them.[561]

411. Other forms of rebate plans have also run afoul of the antitrust laws. For example, a dominant manufacturer's conditioning of rebates on the granting of a certain percentage of display space was held to state a cause of action.[562]

IV. Refusal to Deal[563]

412. "As a general rule, businesses are free to choose the parties with whom they will deal, as well as the prices, terms, and conditions of that dealing."[564] In *United*

559. *Ibid.*, at 155.
560. 509 U.S. 209, 113 S. Ct. 2578, 125 L. Ed. 2d 168 (1993).
561. *Cascade Health Solutions v. PeaceHealth,* 515 F.3d 883, 910 (9th Cir. 2008); *See also, e.g., FTC. v. Church & Dwight Co., Inc.,* 11-5008, 2011 WL 6157620 (D.C. Cir. Dec. 13, 2011) ("*LePage's* is of course not the law of this circuit, and it has been roundly criticized... We need not, however, pass upon the merits of the rule in *LePage's* in order to resolve this case.").
562. *Church & Dwight Co., Inc. v. Mayer Laboratories, Inc.*, C-10-4429 EMC, 2011 WL 1225912 (N.D. Cal. Apr. 1, 2011).
563. This section relates to refusals to deal by a single dominant firm in a market. Joint refusals to deal, or boycotts, are discussed in the Group Boycott section above.
564. *Pac. Bell Tel. Co. v. Linkline Communications, Inc.*, 555 U.S. 438, 448, 129 S. Ct. 1109, 1118, 172 L. Ed. 2d 836 (2009).

States v. Colgate & Co.,[565] the Supreme Court rejected the claim of the government that a refusal to deal with a retailer that discounted the seller's products constituted a violation. It held that:

> [t]he trader or manufacturer ... carries on an entirely private business, and can sell to whom he pleases ... A retail dealer has the unquestioned right to stop dealing with a wholesaler for reasons sufficient to himself, and may do so because he thinks such dealer is acting unfairly in trying to undermine his trade.

In *NYNEX Corp. v. Discon, Inc,*[566] the Court held that a monopolist's decision to switch vendors, even for an improper purpose, was not a per se refusal to deal, as would be the case had multiple players in the market agreed to refuse to deal with a particular entity.

413. Where a monopolist has dealt with an entity in the past and then changes its policy and refuses to deal in the future, a cause of action may arise if the refusal is intended, and can be shown, to harm competition.

414. In *Aspen Skiing Co. v. Aspen Highlands Skiing Corp.,*[567] two different ski resorts within the Aspen area, one controlling three mountains and the other controlling one, had, together, sold a combined single lift-ticket enabling visitors to Aspen to ski on any of the mountains. The dominant firm then unilaterally terminated its participation in the single lift-ticket and began selling tickets limited to its three mountains. The plaintiff was able to adduce considerable evidence of intent by the dominant firm to drive the smaller firm from the market. For example, it refused to sell lift tickets to the smaller firm under any circumstances, had airbrushed the smaller firm's mountain from pictures of Aspen at the Denver airport, and had rejected many reasonable methods of allocating receipts from the joint ticket sales. Moreover, the plaintiff had been able to show consumer harm in that consumers wanted a four mountain ticket and were upset when they learned they were unable to ski at the smaller resort with one lift-ticket as they had formerly been able to do. Under these circumstances, the Court forced the monopolist to deal with the firm as it had in the past.

415. Similarly in *Eastman Kodak Co. v. Image Technical Services, Inc.,*[568] discussed above, the Court held that a monopolist's refusal to continue selling replacement parts of its copiers to independent service companies that had historically serviced its copiers could give rise to a claim under section 2 of the Sherman Act.[569]

416. A recent district court opinion summarized the present state of the law:

565. 250 U.S. 300, 307, 39 S. Ct. 465, 468, 63 L. Ed. 992 (1919).
566. 525 U.S. 128, 135, 119 S. Ct. 493, 498, 142 L. Ed. 2d 510 (1998).
567. 472 U.S. 585, 587, 105 S. Ct. 2847, 2849, 86 L. Ed. 2d 467 (1985).
568. 504 U.S. 451, 112 S. Ct. 2072, 119 L. Ed. 2d 265 (1992).
569. Even an opinion taking a highly restrictive view of the scope of the antitrust laws, recognized that the prior dealing on particular terms was a significant factor to be considered. *See, Queen City Pizza, Inc. v. Domino's Pizza, Inc.*, 124 F.3d 430, 440 (3d Cir. 1997).

> Taken together, Aspen Skiing and Verizon demonstrate that liability under Section 2 can arise when a defendant voluntarily alters a course of dealing and "anticompetitive malice" motivates the defendant's conduct.... When a firm declines to cooperate with a competitor, that decision may have "evidentiary significance" as to the defendant's anticompetitive intent and may give rise to liability under Section 2.[570]

417. A second area where an ongoing duty to deal has been found is where a monopolist controls an "essential facility." The District of Columbia Circuit articulated the doctrine in *Hecht v. Pro-Football, Inc.*:[571]

> The essential facility doctrine, also called the "bottleneck principle," states that "where facilities cannot practicably be duplicated by would-be competitors, those in possession of them must allow them to be shared on fair terms. It is illegal restraint of trade to foreclose the scarce facility."... To be "essential" a facility need not be indispensable; it is sufficient if duplication of the facility would be economically infeasible and if denial of its use inflicts a severe handicap on potential market entrants. Necessarily, this principle must be carefully delimited: the antitrust laws do not require that an essential facility be shared if such sharing would be impractical or would inhibit the defendant's ability to serve its customers adequately. (footnotes omitted)

418. These cases, which derive from an early Supreme Court case, *U.S. v. Terminal R. R. Ass'n of St. Louis*,[572] have significant application to modern issues such as internet neutrality. In *Terminal Railroad*, a number of major railroads created a company that had acquired all of the facilities necessary to move rail traffic across the Mississippi River at St. Louis. The Court imposed a duty to deal fairly on non-discriminatory terms upon all users of the essential facilities held by the terminaling company. *Terminal Railroad* was both a section 1 and section 2 case and it was unclear whether the outcome was dictated by the single firm monopolization or the multi-firm activity to create the exclusive bottleneck that favored their railroads.

419. Subsequent cases have imposed a duty on a single firm monopolist where it controlled an essential facility. *Otter Tail Power Co. v. United States*,[573] required an electric utility to "wheel" electricity purchased from others across its system to municipalities it formerly served that had created municipally owned retail power systems.

420. However, the Supreme Court has been reluctant to give the doctrine broad scope, particularly in a single-actor context. In *Verizon Communications Inc. v. Law Offices of Curtis V. Trinko, LLP*, Justice Scalia, writing for the Court, stated with regard to the essential facilities doctrine in a single-actor context, that, "[w]e have never

570. *Safeway Inc. v. Abbott Laboratories*, C 07-05470 CW, 2010 WL 147988 (N.D. Cal. Jan. 12, 2010).
571. 570 F.2d 982, 992–993 (D.C. Cir. 1977).
572. 224 U.S. 383, 32 S. Ct. 507, 56 L. Ed. 810 (1912).
573. 410 U.S. 366, 373, 93 S. Ct. 1022, 1027, 35 L. Ed. 2d 359 (1973).

recognized such a doctrine ... and we find no need either to recognize it or to repudiate it here."[574]

V. Price Squeeze

421. A price, or margin, squeeze occurs when an integrated firm operating at two levels is a supplier to its downstream competitors and raises its prices as a supplier while holding its price for the downstream product constant, thereby "squeezing" the margins of its competitors. The competitors must pay higher prices for the good or service furnished but are unable to pass on the increased cost to their customers because of competition from their supplier. They are "squeezed." This was long thought to be a basic tool of monopolists and was a basis for Judge Leaned Hand's finding of monopolization in the seminal *Alcoa* case.[575] However, in *Pac. Bell Tel. Co. v. Linkline Communications, Inc.*,[576] the Chief Justice blithely cast this precedent aside in a footnote[577] and the Court has apparently eliminated a price-squeeze as a cause of action absent a showing that the monopolist had a duty to deal – a circumstance the Court stressed was present in only limited circumstances. *Linkline* involved claims by downstream retail internet DSL providers that AT&T, which provided both wholesale and retail internet access and therefore was both their supplier and competitor, had raised wholesale rates while keeping retail rates low, thereby squeezing their margins. However, the plaintiffs' complaint lacked two allegations. It did not claim the AT&T had any duty to deal with them at all, and it did not claim that the low AT&T retail rate was below AT&T's cost.

422. Linkline reasoned that since *Verizon Communications Inc. v. Law Offices of Curtis V. Trinko, LLP*,[578] had held that a firm with no antitrust duty to deal with its rivals is under no obligation to provide those rivals with a "sufficient" level of service, it could not hold that a monopolist was required to provide services at any particular price. Key to the Court's finding was that there was no allegation in *Linkline* that the defendant had a duty to deal with the plaintiffs. The defendant was a DSL provider and under FCC regulations would only have had a duty to deal if it possessed monopoly

574. 540 U.S. 398, 411, 124 S. Ct. 872, 881, 157 L. Ed. 2d 823 (2004).
575. *United States v. Aluminum Co. of Am.*, 148 F.2d 416, 447 (2d Cir. 1945).
576. 555 U.S. 438, 452, 129 S. Ct. 1109, 1120, 172 L. Ed. 2d 836 (2009).
577. *See* , 555 U.S. at 452 n. 3:

Like the Court of Appeals, 503 F.3d, at 880, amici argue that price-squeeze claims have been recognized by Courts of Appeals for many years, beginning with Judge Hand's opinion in United States v. Aluminum Co. of America, 148 F.2d 416 (C.A.2 1945) (Alcoa). In that case, the Government alleged that Alcoa was using its monopoly power in the upstream aluminum ingot market to squeeze the profits of downstream aluminum sheet fabricators. The court concluded: "That it was unlawful to set the price of 'sheet' so low and hold the price of ingot so high, seems to us unquestionable, provided, as we have held, that on this record the price of ingot must be regarded as higher than a 'fair price'" id., at 438. Given developments in economic theory and antitrust jurisprudence since Alcoa, we find our recent decisions in Trinko and Brooke Group more pertinent to the question before us.

578. 540 U.S. 398, 410, 124 S.Ct. 872, 157 L.Ed.2d 823 (2004).

power. However, the Court noted that the FCC had already found that the market for DSL services was competitive.

423. Having reached the conclusion that there was no duty to deal, the Court dissected the price-squeeze claim and found it to be "an amalgamation of a meritless claim at the retail level and a meritless claim at the wholesale level. If there is no duty to deal at the wholesale level and no predatory pricing at the retail level, then a firm is certainly not required to price *both* of these services in a manner that preserves its rivals' profit margins."[579]

424. *Linkline* leaves open the question of whether a price-squeeze claim could be asserted where there is a duty to deal. It recognized that prior decisions had found circumstances where such a duty existed, such as in *Aspen Skiing Co. v. Aspen Highlands Skiing Corp.*.[580] Had the facts of *Eastman Kodak Co. v. Image Technical Services, Inc.*,[581] been such that Kodak had raised the prices on its parts to a level above that which the independent service organizations could pay and still continue to compete against the prices charged by Kodak for servicing copy machines, it is difficult to imagine that the Court would ignore the effect of the "price squeeze" as a tool of the monopolization, regardless of whether the parts or the service were priced at below cost levels at retail.

425. *Linkline* involved facts strikingly similar to those considered by the European Commission in *Deutsche Telekom AG v. Commission*.[582] There, the Commission found a margin squeeze to be an abuse Article 102 TFEU. However, the Supreme Court reached the opposite result under its construction of American antitrust law.

579. 555 U.S. at 452, 129 S. Ct. at 1120.
580. 472 U.S. 585, 608–611, 105 S.Ct. 2847, 86 L.Ed.2d 467 (1985).
581. 504 U.S. 451, 112 S. Ct. 2072, 119 L. Ed. 2d 265 (1992).
582. Case T-271/03 CFI, [2008] ECR II-477.

Chapter 3. Mergers (Concentrations)

§1. Horizontal Mergers

I. History

426. Horizontal merger enforcement has changed significantly since section 7 of the Clayton Act was amended in 1950 by the Celler-Kefauver Act. That Act was passed to address the "fear of what was considered to be a rising tide of economic concentration in the American economy."[583] Section 7 regulates acquisitions of assets or stock. It reaches vertical and conglomerate mergers as well as horizontal mergers and may regulate mergers before they actually harm competition.[584] It regulates mergers the effects of which "*may* be substantially to lessen competition,"[585] that is, "its concern was with probabilities, not certainties."[586]

427. Early cases after the Celler-Kefauver Act amendments to section 7 found that the provision's goal was to combat "not only … accelerated concentration of economic power on economic grounds, but also … the threat to other values a trend toward concentration was thought to pose."[587] Those goals were "to preserve a society of small, independent, decentralized businesses in order to keep economic power dispersed and thereby keep political power diffused."[588] In the 1950s and 1960s, the Supreme Court heeded this mandate and read section 7 to require keeping companies small to preserve the economic structure the Act sought to preserve.[589] It upheld restrictions of horizontal mergers which would have had limited effects on competition. In 1966, in *Von's Grocery*, the Supreme Court upheld an injunction of a merger of two supermarket chains controlling collectively 9% of the Los Angeles market.[590] The Court emphasized that the largest firm in the market already controlled 8% of the market and that the market in general was becoming more highly concentrated.[591]

428. But this view of section 7 eroded in the 1970s and 1980s. The Court's view of the goals of the antitrust laws shifted from that of preserving a particular economic structure of society to that of protecting competition in the market and the Court's

583. *Brown Shoe Co. v. U.S., 370 U.S.* 294, 315 (1962).
584. *Ibid.*, at 315–318.
585. 15 U.S.C. § 18.
586. *Brown Shoe*, 370 U.S. at 323.
587. *Brown Shoe*, 370 U.S. at 316.
588. Eleanor M. Fox & Robert Pitofsky, "United States," in *Global Competition Policy,* ed. Edward M. Graham & J. David Richardson (1997), 236 *available at* <www.iie.com/publications/chapters_preview/56/7iie1664.pdf>.
589. *Brown Shoe*, 370 U.S. at 315–316 ("Other considerations cited in support of the bill [amending Section 7] were the desirability of retaining 'local control' over industry and the protection of small businesses.").
590. *U.S. v. Von's Grocery Co.*, 384 U.S. 270, 281 (1966) (J. White, concurring).
591. *Ibid.*, at 290.

views of economic efficiency, distorted though it may have been from a limited understanding of economics and the limitations of the economic thinking of the era. The focus moved from looking at whether the merger would create a concentration of market power in a small number of entities to economic analyses of the anticipated actual effect of a proposed merger on competition and consumers. The shift can be seen by comparing *United States v. Philadelphia National Bank* decided in 1963 with *United States v. General Dynamics*,[592] decided eleven years later. In *Philadelphia National Bank*, the Court blocked a merger that would have created the largest bank in the Philadelphia area. It held that a high post-merger market concentration warranted a presumption of illegality:

> Th[e] intense congressional concern with the trend toward concentration warrants dispensing, in certain cases, with elaborate proof of market structure, market behavior, or probable anticompetitive effects. Specifically, we think that a merger which produces a firm controlling an undue percentage share of the relevant market, and results in a significant increase in the concentration of firms in that market is so inherently likely to lessen competition substantially that it must be enjoined in the absence of evidence clearly showing that the merger is not likely to have such anticompetitive effects.[593]

429. Eleven years later, in *General Dynamics*,[594] the Court upheld a horizontal merger of coal producers. It found that even though production statistics indicated that the merged company would have a high market concentration, more detailed economic analysis showed that coal reserves were a better measure of future market power than past production.[595] This was because coal producers' main customers were electric utilities that preferred long-term contracts at fixed prices with their suppliers.[596] The utilities would not award contracts based on past performance, but on the reserves available to provide coal in the future.[597] Since the target company in the proposed merger did not have significant coal reserves, even though it currently controlled a high percentage of the market, the Court found the proposed merger to be legal.[598] The Court explained that "statistics concerning market share and concentration, while of great significance, [a]re not conclusive indicators of anticompetitive effects."[599] Since then, the "Supreme Court… has said repeatedly that the economic concept of competition, rather than any desire to preserve rivals as such, is the lodestar that shall guide the contemporary application of the antitrust laws. …"[600] Whether this comports with the Celler-Kefauver Act or even represents a better measure of economic efficiency over

592. 415 U.S. 486, 501 (1974).
593. *U.S. v. Philadelphia Nat'l Bank*, 374 U.S. 321, 363 (1963).
594. 415 U.S. 486, 501 (1974).
595. *Ibid.*
596. *Ibid.*
597. *Ibid.*, at 502.
598. *Ibid.*, at 502–504.
599. *Ibid.*, at 498.
600. *Hospital Corp. of Am.*, 807 F.2d at 1386.

the long-term than measuring concentration remains a serious open question because of the limited knowledge at a given moment and the fluid nature of markets.

430. Antitrust merger enforcement has moved increasingly towards analyses of economic effects rather than market concentration. As late as 1992, the *Horizontal Merger Guidelines* of the Antitrust Division and the FTC, which set out the antitrust agencies' merger enforcement methodologies, began the analyses with market concentration.[601] This had been the agencies' approach since the *Merger Guidelines* were first published in 1968.[602] The 1992 version of the *Guidelines* stated that, "[a] merger is unlikely to create or enhance market power or to facilitate its exercise unless it significantly increases concentration and results in a concentrated market."[603] Under the 1992 *Guidelines,* after analyzing the market structure, the agencies would study, in this order: competitive effects; potential new entry into the market by third parties; efficiencies gained by the merger; and the potential failure of one of the merging parties. The analysis was: How does the market look? Does this market structure mean that the merger will cause harm to competition? Will the market change because of entry or failure? Will the merger provide market efficiencies offsetting any negative effects? The over-riding concern, however, was underlying market structure.

II. Current Enforcement

431. The current *Horizontal Merger Guidelines*, released in 2010, take a more nuanced view. Market structure is subordinated in the analysis to competitive effects: "The measurement of market shares and market concentration is not an end in itself, but is useful to the extent it illuminates the merger's likely competitive effects."[604] Nonetheless, the *Guidelines* continue to use the Herfindal Hirschman Index or, as a basic tool to measure market concentration within the market. The HHI sums the squares of the market shares of individual firms competing in the market, both before and after the proposed merger.[605] The agencies use the HHI to determine whether a market is concentrated and whether the merger would create a small or large change in market concentration.[606] These calculations determine the need for further analysis.

432. A series of standards are set out in the *Guidelines*. An increase of the HHI of less than 100 points is "unlikely to have adverse competitive effects and ordinarily requires no further analysis."[607] By contrast, an increase in the HHI of between 100

601. Fed. Trade Comm'n & U.S. Dep't of Justice, Horizontal Merger Guidelines § 1.0 (1992, revised 1997).
602. U.S. Dep't of Justice, Merger Guidelines §§ 2–3 (1968) ("Within the overall scheme of the Department's antitrust enforcement activity, the primary role of Section 7 enforcement is to preserve and promote market structures conducive to competition. Market structure is the focus of the Department's merger policy chiefly because the conduct of the individual firms in a market tends to be controlled by the structure of that market").
603. Fed. Trade Comm'n & U.S. Dep't of Justice, Horizontal Merger Guidelines § 1.0 (1992, revised 1997).
604. Fed. Trade Comm'n & U.S. Dep't of Justice, Horizontal Merger Guidelines § 4 (2010).
605. *Ibid.*, at § 5.3.
606. *Ibid.*
607. *Ibid.*

and 200 points in a highly concentrated market, i.e. one with an HHI above 2,500, creates a presumption of an enhancement of market power that needs to be rebutted by persuasive evidence that the merger is unlikely to enhance market power.

433. For example, if there is a market with ten sellers each of which has a 10% market share, the HHI would be $10^2+10^2 10^2+10^2+10^2=1{,}000$. If two of the firms were to merge the HHI would be $10^2+10^2 10^2+10^2+20^2=1{,}200$. A more concentrated market might look something like this. Six sellers, one with a market share of 40% another with a market share of 25%, another with a market share of 20% and three with market shares of 5%. The HHI would be calculated as $40^2+25^2+20^2+5^2+5^2+5^2=2{,}700$. It is a highly concentrated market under the *Guidelines*. If the firm with a 20% market share merged with a firm with a 5% market share the HHI would increase to 2,890, i.e., by 190 points. Under the Guidelines it would be presumptively illegal. By contrast if two of the firms having 5% market shares merged the HHI would only increase to 2,750, just fifty points and would be presumptively approved. In this way, the HHI accounts for the sizes of all the firms within a market.

434. An initial matter, before calculating the concentration of the market, is determining what constitutes the actual relevant market. The *Guidelines* utilize what is known as the hypothetical monopolist test to define a market.[608] This test determines whether two products are within the same market by measuring whether a significant number of customers would choose an alternative product if the seller increased prices. Technically, the test asks whether, "a hypothetical profit-maximizing firm, not subject to price regulation, that was the only present and future seller of those products ('hypothetical monopolist') likely would impose at least a small but significant and non-transitory increase in price ('SSNIP') on at least one product in the market."[609] If such a firm would impose a SSNIP, considered a 5%–10% price increase, it is because such a price increase would be profitable, i.e., the firm would not lose significant business to products outside the market because there is something unique about the products included in the market.[610] For example, a rational consumer who prefers blue scissors to red scissors may buy blue scissors so long as the prices of red and blue scissors remained the same or close to each other. But since there is no functional difference between red and blue scissors, a 5%–10% price increase in blue scissors would likely cause a rational consumer to begin buying red scissors. However, if all scissors' prices increase by 5%–10% that rational consumer is much less likely to switch from scissors to knives since there are some functions for which scissors are uniquely suited that insulates them from some competition from outside their market. Red and blue scissors are within the same market, scissors and knives are not. Taking an actual hard example, in the 1970s coconut oil producers encouraged by the Marcos regime, sought to follow OPEC's lead and to cartelize the market for coconut oil. They did so and promptly raised the price of coconut oil significantly only to lose the entire market to competing vegetable oils. Unlike the petroleum sold by OPEC, for which there were no functional substitutes, other vegetable oils were almost perfect substitutes

608. Fed. Trade Comm'n & U.S. Dep't of Justice, Horizontal Merger Guidelines § 4.1 (2010).
609. *Ibid.*, at § 4.1.1.
610. *Ibid.*

for coconut oil and it did not represent a relevant separate product market.[611] The hypothetical monopolist test is not the only test that may be applied to determine relevant market and other tests used are discussed at Part I Chapter 4 §2 above.

435. The *Guidelines* divide the possible anticompetitive effects of a merger into two main categories: unilateral effects and coordinated effects. "Unilateral effects" refer to a lessening of competition from the disappearance of a competitor in the market.[612] If the agencies find that before the merger direct competition between the merging companies led to lower prices, increased output or innovation, or other benefits to customers, the agencies are likely to find the merger anticompetitive.[613]

436. "Coordinated effects" refer to the increased prices, decreased output, or other effects expected from the reduction in the number of competitors in a market caused by the proposed merger.[614] The merger may create too few substantial competitors in the market, may eliminate a competitor that historically has tended to disrupt the market with lower prices, or otherwise may change a market to enable coordinated pricing or other decisions by competitors.[615] For example, by reducing the competitors below a critical number it may facilitate price-fixing or tacit coordination. It may facilitate tacit coordination by allowing more easy detection of price aggression and punishment of deviations that would undermine coordinated interaction.[616]

437. There are many examples of this more sophisticated approach to merger analysis. A good example is Judge Posner's decision in *Hosp. Corp. of Am. v. F.T.C.*[617] As a result of the acquisition at issue, Hospital Corporation of America controlled five of the eleven hospitals in the Chattanooga, Tennessee market and had increased its market share from 11% to 26%. This increase led to further concentration of the overall market. The largest four firms controlled 91% of the market compared to 76% before the merger. While these increases in concentration alone might have provided grounds to block the merger under historic precedent, the FTC had explained why in this particular market the reduction in competition would likely facilitate collusion and higher prices. The sheer number of players was reduced from eleven to seven with four companies controlling almost the entire market. This greatly facilitated coordinated action.

438. New entry was highly unlikely because of regulatory requirements governing hospital construction. Demand for hospital services was inelastic. Sick people needed hospitals. Demand did not decrease if prices increased. Therefore, there was more likelihood that prices would rise through coordinated activity. There was also evidence of a tradition of cooperation between the different hospitals in the market. The hospitals were being pressured to reduce prices by the federal government and insurers, and had an incentive, which they had acted upon, to "present a united front in negotiations

---

611. *See* , James K. Boyce, *The Political Economy of Growth and Impoverishment in the Marcos Era* (Manila, 1993), 208.
612. *Ibid.*, at § 6.
613. *Ibid.*
614. *Ibid.*, at § 7.
615. *Ibid.*, at §§ 2.1.5, 7.1, 7.2.
616. *Ibid.*, at § 7.
617. 807 F.2d 1381 (7th Cir. 1986).

with the third-party payors."[618] These factors together with the changes in market share and concentration provided the basis for concluding the merger was anticompetitive.

439. More recent cases, following this trend of looking beyond simple market share statistics to actual effects, have proven that the number of participants in a market significantly reduces prices to consumers. The FTC, by comparing prices in markets in which there are more players with those in which a single firm dominates, has shown that the presence of multiple competitors reduces prices – exactly what one would expect, but a fact often obscured by hired economic experts seeking to justify mergers.

440. In *Fed. Trade Comm'n v. Staples, Inc.*,[619] the FTC provided dramatic evidence of the unilateral anticompetitive effects of a proposed merger between two office supply superstore chains, Staples and Office Depot. There were three major office supply superstore chains prior to the proposed merger. The FTC showed that in geographic markets in which Staples was the only office supply superstore, it could sustain 13% higher prices than it could in markets also containing its two office supply superstore competitors. The FTC introduced an astonishing exhibit. Staples had identical advertisements in different geographic markets. The only difference between them was that the prices advertised were lower in markets in which Staples faced competition from another office supply superstore.[620]

441. Staples and Office Depot argued for a broader product market definition claiming that they faced competition from mass merchandisers that sold office supplies, like Wal-Mart, K-mart, and Target. But the court found that those stores were in a different market largely because the FTC demonstrated that their presence in a market did not significantly affect the pricing of office supply superstores.[621] In contrast to markets containing multiple office superstores, prices were not lower in markets in which an office superstore was located near a mass merchandiser. These demonstrated effects on prices helped determine the definition of the market as "office supply superstores." When the two companies again tried to merge in 2015, arguing that the market had changed, especially in light of on-line competition, the FTC took a different tack, and persuaded the court that these companies dominance of the business to business bulk sales market, in which on-line competition had not made major.inroads, would be augmented by the merger.[622]

442. The FTC introduced similar evidence in *F.T.C. v. H.J. Heinz Co.*[623] *Heinz* involved a market with three national baby food manufacturers, Heinz, Gerber and Beech-Nut. Gerber was the market leader and Heinz and Beech-Nut sought to merge, allegedly to better compete with Gerber. The Court of Appeals reversed the denial of a preliminary injunction blocking the merger in part on the basis of clear evidence that "where both are present in the same areas, they depress each other's prices as well as

618. *Ibid.*, at 1388–1389.
619. 970 F.Supp. 1066, 1093 (D.D.C. 1997).
620. *See*, Jonathan B. Baker & Robert Pitofsky, "A Turning Point in Merger Enforcement: *Federal Trade Commission v. Staples*," in *Antitrust Stories*, ed. Eleanor M. Fox & Daniel A. Crane (2007), 317.
621. *Staples*, 970 F.Supp. at 1077.
622. *Fed. Trade Comm'n v. Staples, Inc.*, No. CV 15-2115 (EGS), 2016 WL 2899222 (D.D.C. May 17, 2016).
623. 246 F.3d 708 (D.C. Cir. 2001).

those of Gerber …"[624] Even in that case, where HHI numbers began at 4,475 and would increase by 510 points as a result of the merger, the court looked to actual marketplace data as well.

443. In *F.T.C. v. Whole Foods Mkt., Inc.*,[625] the Court of Appeals was again persuaded by hard economic evidence of the effect of existing competition between the merging companies. Two premium natural food supermarket chains, Whole Foods and Wild Oats, sought to merge. As in *Staples*, the hard data on existing pricing served the dual purpose of proving a relevant market and showing the economic harm – higher prices – that would result from the merger:

> Dr. Murphy compared the margins of Whole Foods stores in cities where they competed with Wild Oats. He found the presence of a Wild Oats depressed Whole Foods's margins significantly. …Dr. Murphy showed the opening of a new Whole Foods in the vicinity of a Wild Oats caused Wild Oats's prices to drop, while entry by non-PNOS [premium natural and organic supermarkets] stores had no such effect. Similarly, the opening of Earth Fare stores (another PNOS) near Whole Foods stores caused Whole Foods's prices to drop immediately.[626]

444. As the above quote makes clear, the court was persuaded to define the market as it did, in part, by evidence of competitive effects, including that Whole Foods's and Wild Oats's prices and margins, particularly for high-quality perishables, were affected by the presence of the other PNOS but not by that of conventional supermarkets.[627]

445. Merging firms can alleviate agencies' and courts' concerns with three basic arguments: entry, efficiencies and failure. A SSNIP may induce other firms to enter the market and thereby eliminate the harm to competition posed by the merger.[628] Entry is only considered an effective counteraction to anticompetitive harm if a firm would be likely to do so sufficiently and in a timely manner.[629] A merger could result in efficiencies for the merging firm, enabling it to compete more effectively in the market and thereby reduce prices or increase output for the benefit of customers.[630] The Agencies will not challenge a merger if efficiencies are of a character and magnitude such that the merger is not likely to be anticompetitive in any relevant "market."[631] Another defense to an allegedly anticompetitive merger is failure, i.e., that, absent the merger, one of the merging parties would fail imminently and exit the relevant market.[632] It is very difficult to show imminent failure. It requires showing not merely weakness but all of the following: absent the merger, the firm would be unable to meet its financial

624. *F.T.C. v. H.J. Heinz Co.*, 246 F.3d 708, 718 (D.C. Cir. 2001).
625. 548 F.3d 1028, 1039–1040 (D.C. Cir. 2008).
626. 548 F.3d at 1040.
627. *Ibid.*, at 1039–1040.
628. *Ibid.*, at § 9.
629. *Ibid.*, at § 9.1–9.3.
630. *Ibid.*, at § 10.
631. *Ibid.*
632. *Ibid.*, at § 11.

obligations or reorganize under the Bankruptcy Code, and the failing firm has unsuccessfully tried to form a merger that would pose "less severe danger to competition than does the proposed merger."[633]

§2. Vertical Mergers

446. Vertical mergers have been of less concern to regulators than horizontal mergers. From 1996–2007, the FTC issued a second request for information in 210 horizontal mergers (55%) but in only twenty-five vertical mergers (7%).[634] Since 1984, vertical mergers have not appeared in the agencies' merger guidelines, which the agencies renamed the *Horizontal Merger Guidelines*.[635] Vertical mergers have been the subject of only three Supreme Court cases since 1950.

447. The antitrust agencies' focus has shifted from market share to analysis of the anticompetitive effects of vertical mergers. The *1992 Horizontal Merger Guidelines*, cross-referenced the analysis of vertical mergers in the *1984 Guidelines* but the reference was dropped in the *2010 Guidelines*.[636] The main concerns discussed in the *1984 Guidelines* were with vertical mergers that foreclose entry into a market, facilitate collusion between suppliers (one of whom bought a purchaser) to increase prices in the market, or enable a monopoly public utility to circumvent rate regulation by buying a supplier and inflating the prices it says it pays for inputs from that supplier.[637] The concern with foreclosure was that a vertical merger could harm competition by preventing a competitor from entering one market unless they simultaneously entered a downstream or upstream market, i.e. requiring "two-level entry."[638] Two-level entry would be necessary if the "degree of vertical integration between...two markets [is] so extensive that entrants to one market" would not be able to compete in that market unless they also controlled certain suppliers or purchasers.[639]

448. An example of recent analysis of a vertical merger is the 2011 consent agreement with the Antitrust Division which allowed Google to acquire ITA Software upon certain conditions.[640] Google was the leading search engine provider in the US and ITA Software was the leading independent provider of a technology system powering travel airfare searches, by price, schedule, airline, and other factors.[641] The Antitrust Division alleged that if Google, though not itself a participant in the travel market, were to acquire ITA and use its software to power Google's airfare search

633. *Ibid.*

634. Fed. Trade Comm'n, Horizontal Merger Investigation Data, Fiscal Year 1996–2007, 8 (2008).

635. Fed. Trade Comm'n & U.S. Dep't of Justice, Horizontal Merger Guidelines n.1 (2010) ("These Guidelines do not cover vertical or other types of non-horizontal acquisitions.").

636. Fed. Trade Comm'n & U.S. Dep't of Justice, Horizontal Merger Guidelines (1992) ("Specific guidance on non-horizontal mergers is provided in Section 4 of the Department's 1984 Merger Guidelines, read in the context of today's revisions to the treatment of horizontal mergers.").

637. U.S. Dep't of Justice, Merger Guidelines § 4 (1984).

638. *Ibid.*, at §§ 4.21, 4.211.

639. *Ibid.*, at§ 4.21.

640. Final Judgment, *United States v. Google Inc. and ITA Software, Inc.*, Case No. 1:11-cv-00688 (Oct. 5, 2011), *available at* <www.justice.gov/atr/cases/f275800/275897.pdf>.

641. *Ibid.*, at § I.

results, it would significantly harm competition.[642] Companies currently using ITA's complex software to provide airfare search results would now depend on a rival – Google – to provide access to that critical input, for which there was no adequate substitute.[643] Google would "have an incentive to weaken [competitors] by denying or degrading their access to [ITA's software] because increased profits from driving customers to its new travel service from rival[s]... will likely outweigh any lost profits from reduced licensing revenues."[644] Innovation and consumer choice in the market would diminish.[645] To ameliorate this potential harm to competition, the Antitrust Division required Google, among other things, to continue licensing ITA's software to competitors for a certain period of time on "fair, reasonable, and non-discriminatory 'terms' which includes the right to use ordinary course upgrades" to the software at no additional charge.[646]

449. A second recent example of government intervention in a vertical merger was the Antitrust Division's 2011 consent agreement with Comcast, the huge cable company and the leading video programing distributor in the US. The decree allowed Comcast to take control of NBC, a major content provider, on conditions that included making NBC content available on equal terms to competing on-line content distributors.[647] The Antitrust Division's concern had been that Comcast would foreclose access to an input, NBC's content, that rival distributors depended upon to provide services that would be competitive with that of Comcast.[648]

§3. Market/Product-Extension Mergers

450. Market-extension mergers, as the name implies, involve acquisition of a complementary product manufacturer. Enforcement against market-extension or product-extension mergers are rare in the US.

451. The leading case is *FTC v. Procter & Gamble*,[649] known colloquially as the *Clorox* case. Clorox was the largest manufacturer of household bleach in the US with a dominant market share and little significant competition. It was a single product company at the time. Procter & Gamble was a large, diversified manufacturer of household products, including many cleaning products, but not bleach. It sought to acquire Clorox which would have immediately made Procter and Gamble the dominant liquid bleach marketer and would have raised significant barriers to entry in that market.

642. *Ibid.*, at § III.
643. *Ibid.*, at ¶¶ 29, 37.
644. *Ibid.*, at ¶ 38.
645. *Ibid.*, at ¶ 39.
646. Final Judgment, *United States v. Google Inc. and ITA Software, Inc.*, Case No. 1:11-cv-00688 § IV (Oct. 5, 2011), *available at* <www.justice.gov/atr/cases/f275800/275897.pdf>.
647. Dep't of Justice, "Justice Department Allows Comcast-NBCU Joint Venture to Proceed with Conditions" (Jan. 18, 2011), *available at* <www.justice.gov/atr/public/press_releases/2011/266149.htm>.
648. *Ibid.*, ("The department's complaint alleges that Comcast's traditional and on-line rivals need access to NBCU programming, including the NBC broadcast network, to compete effectively against Comcast.").
649. 386 U.S. 568, 578 (1967).

The Court found that the proposed merger violated section 7 because it eliminated the *potential* competition that Proctor & Gamble presented to Clorox. The Court accepted the argument that the presence of Proctor & Gamble as a potential entrant into the bleach market constrained Clorox's pricing. Allowing the acquisition would have eliminated this price constraint.[650]

452. The *1984 Merger Guidelines* were the last *Guidelines* to discuss conglomerate mergers.[651] They reflected the *Clorox* holding, explaining that a conglomerate merger may be challenged if either (1) the acquirer had been at the edge of entry to the market of the acquired company, and to prevent that entry, participants in that market had been restraining their prices ("perceived potential competition"); or (2) the acquirer could have entered the market in a more pro-competitive manner, such as entry on its own or through the acquisition of a smaller firm ("actual potential competition").[652]

453. The general lack of concern with conglomerate mergers by American regulators, contrasts with the merger policy of the European Commission, which blocked the merger of General Electric and Honeywell which occupied adjacent markets. One was a major manufacturer of jet engines, the other a major avionics manufacturer. The merger, involving two American companies, had been approved by American regulators. The Commission, however, blocked the merger on the basis of a "portfolio effects theory." The portfolio effects theory is that a dominant firm in one market will be able to dominate a complementary market if it is allowed to acquire a participant in that complementary market. This had been one of the grounds for blocking the merger in the *Clorox* case in 1967 but not a ground that American courts and regulators generally considered as a basis for blocking mergers. The *Clorox* Court recognized that the acquisition of Clorox by Procter & Gamble, a large, diversified manufacturer of household products, would raise new barriers to entry in the bleach market. Proctor & Gamble already had huge distribution in the laundry detergent market and vast advertising budgets directed at these related markets.[653] This would represent a major barrier to any third entrant. Portfolio theory has not made much headway in American antitrust law because of the view that the successful entry of a powerful player into a new market is considered efficient, and efficiency is now a

650. *Ibid.*; ABA Section of Antitrust Law, Antitrust Law Developments, 6th edn (2007), 386 ("[L]iability has not been found in any case on this theory [of entrenchment of a dominant firm in another market] since the 1970s. In 1983, the U.S. antitrust agencies eliminated entrenchment as a basis for challenging non-horizontal mergers and, although the Supreme Court has never revisited the issue, its subsequent antitrust decisions make it unlikely that the Court will again apply such theories.").

651. Fed. Trade Comm'n & U.S. Dep't of Justice, Horizontal Merger Guidelines (1992) ("Specific guidance on non-horizontal mergers is provided in Section 4 of the Department's 1984 Merger Guidelines, read in the context of today's revisions to the treatment of horizontal mergers."). The 2010 Horizontal Merger Guidelines do not mention the 1984 Merger Guidelines.

652. U.S. Dep't of Justice, Merger Guidelines § 4.11 (1984). In the 1973 case of *United States v. Falstaff Brewing*, 410 U.S. 526, 93 S.Ct. 1096 (1973) the Supreme Court held that the perceived potential competition theory could be a basis for blocking a market-extension merger. Even if the acquirer had no intention of entering the market of the acquired firm on its own, a merger could be blocked if "Falstaff could be said to be a potential competitor on the fringe of the market with likely influence on existing competition."

653. *Fed. Trade Comm'n v. Procter & Gamble Co.*, 386 U.S. 568, 578 (1967).

defense to a finding that a merger will be anticompetitive.[654] The logic of this theory is open to considerable question especially in light of the many recent cases in which the regulators have introduced evidence that the competition of a multiplicity of actors lowers prices, notwithstanding alleged efficiencies.

§4. Pure Conglomerate Mergers

454. The *Clorox* decision distinguished the merger it was reviewing from a pure conglomerate merger, which it said was one in which there are no economic relationships between the acquiring and the acquired firm.[655] An acquiring firm that does not sell products related to those in the acquired firm's market is unlikely to be an actual or potential competitor in that market, i.e., it will not restrain prices in that market or likely enter the market absent an acquisition. Since American antitrust law currently disfavors theories of leveraging, the dominance of an unrelated market is unlikely to form a basis for finding that a conglomerate merger will be anticompetitive.[656]

§5. Joint Ventures

455. Section 7 of the Clayton Act extends to joint ventures. The same considerations applied to mergers will be applied to joint ventures depending on such things as the structure of the venture, the competitive relationship of the partners to the joint venture and the possible foreclosure effects arising from the venture.

456. The Supreme Court applied section 7 in *United States v. PennOlin Chemical Co.*.[657] It explained that the same criteria were to be applied as in a merger but with consideration for the fact that a new entity was being created:

> The joint venture, like the "merger" and the "conglomeration," often creates anticompetitive dangers. It is the chosen competitive instrument of two or more corporations previously acting independently and usually competitively with one another. The result is "a triumvirate of associated corporations." If the parent companies are in competition, or might compete absent the joint venture, it may be assumed that neither will compete with the progeny in its line of commerce.

654. U.S. Dep't of Justice, Merger Guidelines § 4.135 (1984). The *Procter* Court, in contrast to antitrust law today, refused to consider efficiencies a mitigating factor in its analysis. *Procter & Gamble*, 386 U.S. at 580 ("Possible economies cannot be used as a defense to illegality.").

655. *Procter & Gamble*, 386 U.S. at 577.

656. ABA Section of Antitrust Law, Antitrust Law Developments, 6th edn (2007), 386 ("[L]iability has not been found in any case on this theory [of entrenchment of a dominant firm in another market] since the 1970s. In 1983, the U.S. antitrust agencies eliminated entrenchment as a basis for challenging non-horizontal mergers and, although the Supreme Court has never revisited the issue, its subsequent antitrust decisions make it unlikely that the Court will again apply such theories.").

657. 378 US 158, 12 L Ed 2d 775, 84 S Ct 1710 (1964).

Inevitably, the operations of the joint venture will be frozen to those lines of commerce which will not bring it into competition with the parents, and the latter, by the same token will be foreclosed from the joint venture's market.

This is not to say that the joint venture is controlled by the same criteria as the merger or conglomeration. The merger eliminates one of the participating corporations from the market while a joint venture creates a new competitive force therein.[658]

658. 378 U.S. at 169–170.

Part III. Administrative Procedure

Chapter 1. Administrative Investigations Before The Antitrust Authority

457. This section deals with investigations undertaken by the FTC which is the body that undertakes administrative investigations relating to the antitrust laws. Under American antitrust law investigations are divided between criminal investigations which fall under the jurisdiction of the Antitrust Division of the DOJ and administrative investigations, which may lead to either formal administrative charges or to non-criminal court action, which fall under the jurisdiction of the FTC.[659]

458. The Antitrust Division is not generally considered an administrative body. Its investigations, other than merger review which is dealt with elsewhere in this volume, are generally pursued according to criminal process. Criminal process involves formal criminal procedure, including the issuance of subpoenas by the courts and the convening of grand juries which issue compulsory process and may compel testimony before the grand jury which is subject to confidentiality. It is through such procedures, including also cooperative interviews with prosecutors, often obtained based upon the threat of implementation of formal criminal process, issuance of immunity to potential witnesses during the investigative process and other prosecutorial tools that such investigations of potential criminal conduct are pursued.

§1. Initiative

I. General Sectors Inquiries

459. The FTC will often undertake investigations of the conduct of different industries either upon its own initiative or upon the request of another branch of government. Investigations may be undertaken in conjunction with the FTC's rulemaking authority in order to establish an adequate record for informed rulemaking in a particular area. Congressmen or senators may suggest the propriety of an investigation into particular sectors of the economy and the FTC will often undertake an investigation upon such a request. Sometimes legislation calls for formal periodic review by the

659. The Antitrust Division does also initiate occasional civil litigation in courts, primarily involving mergers.

FTC of particular industries, or sectors within industries. For example, in 2005 the FTC was asked by three prominent senators and the congressman who sponsored the primary legislation governing generic drug marketing in the US to examine the competitive effects of authorized generic drugs, i.e. generic drugs manufactured by, or under license from, the pharmaceutical company holding the patent on the branded drug. The agency conducted a five-year study, the results of which were published in 2011.[660] An example of legislatively mandated studies or reports is the annual report relating to the ethanol markets in the US. The Energy Policy Act of 2005,[661] requires the FTC each year to "perform a market concentration analysis of the ethanol production industry using the ['HHI'] to determine whether there is sufficient competition among industry participants to avoid price-setting and other anticompetitive behavior." The statute also requires the FTC to consider all marketing arrangements among industry participants in preparing its analysis.[662]

460. The FTC may also undertake studies on its own initiative. For example, in 2010 it studied "reverse payment" settlements in pharmaceutical patent litigation with generic manufacturers. Under these settlements, payments were made to generic manufacturers in conjunction with agreements by the generic manufacturers to drop their patent challenges and to refrain from entering the market for a period of time. The FTC was concerned with the cost such settlements imposed upon consumers. It concluded that congress "should pass legislation to protect consumers from such anticompetitive agreements."[663]

II. Ex Officio Investigations

461. There is no formal concept of ex officio investigations. The FTC has detailed formal procedures as to how investigations are undertaken.[664] The investigations can be formal investigations of the Commission itself or lower level staff studies not containing the imprimatur of the full Commission, but simply representing a study by the agency's economists. For example, in contrast to the study of authorized generic drugs which extended over several years, involved use of formal process, and bore the final authority of the full Commission, a study entitled "Gasoline Price Changes and the Petroleum Industry: An Update" was prompted by a spike in petroleum prices between September 2010 and late June 2011 and was published in September 2011 – i.e., in just a few months. It bears a statement that it represents the views of FTC Staff, rather than the Commission, but that the Commission authorized its publication.

660. "Authorized Generic Drugs: Short-Term Effects and Long-Term Impact," *available at* <www.ftc.gov/os/2011/08/2011genericdrugreport.pdf> (last visited Dec. 30, 2011).

661. 42 U.S.C. § 7545(o).

662. The most recent of such reports, "2011 Report on Ethanol Market Concentration" is *available at* <www.ftc.gov/os/2011/12/111213ethanolreport.pdf> (last visited Dec. 30, 2011).

663. "Pay-for-Delay: How Drug Company Pay-Offs Cost Consumers Billions Federal Trade Commission, An FTC Staff Study, January 2010" *available at* <www.ftc.gov/os/2010/01/100112payfordelayrpt.pdf> (last visited Dec. 30, 2011).

664. These procedures are detailed in Chapter 3 of the "Operating Manual of the Federal Trade Commission."

III. Complaints

462. The Operating Manual of the FTC explains that an investigation "may be started as a result of public complaints, reports, or studies by staff…by congressional mandate, referral by another government agency or Commission directive."[665] Complaints to the FTC may come from a variety of quarters. The Operations Manual describes a process of investigation beginning with initial material obtained from the complaining party, informal contacts, and public source documents obtained by the staff. An initial phase investigation involving matters of competition must also be cleared with the DOJ before a potential respondent can be contacted. More formal forms of information gathering are not generally employed until a formal investigation is authorized.

463. A formal administrative complaint is not issued until a very late stage in the investigative process, after efforts at resolution with the potential respondent have been exhausted. The formal complaint must be authorized by the Commission itself, i.e. the five Commissioners by formal vote. Commission Rule 3.11(b)(2) requires that a complaint contain a "clear and concise statement sufficient to inform each respondent with reasonable definiteness of the type of acts or practices alleged to be in violation of the law."[666]

§2. Powers

I. Requests for Information

464. The FTC Rules provide for requests for voluntary furnishing of information. Voluntary methods may include interviews and written requests for submission of facts and data, including surveys and questionnaires. Rule 2.6 requires that any person under investigation requested to furnish information be advised of the purpose and scope of the investigation, the nature and conduct constituting the alleged violation and the applicable provision of law.[667]

II. Investigation and Search Powers

465. Beyond voluntary procedures the agency may issue subpoenas or civil investigative demands, commonly known as CIDs. It may also obtain Access Orders allowing the agency to enter the premises of an entity to obtain evidence. All of these formal compulsory procedures must be signed by a Commissioner acting under a resolution of the Commission authorizing compulsory process. These processes may be used in formal investigations of violations as well as in connection with other forms of investigation.

665. *Ibid.*, at 1.3.3.

666. The procedures for issuing and drafting a complaint are set out in Chap. 4 of the FTC Operating Manual.

667. *Ibid.*, at 3.2.3.2.

466. For example, as part of the investigation into the marketing of authorized generic drugs described above, formal requests requiring very detailed information and production of extensive documents were issued by the FTC pursuant to a formal resolution. They were served on close to a hundred companies and required thirty categories of information.[668]

III. Cooperation with Other State Institutions

467. Before an FTC investigator can contact a potential respondent it must obtain clearance from the DOJ. This reflects a policy of extensive cooperation between the FTC and other federal and state institutions. The FTC conducts investigations – or at least provides significant advice – to state as well as federal legislative and administrative bodies.[669]

468. The FTC has formal procedures for referring to state authorities matters it believes are more appropriately undertaken by state, rather than federal, agencies and will, to the extent possible, share investigative material with them.[670] A formal protocol governs concurrent state and federal reviews of mergers.[671]

---

668. *See* , "Authorized Generic Drugs: Short-Term Effects and Long-Term Impact," at appendices c though f, *available at* <www.ftc.gov/os/2011/08/2011genericdrugreport.pdf> (last visited Dec. 30, 2011).

669. *See,* for example the letter of the FTC staff to New York State Senator James L. Seward responding to his request for comment on proposed New York legislation governing mail order pharmacies:

FTC staff recognize that the Bill seeks to enhance New York consumers' ability to choose how and where their prescriptions are filled. We are concerned, however, that the Bill will have the unintended consequence of harming consumers. By reducing competition between pharmacies, this legislation likely will raise prices for, and reduce access to, prescription drugs, which are an increasingly important component of medical care.

The Bill will limit a health plan's ability to steer beneficiaries to a lower cost mail order vendor of maintenance drugs via financial incentives or other terms of coverage, whenever a competing retail pharmacy is willing to fill prescriptions at "comparable" prices. By restricting a health plan's ability to offer favorable treatment to a low-cost mail order pharmacy, the Bill undercuts pharmacies' incentives to bid aggressively for a share of that health plan's business. Reducing those incentives is likely to raise the prices that consumers pay for the prescription drugs that their health plans cover. Some cost increases may be passed on to plan beneficiaries in the form of higher out-of-pocket prices. In some cases, plans may respond to higher costs by reducing the scope of prescription drug coverage, or by eliminating prescription drug coverage entirely. For those reasons, FTC staff recommend that the Bill not be enacted.

Available at <http://ftc.gov/os/2011/08/110808healthcarecomment.pdf> (last visited Dec. 30, 2011).

670. These procedures are set out in detail in Chap. 15 of the FTC Operating Manual.

671. *See* , <http://ftc.gov/os/1998/03/mergerco.op.htm> (last visited Dec. 30, 2011).

§3. Right of Defense

I. Content and Notification of Opening Decisions

469. The Commissioners of the FTC determine by vote whether to commence an administrative proceeding. A proceeding is commenced by the filing of a complaint.[672] The complaint must specify the statutory provisions allegedly violated, provide "[a] clear and concise factual statement sufficient to inform each respondent with reasonable definiteness of the type of acts or practices alleged to be in violation of the law," and give the respondent notice of the time and place of the evidentiary hearing.[673]

470. The respondent must file an answer within fourteen days of being served with the complaint.[674] If the respondent contests the allegations, the answer must concisely state the facts providing each ground of defense and must respond specifically to each fact alleged in the complaint by either admitting, denying, explaining, or stating lack of knowledge sufficient to respond.[675] "Allegations of a complaint not thus answered shall be deemed to have been admitted."[676] If the respondent chooses not to contest the allegations, the answer must state that the respondent admits that the allegations are true.[677] Such an answer waives a hearing and provides a basis on which the FTC issues a final decision.[678]

II. The Proceedings: Hearings, Access to File, Briefs

471. Administrative hearings within the FTC are heard by Administrative Law Judges (ALJ), who are "independent decision makers" but officially employees of the FTC.[679] These hearings have much in common with trials in federal district courts, though they are governed by the FTC Rules of Practice,[680] not the Federal Rules of Civil Procedure or Federal Rules of Evidence. The parties are required to meet no later than five days after the answer is filed or, if there are multiple respondents, the answer of the last answering respondent is filed, to discuss the claims, defenses, possibilities of settlement, proposed discovery plans, and estimates of the time required for an

672. 16 C.F.R. § 3.11(a).
673. *Ibid.*, at § 3.11(b). Unless the Commission votes to hold the hearing at a different time, it is held five months from the date of the administrative complaint when the FTC also seeks a preliminary injunction against the alleged antitrust violation in federal district court and eight months from the date of the administrative complaint when the FTC does not. *Ibid.*, at 3.11(b)(4).
674. *Ibid.*, at § 3.12(a). Failure to respond within 14 days constitutes a default, that is, a waiver of the right to a hearing to contest the allegations. *Ibid.*, at § 3.12(c).
675. *Ibid.*, at § 3.12(b).
676. *Ibid.*, at § 3.12(b)(1)(ii).
677. *Ibid.*, at § 3.12(b)(2).
678. *Ibid.*,
679. FTC, *About the Office of Administrative Law Judges*, <www.ftc.gov/ftc/alj.shtm> (last visited Dec. 19, 2011).
680. 16 C.F.R. Part 3 (these rules are often called simply "Part 3").

evidentiary hearing.[681] Within ten days after the answer is filed, the ALJ is required to hold a scheduling conference with the parties to discuss the factual and legal theories, motions, proposed hearing schedules, anticipated discovery, and potential agreements to narrow the issues in dispute or otherwise to "aid in the just and expeditious disposition of the proceeding and to avoid unnecessary cost."[682] Within two days of the scheduling conference, the ALJ is required to enter an order setting forth the proceeding schedule and other results of the conference.[683] There is also a required final prehearing conference with the ALJ to deal with any final discovery and hearing issues, as well as a required meeting between the parties to prepare for that conference.[684]

472. The parties learn information about the conduct at issue, and the FTC's investigation of that conduct, through discovery. Discovery includes the production of documents or things, the exchange of written interrogatories, requests for admission, and depositions by oral examination or written answers.[685] Generally, any information that reasonably can be expected to yield information relevant to the allegations, proposed relief, or defenses is within the scope of discovery.[686] There are limitations on discovery, such as privileged information or requests that impose an undue burden or cost.[687]

473. If a party refuses to disclose information, the party seeking the information can ask the ALJ to order disclosure.[688] The ALJ can take a wide range of disciplinary actions to enforce compliance.[689]

III. Statement of Objections

474. A party may file a motion to dismiss the proceedings or to obtain a summary decision before a hearing.[690] The Commission itself rules on these motions, but may refer the motion to the ALJ.[691] The party opposing the motion must file an answer within ten days of service or "shall be deemed to have consented to the granting of the relief asked for in the motion."[692]

475. Interlocutory appeals may be taken to the Commission itself in limited circumstances if allowed by the Commission, which means that a party can ask the Commission to rule on a decision of the ALJ before it takes effect.[693]

476. If the case is not dismissed following the preliminary motion, it continues through discovery and final hearing.

681. 16 C.F.R. § 3.21(a).
682. *Ibid.*, at § 3.21(b).
683. *Ibid.*, at § 3.21(c)(1).
684. *Ibid.*, at § 3.21(d)–(e).
685. *Ibid.*, at § 3.31(a).
686. *Ibid.*, at § 3.31(c)(1).
687. *Ibid.*, at § 3.31(c)(2)–(4).
688. *Ibid.*, at § 3.38(a).
689. *Ibid.*, at § 3.38(a)–(b).
690. *Ibid.*, at § 3.22(a).
691. *Ibid.*
692. *Ibid.*, at § 3.22(d).
693. *Ibid.*, at § 3.23.

IV. Final Hearing and Decision

477. There are strict time limitations of the length of hearings: they must "proceed with all reasonable expedition" and "should be limited to no more than 210 hours."[694] All parties have the right to due notice, to cross-examination of witnesses, to present evidence, object, file motions, and to present arguments.[695] The FTC's Administrative Part 3 rules provide rules of evidence, the burdens of proof, reporting and transcription, and the extent of confidentiality.[696]

478. After the close of the hearing, the parties have the right to file for the ALJ's consideration, "proposed findings of fact, conclusions of law, and rule or order, together with reasons therefor and briefs in support thereof."[697] The ALJ then issues an initial decision, based on the entire record and supported by reliable and probative evidence.[698] The decision must include a statement of findings of fact and conclusions of law.[699]

479. The ALJ's decision is not considered a final administrative remedy and so is not directly reviewable by a court.[700] Instead, the decision can be appealed to the Commission, which will consider briefs and oral arguments by both parties.[701] The Commission considers the record and issues as if it had been the initial decision-maker.[702] The Commission then renders a decision which can be appealed to a federal Court of Appeals and then to the Supreme Court.[703]

694. *Ibid.*, at § 3.41(b).
695. *Ibid.*, at § 3.41(c).
696. *Ibid.*, at §§ 3.43-3.45.
697. *Ibid.*, at § 3.46(a).
698. *Ibid.*, at § 3.51(c).
699. *Ibid.*
700. *Ibid.*, at § 3.51(b).
701. *Ibid.*, at § 3.52(a).
702. *Ibid.*, at § 3.54.
703. *Ibid.*, at § 3.71.

Chapter 2. Voluntary Notifications and Clearance Decisions

480. The notification procedures and merger clearance provisions relating to mergers are discussed in Chapter 3 below. The government also has a voluntary amnesty program which is discussed at Part I Chapter 5 §3.III.B above.

Chapter 3. Merger Control

§1. Preliminary Filing Obligations

481. The Hart-Scott-Rodino (HSR) Antitrust Improvements Act of 1976,[704] requires that companies seeking to merge file a "Notification and Report Form for Certain Mergers and Acquisitions," or, as it is more commonly known, an HSR form, with the Antitrust Division and the FTC. The HSR form requires detailed information about the proposed merger and merging companies, including, "all studies, surveys, analyses and reports which were prepared by or for any officer(s) or director(s) ... for the purpose of evaluating or analyzing the acquisition with respect to market shares, competition, competitors, markets, potential for sales growth or expansion into product or geographic markets."[705]

I. Criteria and Thresholds

482. If a merger transaction is valued at over USD 200 million, as adjusted for inflation (USD 263.8 million in 2011),[706] the merging parties must file an HSR form. If the merger transaction is valued at over USD 50 million, as adjusted for inflation (USD 66 million in 2011), but under USD 200 million, as adjusted, the merging parties only need to file if at least one merging company has at least USD 100 million in annual net sales or total assets, as adjusted for inflation (USD 131.9 million in 2011) and the other company has at least USD 10 million, as adjusted (USD 13.2 million in 2011).

II. Turnover Calculation

483. Turnover is not an issue in antitrust analysis in the US.

III. Market Share Calculation

484. Market share calculation is not a requirement of the HSR form, but it plays a very significant role in the agencies' review and in the courts' determinations of

704. 15 U.S.C. § 18A.
705. Dep't of Justice and Federal Trade Comm'n, Antitrust Improvements Act Notification and Report Form for Certain Mergers and Acquisitions, Item 4(c)<www.ftc.gov/os/2004/03/premergerfrninsrtuctions.pdf> (last visited Sept. 6, 2012).
706. Fed. Trade Comm'n, Revised Jurisdictional Thresholds for s. 7a of The Clayton Act, 76 Fed. Reg. 4349, 4350 (Jan. 25, 2011), *available at* <www.ftc.gov/os/fedreg/2011/01/110121clayton7afrn.pdf>.

whether a proposed merger would violate the antitrust laws. The role of market share in antitrust analysis is discussed in depth in the "Mergers" section above.

IV. Other Relevant Notions

485. The Hart-Scott-Rodino Act exempts from filing mergers that are unlikely to violate antitrust law. These exemptions include acquisitions of goods or property in the ordinary course of business, acquisitions of non-voting securities, transfers to or from a government agency, and acquisitions for investment purposes only.[707]

§2. Structure of Proceedings

486. The Antitrust Division and the FTC have concurrent jurisdiction over antitrust merger review. They decide which agency will review a merger at the time the HSR form is filed, based on which agency has greater experience relevant to the particular merger. The process of determining which agency will review a merger can be adversarial between the agencies and take a substantial portion of the statutory waiting period, especially for high-profile mergers that both agencies are interested in reviewing.[708] Once either the Antitrust Division or the FTC obtains authority to review a merger, the agency will follow standard procedures. The Hart-Scott-Rodino Act provides statutory time limits for merger review, and the agencies' *Horizontal Merger Guidelines*, jointly issued by the FTC and the Antitrust Division explain the substantive criteria that the agencies will use to evaluate the legality of a proposed merger.

I. Preliminary Assessment and Full Investigation

487. The Hart-Scott-Rodino Act provides a thirty-day waiting period between filing an HSR form and consummating a merger. An agency can decrease the waiting period if a filing company requests an early termination and the agency determines within a shorter period of time than the statutory waiting period that the proposed merger should not be blocked. Most companies request and receive early termination. In fiscal year 2010, early termination was requested in 84% of the transactions reported and of those requests, 74% were granted.[709]

488. An agency can increase the waiting period by making a "second request" for additional information after determining that the proposed merger requires closer

707. 15 U.S.C. § 18A(c).

708. For a description of the problems with the process of determining which agency reviews a merger *see*, Timothy Muris, *Comments on the FTC-DOJ Clearance Process Before the Antitrust Modernization Commission* (Nov. 3, 2005), *available at* <http://govinfo.library.unt.edu/amc/commission_hearings/pdf/Muris_Statement.pdf>.

709. Dep't of Justice and Fed. Trade Comm'n, *Hart-Scott-Rodino Annual Report: Fiscal Year 2010*, 5 (2010), *available at* <www.ftc.gov/os/2011/02/1101hsrreport.pdf>.

review. A "second request" serves as a full investigation into the merger. It greatly extends the waiting period since it extends the review period until thirty days after the agency is satisfied that all the information requested in the "second request" has been provided. The attorneys representing the merging parties and the reviewing agency usually negotiate the scope of a "second request," though the agency has final say. During a "second request" investigation, an agency will often use its full investigative powers, and may require senior executives of the merging companies to provide sworn testimony. A typical second request form requires the companies to provide detailed information regarding their products, customers, competitors, pricing, sales, strategies, and other studies of the market.[710] Agencies use customer and competitor lists to find market participants who can provide further information regarding the market and input regarding the proposed merger's effect on competition. Within agencies, attorneys typically work closely with economists to understand the competitive effects of a proposed merger, and sometimes will consult with experts in other fields. Agencies will usually give attorneys representing the merging parties the opportunity to present their arguments that the proposed merger will not harm competition.

II. Time Framework

489. The Hart-Scott-Rodino Act provides that a covered merger cannot be consummated for thirty days following filing of the HSR form.[711] During that "waiting period," the reviewing agency may issue a "second request" for additional information, further extending the waiting period until thirty days after the agency determines that it has received all the additional information. Reviewing agencies can allow mergers to close by allowing the waiting period to expire or by granting early termination of the waiting period.

490. Before the end of the second waiting period the reviewing agency can decide to allow the merger, to seek injunctive relief to block the merger, or agree with the merging parties on a consent decree that will allow the merger to proceed on specified conditions.

III. Right of Defense

491. If an agency pursues an enforcement action against the merger, the parties have a right to defend their merger in an administrative proceeding or in federal court, depending upon how the agencies proceed.

492. During the administrative review process, prior to the filing of a complaint in court, merging parties have a number of protections. After exhausting "reasonable efforts," parties can appeal either the agency's decision to issue a "second request" or an agency finding that the parties have not substantially complied with the "second

710. *See,* Fed. Trade Comm'n Premerger Notification Office, Introductory Guide III: Model Request for Additional Information and Documentary Material (Second Request) (2010), *available at* <www.ftc.gov/bc/hsr/introguides/guide3.pdf>.

711. 15 days, if the mergers are to be done by cash-tender offer.

request."[712] A reviewing agency typically provides the merging parties' attorneys with opportunities to argue their clients' positions. The FTC states that its "[s]taff will typically offer, or be willing, to confer with counsel to discuss the focus of the investigation" and it "has a policy of convening a 'second request conference' within five business days of issuance of the second request."[713] The Antitrust Division also has a policy of holding "[e]arly conferences with the merging parties to identify competitive issues."[714] The merging parties' counsel typically have the opportunity to negotiate the scope of "second requests" and to present their analyses of the competitive effects of the proposed merger.

493. If the reviewing agency determines that the merger would violate antitrust law, it cannot block the merger on its own, but must bring an action in federal court to enjoin the merger or, in the case of the FTC, the FTC may bring an administrative proceeding. It is at that point that the parties to the proposed merger have a formal right to defend their proposed merger.

§3. CLEARANCE AND CONDITIONAL CLEARANCE

I. Conditions and Undertakings

494. When an agency files suit to challenge a merger, the merging parties and the agency will often agree upon a consent order that allows the merger to proceed on certain conditions.[715] The typical outcome when an agency files suit and no consent order is reached is that the parties abandon their proposed merger because of the delays involved.[716]

A. Content

495. Consent orders provide conditions under which the agency will approve a proposed merger. These conditions usually involve divestiture or, less often, restrictions on post-merger conduct in areas of the business in which the agency finds that the

712. 66 Fed. Reg. 8721 (2001) (allowing recipients of "second requests" to petition the FTC's General Counsel to hear an appeal about the issue); Dep't of Justice, *Second Request Internal Appeal Procedure* (Jun. 2001), *available at* <www.justice.gov/atr/public/8430.pdf> (providing a similar procedure for appealing to a Deputy Assistant Attorney General).

713. Fed. Trade Comm'n, *Guidance for Federal Merger Investigations and Complying with "Second Requests"* 17 (Dec. 2000) *available at* <www.ftc.gov/bc/bestpractices/mergerguidelines.pdf>.

714. Dep't of Justice, Press Release (Apr. 6, 2000), *available at* <www.justice.gov/opa/pr/2000/April/181at.htm>.

715. The FTC calls these "consent orders," while the Antitrust Division calls them "consent decrees." For the sake of simplicity, the term "consent orders" will be used throughout this text.

716. *Annual Report 2010* (reporting that the merging parties abandoned the three transactions that the FTC challenged and did not resolve by consent order and eight of the nine that the Antitrust Division challenged and did not resolve by consent order).

merger would provide the post-merger company with too much market power.[717] The agencies emphasize that each consent order is tailored to address the particular market harm that a merger would cause if it were allowed to consummate free of any conditions.[718]

496. Of the twenty-nine consent orders that the FTC and Antitrust Divisions reached with merging companies in fiscal year 2010, twenty-four required divestiture of portions of the merging companies' businesses, while seven required the post-merger firm to act in specified ways. The required actions included granting licenses to the merged companies' products, installing firewalls to protect competitor data, restructuring business agreements, continuing to offer a product, and offering discounts on a product to customers.[719]

497. Consent orders usually also require that merged companies report the status of their compliance with the orders to the agencies and to provide agency access to their employees and documents for a certain period of time.[720]

B. Timing

498. Consent orders typically require divestitures and other remedies within short periods of time, but tend to provide restrictions on the merged companies' conduct for ten years or longer. The Antitrust Division explains that a typical consent order's "prohibition on reacquisition of assets is the key reason that the term of the decree in merger cases exceeds the completion of the divestiture. The typical term of Division merger decrees is 10 years."[721] The agencies shape the duration of a consent order to the specific remedy it is intended to provide. For example, in a 2010 settlement between the FTC and the Coca-Cola Company, the agency allowed the company to obtain an exclusive distribution license of a competitor's products provided that, among other restrictions, the Coca-Cola Company establish a firewall to prevent its access to the competitor's commercially sensitive information. The term of the license agreement was twenty years, so the term of the consent order was also twenty years.[722]

499. Regardless of a consent order's term, any divestiture required by the consent order usually must be completed within two to six months of the date the parties sign

717. *Annual Report 2010.* at 2–3 (reporting that the FTC resolved nineteen of the twenty-two transactions it challenged, and the Antitrust Division resolved ten of the nineteen transactions it challenged, in fiscal year 2010 with consent orders).
718. Fed. Trade Comm'n, *Frequently Asked Questions About Merger Consent Order Provisions* (hereinafter "*FTC Consent Order FAQs*"), *available at* <www.ftc.gov/bc/mergerfaq.shtm> ("Every order in a merger case has the same goal: to preserve fully the existing competition in the relevant market or markets …[T]here is no 'magic formula' to achieve that goal and developing appropriate merger remedies is a very fact-specific inquiry.").
719. *Ibid.*, at 8–17.
720. *FTC Consent Order FAQs*, *supra* n. 691.
721. Dep't of Justice, *Antitrust Division Policy Guide to Merger Remedies* 35 n.48 (Oct. 2004).
722. Fed. Trade Comm'n, *In the Matter of The Coca-Cola Company; Analysis of Agreement Containing Consent Order to Aid Public Comment*, 75 Fed. Reg. 61141 (Oct. 4, 2010), *available at* <www. ftc.gov/os/fedreg/2010/october/101004cocacolaanal.pdf>.

the order.[723] The agencies require divestitures so quickly in order to limit competitive harm and the deterioration of assets before they are sold. According to the FTC, "[o] ur experience confirms that firms can, with some rare exceptions, complete divestitures in less than six months."[724]

§4. Relations with Other Merger Control Authorities

500. The Antitrust Division and FTC regularly collaborate with other federal, state, and international government agencies on merger review.

I. Other Authorities within the Local Jurisdiction

A. Federal Agencies

501. Depending on the industry in which a merger is occurring, federal agencies other than the FTC and Antitrust Division may have authority to review the merger, either instead of, or in addition to, the antitrust agencies.

502. FCC has authority to review proposed mergers between "common carriers engaged in wire or radio communication or radio transmission of energy."[725] The FCC usually conducts its merger reviews under the separate authority of the Communications Act of 1934, which provides a "public interest" standard of review.[726] The FCC tends to apply the "public interest" standard by, first, conducting an antitrust review similar to that conducted by the FTC and Antitrust Division, and then looking at wide-ranging transaction-specific public effects of the merger, such as effects on prices and service coverage.[727] Because the FCC and the antitrust agencies review mergers based on similar criteria (though the FCC standard is more stringent in that it looks for public benefits, not just lack of public harm), the agencies often find it useful to coordinate their reviews.

503. Other industries in which non-antitrust federal agencies have authority to review mergers include electric power (review conducted by the FERC and sometimes the Securities and Exchange Commission), national banks (Office of Comptroller of the Currency), "federally-insured, state-chartered banks that are not members of the Federal Reserve System" (Federal Deposit Insurance Corporation), "bank holding companies and state-chartered banks that are members of the Federal Reserve System" (Board of Governors of the Federal Reserve System), and "savings and loan companies

723. Dep't of Justice, *Antitrust Division Policy Guide to Merger Remedies* 29 (Oct. 2004) (setting out the Antitrust Division's policy of usually requiring divestiture within 60–90 days); *FTC Consent Order FAQs, supra* n. 101(explaining the FTC's policy of usually requiring divestiture within three to six months).

724. *FTC Consent Order FAQs, supra* n. 691.

725. 15 U.S.C. § 21.

726. 47 U.S.C. §§ 214(a), 310(d).

727. Congressional Research Service, *CRS Report for Congress: Merger Review Authority of the Federal Communications Commission* 4–6 (Aug. 20, 2008).

and savings associations" (Office of Thrift Supervision).[728] The Clayton Act gives the Department of Transportation exclusive authority to review mergers of "air carriers."[729] In addition, the Surface Transportation Board has exclusive jurisdiction over railroad mergers. In such mergers, the antitrust agencies play only an advisory role.[730]

B. State Agencies

504. In addition to the federal government, state government agencies have authority to review many mergers. State attorneys general, who are the chief law enforcement officers of their states, have authority under state laws and some federal laws to review mergers of companies that do business in their states. Attorneys general may collaborate with the FTC or Antitrust Division to enforce merger laws, but they may also enforce antitrust policies that differ from those of the federal agencies.

505. As in the federal system, state regulatory agencies may also review mergers based on the industries of the merger parties. For example, state public service commissions review mergers of energy companies.[731]

506. A formal protocol governs coordination of state and federal merge enforcement.

II. International Coordination

507. Since most large corporations now operate in multiple countries, their mergers often face review by antitrust regulators in multiple jurisdictions. The importance of international coordination was demonstrated when the European Commission blocked the merger between General Electric Company (GE) and Honeywell, which would have been the largest industrial merger in history, after the Antitrust Division approved it, subject to divestitures.[732] Since GE and Honeywell are American corporations, American officials, including its antitrust authorities, expressed outrage at the European Commission's decision.[733]

508. Over the years, the FTC and Antitrust Division have increased their collaboration with the European Commission and other foreign antitrust authorities. The agencies have departments that focus exclusively on international coordination of antitrust enforcement: the FTC has an International Antitrust Program within its Office of International Affairs and the Antitrust Division has an International Program.

---

728. Dep't of Justice, *Annex 3-B: The Relationship Between the Antitrust Agencies and Sectoral Regulators*, *available at* <www.justice.gov/atr/icpac/3b.pdf>.

729. 15 U.S.C. § 21.

730. Dep't of Justice, *Annex 3-B: The Relationship Between the Antitrust Agencies and Sectoral Regulators*, *available at* <www.justice.gov/atr/icpac/3b.pdf>.

731. *Ibid.*

732. Eleanor M. Fox & GE. Honeywell, "The U.S. Merger that Europe Stopped – A Story of the Politics of Convergence," *Antitrust Stories*, ed. Eleanor M. Fox & Daniel A. Crane (2007), 331, 338.

733. *Ibid.*, at 332.

509. The agencies have bilateral cooperation agreements with the antitrust authorities of the European Community, Germany, Australia, Canada, Israel, Japan, Brazil and Mexico through which parties to an agreement inform each other of planned antitrust actions that would affect the other's important interests, hold consultations to resolve concerns, and cooperate on antitrust enforcement.[734] The agreements do not override national interests or domestic prohibitions on sharing confidential business information. The US also has an agreement with the European Commission and with Canada under which each country's antitrust authorities can request that the other enforce antitrust law against a corporate action.

510. Under the International Antitrust Assistance Act of 1994,[735] the FTC and Antitrust Division may form bilateral international agreements under which the antitrust authorities may collaborate even more closely. The US has such agreements, termed Mutual Legal Assistance Treaties, with Canada and Australia. Under these agreements, the antitrust authorities may share otherwise confidential business information and use their investigative tools to aid the other country's antitrust investigations.[736]

734. John J, Parisi, "U.S. Federal Trade Commission," *Enforcement Cooperation among Antitrust Authorities* (Aug. 2010), 4–5 *available at* <http://ftc.gov/oia/speeches/1008enforementantitrust.pdf>, *available at* <http://ftc.gov/oia/speeches/1008enforementantitrust.pdf>.

735. 15 U.S.C. §§ 6201–6212.

736. John J, Parisi, "U.S. Federal Trade Commission," *Enforcement Cooperation among Antitrust Authorities* (Aug. 2010), 6.

Chapter 4. Challenging of the Administrative Decision

§1. Competent Courts

511. Any final order of the FTC is subject to review in a federal Court of Appeals. The case may be brought either in the Court of Appeals in which the violation occurred or in which the party resides. The review is governed by 15 U.S.C.A. § 21 which reads:

> Any person required by such order of the commission, board, or Secretary to cease and desist from any such violation may obtain a review of such order in the court of appeals of the United States for any circuit within which such violation occurred or within which such person resides or carries on business, by filing in the court, within sixty days after the date of the service of such order, a written petition praying that the order of the commission, board, or Secretary be set aside. A copy of such petition shall be forthwith transmitted by the clerk of the court to the commission, board, or Secretary, and thereupon the commission, board, or Secretary shall file in the court the record in the proceeding, as provided in Section 2112 of Title 28. Upon such filing of the petition the court shall have jurisdiction of the proceeding and of the question determined therein concurrently with the commission, board, or Secretary until the filing of the record, and shall have power to make and enter a decree affirming, modifying, or setting aside the order of the commission, board, or Secretary, and enforcing the same to the extent that such order is affirmed, and to issue such writs as are ancillary to its jurisdiction or are necessary in its judgment to prevent injury to the public or to competitors pendente lite. The findings of the commission, board, or Secretary as to the facts, if supported by substantial evidence, shall be conclusive. To the extent that the order of the commission, board, or Secretary is affirmed, the court shall issue its own order commanding obedience to the terms of such order of the commission, board, or Secretary. If either party shall apply to the court for leave to adduce additional evidence, and shall show to the satisfaction of the court that such additional evidence is material and that there were reasonable grounds for the failure to adduce such evidence in the proceeding before the commission, board, or Secretary, the court may order such additional evidence to be taken before the commission, board, or Secretary, and to be adduced upon the hearing in such manner and upon such terms and conditions as to the court may seem proper. The commission, board, or Secretary may modify its findings as to the facts, or make new findings, by reason of the additional evidence so taken, and shall file such modified or new findings, which if supported by substantial evidence, shall be conclusive, and its recommendation, if any, for the modification or setting aside of its original order, with the return of such additional evidence. The judgment and decree of the court shall be final, except that the same shall be.

§2. Time Limits

512. As the above quoted statute makes clear, a petition must be filed within sixty days of the FTC order.

§3. Judicial Scope of Review

513. The statute sets out the scope of review. It is a highly deferential standard: "The findings of the commission, board, or Secretary as to the facts, if supported by substantial evidence, shall be conclusive." The appraisal of the evidence and the inferences to be drawn from it are for the Commission, not the courts.[737] As Judge Richard Posner explained in applying this standard to the economic effects of a proposed merger:

> [T]the substantial evidence rule ... applies to ultimate as well as underlying facts, including economic judgments. This is implicit in the many cases that hold that the ultimate question under the Clayton Act – whether the challenged transaction may substantially lessen competition – is governed by the substantial evidence rule. [Citations] Hospital Corporation has argued the case to us as if we were the FTC, which assuredly we are not. Our only function is to determine whether the Commission's analysis of the probable effects of these acquisitions on ... competition ... is so implausible, so feebly supported by the record, that it flunks even the deferential test of substantial evidence.[738]

737. *Fed. Trade Comm'n v. A.E. Staley Mfg. Co.*, 324 U.S. 746, 760, 65 S. Ct. 971, 977, 89 L. Ed. 1338 (1945).

738. *Hosp. Corp. of Am. v. F.T.C.*, 807 F.2d 1381, 1385 (7th Cir. 1986).

Selected Bibliography

Ariel Ezrachi, *EU Competition Law, An Analytical Guide to the Leading Cases*. 2d ed. (Hart, Oxford and Portland, Oregon 2010).
Eleanor Fox & Daniel Crane, *Antitrust Stories* (Foundation, New York 2007).
Ernest Gellhorn, William Kovacic & Stephen Calkins, *Antitrust Law and Economics*. 5th ed. (West, St. Paul 2004).
Earl W. Kintner, et al., *Federal Antitrust Law* (2011).
Herbert Hovenkamp, *Federal Antitrust Policy, The Law of Competition and Its Practice*. 4th ed. (West, St. Paul 2011).
John J. Flynn, Harry First & Darren Bush, *Antitrust: Statutes, Treaties, Regulations, Guidelines, Policies* (West, St. Paul 2011).
Lawrence A. Sullivan & Warren S. Grimes, *The Law of Antitrust: An Integrated Handbook*. 2d ed. (West, St. Paul 2006).
Phillip E. Areeda & Herbert Hovenkamp, *Antitrust Law: An Analysis of Antitrust Principles and Their Application*. 3d ed. (Wolters Kluwer 2011).
Richard A. Posner, *Antitrust Law*. 2d ed. (University of Chicago, Chicago 2001).

Selected Bibliography

Table of Cases

The bold numbers here refer to paragraph numbers.

Table of Cases

Ethyl Gasoline Corp. v. United States, 309 U.S. 436, 60 S. Ct. 618, 84 L. Ed. 852 (1940), **360**

F. Hoffmann-La Roche Ltd. v. Epigram S.A., 542 U.S. 155, 124 S. Ct. 2359 (2004), **40**
F.T.C & U.S. Dep't of Justice, Horizontal Merger Guidelines (2010), **74**
F.T.C. v. Actavis, Inc., 133 S. Ct. 2223 (2013), **367, 368**
F.T.C v. Arch Coal, Inc., 329 F. Supp. 2d 109 (D.D.C. 2004), **203**
F.T.C v. CCC Holdings Inc., 605 F. Supp. 2d 26 (2009), **203**
F.T.C. v. Church & Dwight Co., Inc., 11-5008, 2011 WL 6157620 (D.C. Cir. Dec. 13, 2011), **410**
F.T.C. v. H.J. Heinz Co., 246 F.3d 708 (D.C. Cir. 2001), **199, 442**
F.T.C. v. Indiana Fed'n of Dentists, 476 U.S. 447, 106 S. Ct. 2009, 90 L. Ed. 2d 445 (1986), **71, 254, 355**
F.T.C v. Laboratory Corp. of America, 2011 WL 3100372 (C.D. Cal., Mar. 11, 2011), **203**
F.T.C v. Morton Salt Co., 334 U.S. 37, 68 S. Ct. 822, 92 L. Ed. 1196 (1948), **384**
F.T.C v. Motion Picture Advertising Serv. Co., 344 U.S. 392 (1953), **135**
F.T.C. v. Phoebe Putney Health System, Inc., 133 S. Ct. 1003 (2013), **44, 48**
F.T.C. v. Procter & Gamble, 386 U.S. 568 (1967), **451**
F.T.C. v. Schering-Plough Corp., 126 S. Ct. 2929 (No. 05-273), 2005 WL 2105243 (U.S. Aug. 29, 2005), **130**
F.T.C v. Schering-Plough Corp., 126 S. Ct. 2929 (No. 05-273), 2006 WL 1358441 (U.S. May 17, 2006), **130**
F.T.C v. Sperry & Hutchinson Co., 405 U.S. 233 (1972), **29**
F.T.C. v. Staples, Inc., 970 F. Supp. 1066 (D.D.C. 1997), **75, 82, 87, 95, 203**
F.T.C. v. Superior Court Trial Lawyers Ass'n, 493 U.S. 411, 110 S. Ct. 768, 107 L. Ed. 2d 851 (1990), **273, 274**
F.T.C. v. Swedish Match, 131 F. Supp. 2d 151 (D.D.C. 2000), **203**
F.T.C. v. Whole Foods Market., Inc., 548 F.3d 1028 (D.C. Cir. 2008), **82, 87, 202, 443**
Fashion Originators' Guild of Am. v. F.T.C., 312 U.S. 457, 61 S. Ct. 703, 85 L. Ed. 949 (1941), **273**
F.T.C. v. A.E. Staley Mfg. Co., 324 U.S. 746, 65 S. Ct. 971, 89 L. Ed. 1338 (1945), **513**
F.T.C. v. Procter & Gamble Co., 386 U.S. 568 (1967), **453**
F.T.C. v. Staples, Inc., 970 F. Supp. 1066 (D.D.C. 1997), **440**
F.T.C. v. Staples, Inc., No. CV 15-2115 (EGS), 2016 WL 2899222 (D.D.C. May 17, 2016), **87, 441**
F.T.C. v. Whole Foods Mkt., Inc., 548 F.3d 1028 (D.C. Cir. 2008), **75**
Flat Glass Antitrust Litigation, In re, 385 F.3d 350 (3d Cir. 2004), **231, 233, 238, 293**
Flonase Antitrust Litig., In re, 692 F. Supp. 2d 524 (E.D. Pa. 2010), **176**
Fontana Aviation, Inc. v. Cessna Aircraft Co., 617 F.2d 478 (7th Cir. 1980), **173**
France Telecom SA v. Commission, Case C-202/07 (Apr. 2, 2009), **393**
Freeman v. San Diego Ass'n of Realtors, 322 F.3d 1133 (9th Cir. 2003), **316**

Gen. Motors Corp., 103 F.T.C. 374 (1984), **317**
Gen. Motors Corp., et al., In the Matter of, 116 F.T.C. 1276 (1993), **317**

Table of Cases

Gen. Talking Pictures Corp. v. W. Elec. Co., 305 U.S. 124, 59 S. Ct. 116, 83 L. Ed. 81 (1938), **360**
General Leaseways v. National Truck Leasing Association, 744 F.2d 588 (7th Cir. 1984), **102, 266, 314**
George Haug Co., Inc. v. Rolls Royce Motor Cars Inc., 148 F.3d 136 (2d Cir. 1998), **384**
George Lussier Enterprises, Inc. v. Subaru of New England, Inc., 286 F. Supp. 2d 86 (D.N.H. 2003) aff'd, 393 F.3d 36 (1st Cir. 2004), **356**
Glaberson v. Comcast Corp., 2013 WL 5988966 (E.D. Pa. Nov. 12, 2013), **193**
Goldfarb v. Virginia State Bar, 421 U.S. 773, 95 S. Ct. 2004, 44 L. Ed. 2d 572 (1975), **251, 252**
Gulf Oil Corp. v. Copp Paving Co., 419 U.S. 186 (1974), **52**

Hanover Shoe, Inc. v. United Shoe Machinery Corporation., 392 U.S. 481, 88 S. Ct. 2224, 20 L. Ed. 2d 1231 (1968), **173**
Hartford Fire Ins. Co. v. California, 509 U.S. 764, 113 S. Ct. 2891, 125 L. Ed. 2d 612 (1993), **281**
Hawaii v. Standard Oil Co. of Cal., 405 U.S. 251, 92 S. Ct. 885, 31 L. Ed. 2d 184 (1972), **160**
Hecht v. Pro-Football, Inc., 570 F.2d 982 (D.C. Cir. 1977), **417**
High Fructose Corn Syrup Antitrust Litig, In re, 295 F.3d 651 (7th Cir. 2002), **184, 231, 235**
Hosp. Corp. of Am. v. F.T.C., 807 F.2d 1381 (7th Cir. 1986), **437**, **513**
Hydrogen Peroxide Antitrust Litig., In re, 552 F.3d 305 (3d Cir. 2008), **192**

ILC Peripherals Leasing Corp. v. IBM Corp., 458 F. Supp. 423 (N.D. Cal. 1978), **398**
Illinois Brick Co. v. Illinois, 431 U.S. 720, 97 S. Ct. 2061, 52 L. Ed. 2d 707 (1977), **172**
Illinois Tool Works Inc. v. Indep. Ink, Inc., 547 U.S. 28, 126 S. Ct. 1281, 164 L. Ed. 2d 26 (2006), **69, 364, 400**
Image Technical Services, Inc. v. Eastman Kodak Co., 125 F.3d 1195 (9th Cir. 1997), **354**
Indep. Gasoline Antitrust Litig., In re, 79 F.R.D. 552 (D. Md. 1978), **245**
Indus. Gas Antitrust Litig., In re, 100 F.R.D. 280 (N.D. Ill. 1983), **263**
Int'l Raw Materials, Ltd. v. Stauffer Chem. Co., 978 F.2d 1318 (3d Cir. 1992), **42**
Int'l Salt Co. v. United States, 332 U.S. 392, 68 S. Ct. 12, 92 L. Ed. 20 (1947), **400**

J. Truett Payne Co., Inc. v. Chrysler Motors Corp., 451 U.S. 557, 101 S. Ct. 1923, 68 L. Ed. 2d 442 (1981), **186, 383**
Jefferson Parish Hosp. Dist. No. 2 v. Hyde, 466 U.S. 2, 104 S. Ct. 1551, 80 L. Ed. 2d 2 (1984), **400–402, 404**

Kaiser Steel Corp. v. Mullins, 455 U.S. 72, 102 S. Ct. 851, 70 L. Ed. 2d 833 (1982), **179**
Kay Elec. Cooperative v. Newkirk, 647 F.3d 1039 (10th Cir. 2011), **48**

K-Dur Antitrust Litigation, In re, 10-2077, 2012 WL 2877662 (3d Cir. Jul. 16, 2012), **367**
K-Dur Antitrust Litig., In re, No. 01-CV-1652-SRC/CLW, 2016 WL 755623 (D.N.J. Feb. 25, 2016), **368**
Kelly v. Kosuga, 358 U.S. 516, 79 S. Ct. 429, 3 L. Ed. 2d 475 (1959), **179**
King Drug Co. of Florence, Inc. v. Cephalon, Inc., No. 2:06-CV-1797, 2015 WL 5783603 (E.D. Pa. Oct. 5, 2015), **368**
King Drug Co. of Florence v. Cephalon, Inc., 88 F. Supp. 3d 402 (E.D. Pa. 2015), **368**
Kingray, Inc. v. NBA, Inc., 188 F. Supp. 2d 1177 (S.D. Cal. 2002), **42**

Laumann v. Nat'l Hockey League, 907 F. Supp. 2d 465 (S.D.N.Y. 2012), **42, 72**
Law v. National Collegiate Athletic Association, 134 F.3d 1010 (10th Cir. 1998), **55, 72, 195, 257, 258**
Leaseways, Inc. v. Nat'l Truck Leasing Ass'n, 744 F.2d 588 (7th Cir. 1984) (Posner, J.), **261**
Leegin Creative Leather Products, Inc. v. PSKS, Inc., 551 U.S. 877, 127 S. Ct. 2705, 168 L. Ed. 2d 623 (2007), **39, 54, 69, 327, 328, 330, 334–336, 360**
LePage's Inc. v. 3M, 324 F.3d 141 (3d Cir. 2003), **110, 345, 376, 409**
Linerboard Antitrust Litig., In re, 305 F.3d 145 (3d Cir. 2002), **53, 174, 177, 184, 191, 192, 266, 269**
Linerboard Antitrust Litig., In re, 292 F. Supp. 2d 644 (E.D. Pa. 2003), **194**
Linerboard Antitrust Litig., In re, 321 F. Supp. 2d 619 (E.D. Pa. 2004), **161, 197**
Lipitor Antitrust Litig., In re, 46 F.Supp.3d 523 (D.N.J. 2014), **368**
Loeb v. Eastman Kodak, 183 F. 704 (3d Cir. 1910), **171**
Loestrin 24 Fe Antitrust Litig., In re, 814 F.3d 538 (1st Cir. 2016), **368**
Lower Lake Erie Iron Ore Antitrust Litig., In re, 998 F.2d 1144 (3d Cir. 1993), **168, 187**

Maple Flooring Manufacturers Association v. U. S., 268 U.S. 563, 45 S. Ct. 578, 69 L. Ed. 1093 (1925), **290**
Massachusetts School of Law at Andover v. American Bar Ass'n, 107 F.3d 1026 (3d Cir. 1997), **305**
Matsushita Elec. Indus. Co., Ltd. v. Zenith Radio Corp., 475 U.S. 574, 106 S. Ct. 1348, 89 L. Ed. 2d 538 (1986), **19, 394**
MCI Communications Corp. v. Am. Tel. & Tel. Co., 708 F.2d 1081 (7th Cir. 1983), **45, 47, 188, 398**
Meat Cutters v. Jewel Tea, 381 U.S. 676 (1965), **43**
Memorex Corp. v. IBM Corp., 636 F.2d 1188 (9th Cir.1980), *cert. denied*, 452 U.S. 972, 101 S. Ct. 3126, 69 L. Ed. 2d 983 (1981), **398**
Monsanto Co. v. Spray-Rite Serv. Corp., 465 U.S. 752, 104 S. Ct. 1464, 79 L. Ed. 2d 775 (1984), **68, 335**
Morton Salt Co. v. G. S. Suppiger Co., 314 U.S. 488, 62 S. Ct. 402, 86 L. Ed. 363 (1942), **400**

N.A.A.C.P. v. Claiborne Hardware Co., 458 U.S. 886, 102 S. Ct. 3409, 73 L. Ed. 2d 1215 (1982), **274**

Table of Cases

N. Carolina State Bd. of Dental Examiners v. F.T.C., 135 S. Ct. 1101 (2015), **44, 48**
NASDAQ Mkt.-Makers Antitrust Litig., In re, 169 F.R.D. 493 (S.D.N.Y. 1996), **192**
NASDAQ Mkt.-Makers Antitrust Litig., In re, 187 F.R.D. 465 (S.D.N.Y. 1998), **161**
National Collegiate Athletic Association v. Board of Regents of University of Oklahoma, 468 U.S. 85, 104 S. Ct. 2948, 82 L. Ed. 2d 70 (1984), **55, 71, 72, 88, 90, 253, 259**
National Society of Professional Engineers v. United States, 435 U.S. 679, 98 S. Ct. 1355, 55 L. Ed. 2d 637 (1978), **71, 72, 249, 252, 254, 259**
Nexium (Esomeprazole) Antitrust Litig., In re, 968 F. Supp. 2d 367 (D. Mass. 2013), **368**
Nexium (Esomeprazole) Antitrust Litigation, In re, 42 F. Supp. 3d 231 (D. Mass. 2014), **368**
North Texas Specialty Physicians v. F.T.C., 528 F.3d 346 (5th Cir. 2008), **257**
Northwest Wholesale Stationers, Inc. v. Pac. Stationery & Printing Co., 472 U.S. 284, 105 S. Ct. 2613, 86 L. Ed. 2d 202 (1985), **276, 277, 279, 280, 319**
NYNEX Corp. v. Discon, Inc., 525 U.S. 128, 119 S. Ct. 493, 142 L. Ed. 2d 510 (1998), **412**

Official Airlines Guides v. FTC, 630 F.2d 920 (2d Cir. 1980), **29**
Otter Tail Power Co. v. United States, 410 U.S. 366, 93 S. Ct. 1022, 35 L. Ed. 2d 359 (1973), **47, 419**

Pacific Bell Telephone Co. v. Linkline Communications, Inc., 129 S. Ct. 1109 (2009), **39, 47, 377, 412, 421**
Palmer v. BRG of Georgia, Inc., 498 U.S. 46, 111 S. Ct. 401, 112 L. Ed. 2d 349 (1990), **53, 265**
Paramount Famous Lasky Corp. v. United States, 282 U.S. 30 (1930), **96**
Payment Card Interchange Fee & Merch. Disc. Antitrust Litig., In re, 562 F. Supp. 2d 392 (E.D.N.Y. 2008), **94**
Phillips v. Crown Cent. Petroleum Corp., 602 F.2d 616 (4th Cir. 1979), **245**
Plywood Antitrust Litig., In re, 655 F.2d 627 (5th Cir. 1981), **196, 184, 248**
Professional Real Estate Investors v. Columbia Pictures, Inc., 508 U.S. 49 (1993), **45, 46**

Queen City Pizza, Inc. v. Domino's Pizza, Inc., 124 F.3d 430 (3d Cir. 1997), **351, 354–356, 415**

Radiant Burners, Inc. v. Peoples Gas Light & Coke Co., 364 U.S. 656, 81 S. Ct. 365, 5 L. Ed. 2d 358 (1961), **270, 308**
Rambus Inc. v. FTC, 522 F.3d 456 (D.C. Cir. 2008), **311, 312**
Research In Motion Ltd. v. Motorola, Inc., 644 F. Supp. 2d 788 (N.D. Tex. 2008), **312**
Rochester Drug Co-Operative, Inc. v. Braintree Laboratories, CIV. 07-142-SLR, 2011 WL 2669208 (D. Del. Jul. 7, 2011), **204**
Rossi v. Standard Roofing, Inc., 156 F.3d 452 (3d Cir. 1998), **279**
Rothery Storage & Van Co. v. Atlas Van Lines, Inc., 792 F.2d 210 (D.C. Cir. 1986), **104, 261, 314**

Table of Cases

Table of Cases

Index

The number refers to paragraph numbers.

Index

Index

Made in the USA
Monee, IL
16 September 2026

63296741R00116